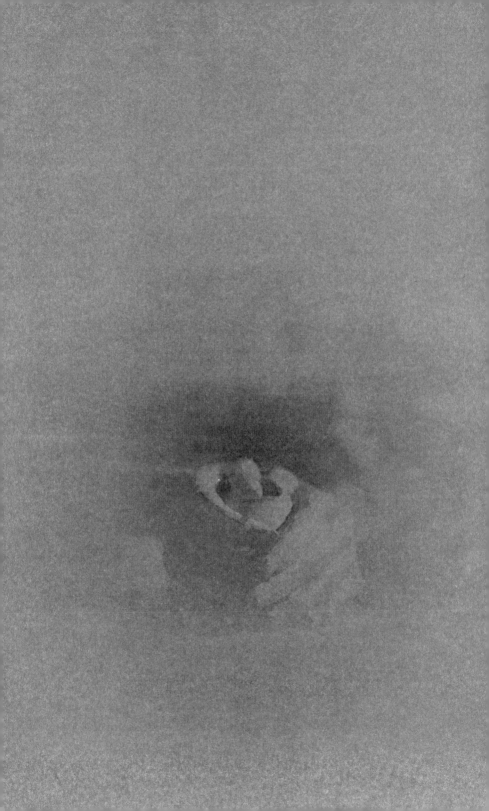

"In a year apart from everyone she loves, Tracy Franz reconciles her feelings of loneliness and displacement into acceptance and trust. Keenly observed and lyrically told, her journal takes us deep into the spirit of Zen, where every place you stand is the monastery."

KAREN MAEZEN MILLER, author of *Paradise in Plain Sight: Lessons from a Zen Garden*

"Crisp, glittering, deep, and probing."

DAI-EN BENNAGE, translator of *Zen Seeds*

"Tracy Franz's *My Year of Dirt and Water* is both bold and quietly elegant in form and insight, and spacious enough for many striking paradoxes: the intimacy that arises in the midst of loneliness, finding belonging in exile, discovering real freedom on a journey punctuated by encounters with dark and cruel men, and moving forward into the unknown to finally excavate secrets of the past. It is a long poem, a string of koans and startling encounters, a clear dream of transmissions beyond words. And it is a remarkable love story that moved me to tears."

BONNIE NADZAM, author of *Lamb* and *Lions*, co-author of *Love in the Anthropocene*

"A remarkable account of a woman's sojourn, largely in Japan, while her husband undergoes a year-long training session in a Zen Buddhist monastery. Difficult, disciplined, and interesting as the husband's training toward becoming a monk may be, it is the author's tale that has our attention here."

JOHN KEEBLE, author of seven books, including *The Shadows of Owls*

"Franz matches restraint with reflexiveness, crafting a narrative equally filled with the luminous particular and the telling omission. Death and impermanence—Zen's secret heart—are very present. . . . [The memoir] incorporates Zen, pottery, living abroad, and Franz's past and present with skillful delicacy, connecting these elements as if by analogy. Traversing territory defined by lack, *My Year of Dirt and Water* offers the singular pleasure of a story that 'obscures but is not obscured.'"

LETITIA MONTGOMERY-RODGERS, *Foreword Magazine*

My Year of Dirt and Water

JOURNAL OF A ZEN MONK'S WIFE IN JAPAN

Tracy Franz

Stone Bridge Press • Berkeley, California

Published by
Stone Bridge Press
P. O. Box 8208, Berkeley, CA 94707
sbp@stonebridge.com • www.stonebridge.com

Text © 2018 Tracy Franz.

The lines quoted from the poem by Ryokan are from a translation by Edward Seidensticker (https://www.nobelprize.org/nobel_prizes/literature/laureates/1968/kawabata-lecture.html).

Map artwork from Free Vector Maps, http://freevectormaps.com.

Cover design by Linda Ronan incorporating a photograph by Ekaterina Dema/Shutterstock.com. Book design by Peter Goodman.

All rights reserved.

No part of this book may be reproduced in any form without permission from the publisher.

Printed in the United States of America.

10 9 8 7 6 5 4 3 2   2022 2021 2020 2019 2018

p-ISBN: 978-1-61172-042-6
e-ISBN: 978-1-61172-930-6

for
Koun

Contents

My Year of Dirt and Water

Japan, Kyushu,
and Kumamoto City

Sunday, February 29, 2004

Today marks a leap year—a day that does and does not exist. And so I am and am not on the island of Kyushu, Japan, driving the toll roads through night away from the Oita Ferry Terminal and toward the outskirts of Kumamoto City, my mind returning to one image superimposed on the rush of blacktop: my husband—a tall, shorn-headed American with his hand in the air, black monk's robes jerking in the wind around his body. The sun swiftly sliding into the Inland Sea. The ship receding to a single dot of light and then, finally, extinguished.

Spring

MARCH
Beginnings

Monday, March 1

"Why are you here?"
"For shugyo."
"What is shugyo?"
"It is training in the way of Master Dogen Zenji."
"Go away. You need to think about it some more."

~

I wake from my dreams to frigid air and a growing expansiveness in the center of my chest. Lying there, feeling it—the morning cold and also that diffusive emotion. Breathing it in and then out again. The breath visible in the morning light of a cold room. Outside, it is overcast and snowing white petals that dissolve on contact. Early plum blossoms bloom like fire along gnarled branches in the courtyard below the townhouse. It is spring in Kumamoto.

In the weeks and months before he left to enter the monastery, my husband Koun and I gathered bits of knowledge from his teacher and other priests in the Soto Zen lineage. We learned what would be expected of him, what his life was about to become. I wonder now, how many hours has he had to wait at the gates of Zuioji this morning, ritually asking to enter, ritually being rejected? How many hours standing in formal *shashu*—his elbows raised high and out, left fist against his chest, right hand on top, gaze unwavering? I imagine him already admitted into *tanga-ryo*, the "waiting area," a small room within the monastery where new monks remain for at least a week. The random visits by senior monks, the limited sleep, and the constant and rigid stillness will test their sincerity and resolve before they are allowed to officially enter and be called by their Buddhist names, rather than simply *anata*, "you."

From now on, he'll likely wake at 3:00 a.m. to sit in zazen— the cross-legged posture of meditation—or to kneel in formal *seiza*, his legs tucked beneath his body and pressed against cold tatami, while he silently memorizes ancient sutras. The only sound his breathing and the breathing of the other three or four new monks in the room. Bouts of shivering will come and go in gusts, like the snow drifting through the cracks between the warped fusuma sliding doors. After, he will take his bowl of rice gruel, a small warm coal in the belly. Much of this will be the same again until lunch, until dinner, until bedtime at 9 p.m., and even then, in his futon, he will never get warm. In this way, the hours and days and weeks will cycle through a pattern, and later he will enter other patterns.

The cold will eventually give them all chilblains—darkened and bleeding earlobes, cracked knuckles, split feet and knees. But by then they won't mind so much, the cold having become just another process of the body, like respiration.

I rise from the futon to dress for the day, and close the gray curtains against gray light, but I leave the portable kerosene heaters untouched. Better to feel the chill this morning. Those bright red blossoms burn through everything.

~

The Japanese school year has just ended, and it is quiet in the halls of Shokei Daigaku, the small women's university where I teach English. Inside my office, I sit at a desk with a pencil worrying between my teeth—that gray light still in the wall of windows behind me. My grades and stack of year-end paperwork have already been turned in, but there is now the matter of our soon-to-expire visas to attend to.

Three days ago, Koun and I went together to Immigration, a dismal office smelling of paper and stale cigarette smoke. Behind the counter, sour-faced government workers riffled leisurely through stacks of documents—their sole job, seemingly, to produce as much red tape as possible.

Koun cleared his throat as he approached the counter, and then he explained in humble Japanese, "I'm very sorry to trouble you, but it is important that we complete this paperwork today. It will be difficult for me to return later." As added emphasis, I stood beside him and smiled in what I hoped was an ingratiating way.

"Impossible," grunted Mr. Sour-face.

"I'll be cloistered in a Zen monastery, you see. I won't be allowed correspondence of any kind for at least three months."

"Sit down," replied Mr. Sour-face as he thumbed angrily through our paperwork and passports.

We sat. He paced, smoked. Paced and smoked. Where, I wondered, was that Japanese politeness I had grown so used to? After a full hour had passed, he appeared to be taking a renewed interest in our documents.

"Franz-san! Come!" We stood and approached the counter again. "It says here you're asking for 'dependent' status—but you won't be living together for a year or more?"

"That's right," said Koun. "I'll be at the monastery. In Shikoku."

"Well, will she be sending you money?"

"No. That won't be necessary. The monks engage in formal begging and the local farmers donate vegetables sometimes."

Long silence. "Well, you both need to think carefully about what 'dependent' means. You may sign the papers now, but I can't guarantee anything."

We were dismissed curtly, again without the usual Japanese politeness.

Today, Takahashi-sensei, the head of the English Department, calls Immigration on my behalf and then tells me gravely that I'll need to write up a statement explaining

(1) What *Exactly* Koun Is Doing, and
(2) Why He Is Doing It

This, I already know, is no easy task. After all, we haven't yet been able to explain it adequately to anyone, not even to our friends and family who tend (usually, at least) to be sympathetic listeners. How then to present it to bureaucrats in all its official glory? I spend something like three hours at my desk writing up possibilities before finally settling on this statement:

(1) Learning the values, traditions, and lineage of Zen Buddhism as set forth by Soto monasteries/temples throughout Japan

(2) In order to obtain the necessary licensure and training to become a full priest in the Soto Zen tradition so that he, Koun Garrett Franz, may one day be of service to the Japanese/Buddhist community at large (on the advisement of his master, Reverend Honda Kosoku of Ganzoji of Takamori, Aso)

What I want to write:

(1) Saving all beings (infinite), ending all delusions (inexhaustible), realizing truth (incomprehensible), following the path of Buddha (unsurpassable)

(2) No special reason

Or:

(1) Seeking enlightenment

(2) To obtain enlightenment

Or better still:

(1) *Shugyo*

(2) I don't know

Tuesday, March 2

Just before 8 p.m. nearly every Tuesday, I drive the ten

minutes to my pottery teacher's house and leave my car in an adjacent grocery store parking lot. I have never seen the inside of her home, save for the receiving room that I always enter through the open-air garage stacked high with fat bags of clay, walking past the enclosed workroom and adjacent kilns and then sliding open the glass door to a cozy tatami room walled with shelves and cupboards. Each shelf displays pottery—*yaki-mono*, literally "fired things."

Tonight, the pottery ladies are in good form, the four of them deep in conversation as I slip off my shoes and bow into the room. In many ways, we are typical of the women who make up such groups around the traditional Japanese arts: my teacher, Nishida-sensei, in her mid-fifties, a housewife and at-home pottery teacher with three artistic daughters; Baba-san, in her sixties, a well-traveled housewife with a salaryman son; Megumi-san, a newly married city hall office worker in her early thirties; Yoko-san, in her seventies, a housewife and an avid student of English with one daughter and two grand-children; and me, the token foreigner, married, thirty years old, childless (a point frequently noted by all in the room), and harboring a vague desire to dive into something "authentically Japanese."

We greet each other as Sensei sets a cup of green tea and an assortment of delicate rice crackers at my place on the *kotatsu*, the low heated table under which we collectively tuck our chilled legs and hands. Thoughtfully, Sensei slows her speech and simplifies her vocabulary and dialect so I can participate in conversation.

"*Koun-san mo otera ni iru?*" (Is Koun already in the temple?)

"*Hai, so desu.*" (Yes.)

"*Aa, so. Taihen ne. . . Bangohan mo tabeta?*" (Ah, that's rough. . . Have you already eaten dinner?)

"*Ee.*" (Yes.)

"*Nani o tabeta?*" (What did you eat?)

"*Chili o tabemashita.*" (I ate chili.)

"What?!" asks Yoko-san loudly in English. "*Chiri?* You ate dust?"

"No—ah—it's Mexican food, kind of like a soup. Beans,

tomatoes, taco spices. Usually it has ground beef, but I'm basically a vegetarian so I leave that out."

"*Tako?* It has octopus?"

"*Tako-SU,*" corrects Sensei—indicating the popular Mexican dish as opposed to the Japanese word for the eight-armed sea creature. She continues, "*Hitori de tabeta?*" (Did you eat alone?)

"*Hai.*" (Yes.)

"*Aa, sabishii, nee.*" (Ah, that's lonely. . . .)

The conversation lulls and we sip our tea, contemplating the gravity of my new situation: alone in an empty kitchen, eating dust-and-octopus soup.

"Well, I for one am grateful when my husband is gone," says Baba-san in a burst of local dialect. Giggles in agreement all around. "But the young couples these days, maybe it's different for them. . . ."

Yoko-san nudges my side and cocks her head, that common Japanese gesture indicating an attempt to understand. "*Nani? Tako-SU??*"

The two ladies across from me begin to laugh again into their now-empty cups, but Sensei cuts them off abruptly: "*Jaa, hajimemashoka?*" (Shall we begin?)

Sensei stands, paces decisively across the room to slide open the door, and beckons us all out onto the covered patio that shelters her kilns and shelves of pots awaiting glaze. She points me toward the tiny workroom that is, thankfully, warm because of the one portable kerosene heater set in a corner nearest my stool. A boiling kettle of water sits atop the heater, giving off steam. On my electric pottery wheel, a lump of freshly kneaded gray clay has already been set out for me, a gift that always makes me feel more than a little incompetent. As I wait for the others, I tie my hair back and lean into the warmth of the heater, watching the labor of the women through the sliding glass door. The four of them stand around an old wooden table and cut thick slices of gray and brown clay from fat blocks, which they then quickly and powerfully knead into shape before entering the room one by one, squeezing around and over buckets of water, tables, tool boxes, works in progress, and the five big pottery wheels. Once settled in, it's amazing we're ever able to extract ourselves. "Like sardines," giggles Baba-san, getting in one last joke before the work begins.

I take in a long breath and then exhale as I lay my hands across the gray lump before me. Despite the warmth of the room, the clay is still cool—a surprise. I lift it and throw it down with a loud slam onto the approximate center of the wheel, adhering it to the metal. I flick on the power, dip my hands in the water bucket, and then run my wet fingers over the surface of the mound while pushing cautiously on the pedal with my right foot. The clay spins and wobbles with possibility. After nearly six months of lessons with Nishida-sensei, I still have only rare glimpses of that felt-sense of creating something purposefully. What, I wonder, will I accidentally make today?

Bracing my elbows against my thighs, I begin to work—first applying firm pressure to the sides of the clay, then coaxing it in and up into a tall, slender cylinder, then forcing it all back down again with one hand pushing against the top and the other cupping the back. Repeating this several times will center the clay and, I am told, remove the potential for faults and air bubbles when the form is heated in the kiln. I finish this process with a squat cylinder, pause to wet my fingers again, and—taking in a quick breath—push both thumbs firmly into the center and out as the wheel spins too fast, then too slow. The fingertips of one hand begin to trace inside the vessel, and the fingertips of the other hand are on the outside, working in tandem to thin and lift. In this way, the beginning of a bowl appears, but my hands-the-clay-my-hands-the-clay seem unyielding and awkward. I pause again, the wheel coming to a full stop as I consider the tools on the table and then select and soak a two-by-two-inch square of chamois in water. My foot pushes down gently on the pedal, and I press the sodden cloth against the interior of the form. Mud spits across my fleece vest, up along my arms to the elbows. I push away a bit of flyaway hair in frustration and streak gray sludge across my forehead. My bowl is a damp, lopsided mess.

When she sees what I've done, Sensei nudges me off my stool and takes my place. She pushes down hard on the foot pedal and inserts a sponge into the center of spinning clay. The excess water disappears, and then she balances and shapes the bowl— all of this in under thirty seconds. I try to track her hands with my eyes, to break it down into plausible steps—press and then pull and then lift and then—but I can't follow her fast, sure fingers. First, a twisted, ugly lump. Then—perfection.

She cuts the bowl off the hump with one quick slice of a string held taut, and then she makes another identical bowl while I watch, still unable to comprehend. Finally, she centers the mass that is left, drawing it up into a balanced cone. We switch places. I try once more, but my next attempt folds in on itself, a victim of the weight of water.

Wednesday, March 3

I'm eating my lunch alone in the kitchen when a crushed box from Thailand arrives three days too late. Inside are bargain-rate monk's clothes—casual *samu-e* for work, flowing formal robes, traditional undergarments. Each item must be carefully refolded into a new box before I can send it on to Koun tomorrow.

These few new belongings will supplement all that he carried on his back and in his hands to the monastery:

okesa (quilted toga-like vestment)
kasa (bamboo hat used for anonymity when begging for alms)
kyahan (white shin guards used for begging)
teko (hand and forearm guards also used for begging)
waraji (straw rope sandals)
zafu (cushion for seated meditation)
Shobogenzo (a book of teachings by Dogen, the founder of Soto Zen)
ketchimyaku (lineage chart tracing back to the original Buddha)
ryutenjiku (scroll for protection of the lineage)
oryoki (lacquered, nested bowls)

one pair of underwear (to be worn after the bath marking
the end of the stay in *tanga-ryo*)
razor (to be used after the end of the stay in *tanga-ryo*)
toothbrush and toothpaste (to be used daily)
small white towel (for bathing or protecting the head
from the sun while working)
bessu (white, woven socks with fasteners; to be used on
special occasions)
U.S. passport
10,000 yen (approximately 100 dollars for funeral money
in case of the monk's death, so disposing of the body
won't be too much trouble)

In addition to all of this gear is what Koun wore when he
left home—the standard semi-formal monk's costume, the layers of which reflect the movement of Buddhism across Asia:

on top, the *rakusu*, a much smaller version of the *okesa*
(origin: India)
beneath that, the wing-sleeved, flowing robes of the
jikitotsu (origin: China)
beneath that, the more form-fitting *kimono* and *jiban*
(origin: Japan)

And thus, at any given moment, an American Zen monk
undressing and dressing in a cold room pays homage to his
lineage.

Thursday, March 4

While I wait for my number to be called at the post office,
one of the women sitting next to me leans in close and tells a
story as a way of practicing her English:

"When I was child, my mother opened all window and door
of our house. It is for spring cleaning. She told me pick up everything off a tatami and put outside. So I do it—even little brown
songbird in cage. It sing so happy always, even when I put in

driveway next to *kotatsu* and book and other stuffs. All day long we listen to happy song of bird and cleaned while the sun is moving across sky. A beautiful spring day. After a while, I remember so quiet and peaceful. No more singing. When I pick up stuffs and bring back inside, I saw snake had got inside cage and eating songbird. The green body of snake too fat for going outside the cage. After that we had pet snake. I very sorry for songbird."

Some time later, I sit in my office at work, puzzling over my courses for the new school year: Writing, Culture, Debate, Conversation, others. Each topic too big, too weighty to cram into two neat little semesters and once-a-week meetings. Plus I keep thinking about the songbird. Is this a tragedy or a tale of transformation? Is it nothing more than a testament to that Japanese preoccupation with the turning of the seasons? Can any one theme be neatly separated from another? And also: Why is this the third time I have heard this story, always from a different person?

As if in answer, an explosion of sound erupts from the hallway outside my door: laughter, scuffling, a metallic clanging. Stepping out of my office, I see that the doors lining the hallway are open wide and the teachers are cleaning with near-violence. Arau-sensei, the French teacher who wears a fashionable streak of purple in her short black-and-gray hair, passes by with a broom in hand, greeting me respectively in French, Japanese, and English. And then in Japanese, she says, "You know what they say—clean for spring, and it will snow!"

To test her theory, I set aside my syllabi, slide open the windows to chill air, and seek out the necessary equipment from the hall closet. How long has it been since I've really looked at the state of my office? Stacks of books, student papers, drafts of things unfinished. Dust, cobwebs. Brittle brown leaves beneath my overgrown plants. The carcasses of small, blue-winged insects.

By the time I return home, I can't stop cleaning, so I start in on the house. By 2 or 3 a.m., when I finally slip into bed with a dull and righteous ache in the body, I see snow falling behind my eyes and hear nothing. A few hours later, it is dawn and a bird begins to sing.

Saturday, March 6

I am walking down the hill from my home in the early morning to catch the bus into town for my first language lesson since winter break, a 5-foot-3-inch pale, sleepy foreigner bundled thickly in sweaters and scarf, hat, and mittens. A group of farmers—each half a head or more shorter than I—greet me with wide-open grins and *"Ohayo gozaimasu!"* There are three men and four women, all of them surely well into their seventies or older. Their skin is deep brown and wrinkled and they carry their tools across their arched backs and fallen shoulders, the women in wide-brimmed straw hats and mismatched flower prints layered against the chill, the men in baseball caps and old blue and brown *samu-e* and quilted vests. They wear rubber boots that pat out a slow rhythm as they work their way up the narrow street to the vegetable and rice plots tucked around the university grounds.

I wish I could chat with them, but their dialect is too far removed from the clean, polite Tokyo Japanese I am learning. I grin and nod and they grin and nod every Saturday morning, and this small offering of human connection is enough to make me profoundly joyful for the ten minutes or so it takes for the bus to come. And when it does come today, I take my ticket and choose a seat next to the window so I can try to name the objects I spot as quickly as they pass beyond the glass: *ki* (tree), *kumo* (cloud), *otera* (temple). But the language is too fast for me, and it slips by before I can ever hope to capture it.

I remember, some years ago, walking the streets of Kumamoto City on the night of a lunar eclipse, the women coming out of their apartments and teaching me the word for "moon." This was when I was new to Japan, when I had almost no words to call my own. And me wanting to say the new word, *tsuki*, afterward so often because it was the one fragment of language I felt I had earned. It was authentic. Now, some words are eclipsing others in my speech and thinking and even in my dreams, what the linguists call "interlanguage."

When I enter the YMCA this morning, my teacher from the previous semester asks about Koun, and I tell her: "Yes, my *otto* is now in *otera*. *Chotto sabishii*, but I have my *yakimono* lessons, my *shigoto*. Time will pass *hayaku*, *hayaku*. I only hope he is not too *samui*, that he is not too hungry. *Shinpai*, yes. . . But probably *daijobu desu ne*."

Monday, March 8

This evening, Stephen, owner of a local language school and my first boss in Japan, picks me up and we drive together to the Tatsuda Center to engage in seated meditation with our unlikely sangha: Kyoko, office worker and avid student of Japanese tea ceremony; Richard, English professor, musician, haiku expert, and one-time member of the ceremonial guard of the Tibetan teacher Chogyam Trungpa; Sakamoto-san, bank clerk and freakishly acrobatic yoga practitioner (this once demonstrated to us all when he twisted himself into a series of impossible shapes as a way to stretch after zazen); and whoever else finds their way to our little weekly zazenkai. Six months or so ago, we chose the Center because it is near enough to all of us that we can more or less manage to get there by 8 p.m. on Monday evenings, and also because it has proven surprisingly difficult to find a temple nearby that offers zazen regularly.

"Hopefully we'll get a good crowd tonight," Stephen says as we drive. His ever-present cowboy hat rests between us and he wears the requisite well-worn jeans. That long hair and beard of a 70's-era hippie. For as long as I have known him, he has looked like a man out of time. "Has Koun finished with *tanga-ryo* yet?" he asks.

"Yes—that is, if all has gone well." He should officially be *unsui* now—"clouds and water," the designation given novice monks. He is expected to be supple enough to flow.

The parking lot is full when we arrive, and we know the zazen will be interesting. Already commuter trains pass within fifty feet of the building at precisely 8:27 and 8:48 p.m., vibrating its thin walls during our sessions. I remember the terrible jolt of it the first few times we sat together here, the rush of flight-or-fight adrenaline yanking me from my meditative aim.

There was an instinctual sense of indignation: *How dare this beast of a train intrude!* But later, an appreciation of sorts arose, and I embraced that common advice: Do not resent the world moving around one as bothersome distraction; it is simply that which arises naturally, like the internal noise of thought, of memory, of narrative. *Acknowledge it and let it go.*

Sometimes we are given opportunities to practice this concept in unexpected ways. The ever-changing night guard occasionally flicks on the room's lights with the exterior switch, thinking perhaps that we're unaware of their availability. One of us will get up quietly, slide open the fusuma, and turn them off again. And more recently, some well-meaning soul has acquired the habit of passing by our room and, thinking no one inside, switching off the heat we have paid for with 100-yen coins.

Tonight we slip off our shoes and enter the eight-mat tatami room while the jovial laughter of drunken partygoers one room over vibrates the paper fusuma that separates us. Across the hall, a karate lesson is in full swing, each fierce *kiai* shout echoing around us. I cover the low table with a cloth and light two candles, then set out the bell and ringer and travel clock. It's our first night without Koun, and though I'm to take his place as bell-ringer, I can't remember how many times to strike it. I settle on three slow taps to begin, one to signal *kinhin* (walking meditation), three to start zazen again, one to finish.

The neighboring party ends abruptly while we are still sitting, and the fusuma dividing our rooms slides open to the width of a doorway. We hear something about "cleaning up" and the partygoers begin stumbling through the gap with their cushions and folded-up tables. And then there is an audible sucking in of breath as they realize that the darkness is filled with silent, unmoving people. The rapid-fire *"Sumimasen! Sumimasen!"* begins as they back out, followed by apparent confusion when we don't answer. This happens four more times before I hear one partygoer explaining loudly to the others that there appears to be a group of mostly foreign people doing zazen in the adjacent room.

"Bikkuri shimashita!" (It surprised me!), says one woman, giggling loudly.

The train roars past, letting us know that we've got twelve minutes to go.

Tuesday, March 9

In pottery class, two semi-dry bowls from last week sit beneath a damp cloth, waiting to be trimmed and smoothed into the shape that will be fired and made solid in the kiln. I settle into my seat and unveil the first. Sensei gestures at the hard metal wheel, reminding me to spill a few droplets of water over it and lay down a circle of protective green rubber—this will serve as cushioning for the delicate top edge of the bowls. I follow her instructions and then lift the first bowl with two hands, turn it upside down, and lower it onto the green rubber. The first challenge is to center the bowl on the wheel—no easy feat, but it is necessary for trimming the walls to equal thickness. I switch on the power and press my foot cautiously against the pedal. Running a fingertip along one side of the clay as it wobbles and spins, I squint and try to gauge where contact is lost. Again and again, I quickly stop the wheel and ease the bowl into the place where I sensed the gap. But my perception is skewed by the wheel's spin and by my slow reflexes. This process always takes me too long.

Nishida-sensei sighs, reaches across the table, and slaps the hard clay twice as it whirls, sending it into position. The wobble from before is gone.

I stop the wheel and look at her in disbelief. *"Arigato."*

Sensei waves away my thanks, and I begin to affix fresh bits of rolled clay along the edges of the bowl to keep it in place when I begin to cut away the excess with a potter's trimming tool—a loop of sharpened iron embedded in a slender length of wood.

I feel Sensei's disapproving eyes on me as I work. "Cut more!" she says. "More, more, more, more!" Against the instinct of caution, I carve away thick swaths. When I finally lift the bowl off the wheel it is light enough. Sensei plucks it from my fingers, satisfied.

With the second bowl I am not so lucky. Again, I am brave

in my cutting but fail, in the last moment, by slicing clean through the bottom. I spend a good portion of the rest of the class making repairs with wet new clay—a knotted scar against smooth curves.

I finish with a little time to spare and Sensei, perhaps feeling sorry for me, gives me a brush and some off-white slip to apply as decoration. I try for the beautiful *wabi-sabi* "elegant imperfection" of Japanese design, and instead create something that looks as if it has been spit upon.

"*Eh??*" says Sensei. "Did you do that on purpose?"

Wednesday, March 10

At last, it is beginning to smell like spring outside—earthy and organic. I open the screen doors and windows of the townhouse to take in the scent, and from the field beyond the line of trees out back come the joyously amplified sounds of a chorus of singing chipmunks. It is the annual kindergarten *happyokai* performance practice. In the gaps between leaves, I can just make out little bodies in coordinated primary colors being led in a series of dance steps the children have been perfecting for months—their faces, if I could see them, no doubt restrained in this rare moment of deep concentration.

In some ways it will be like this for the *unsui* in the monastery: awkward at first, each movement scripted, contrived. Eventually, the body will learn the motion, will become the motion so effortlessly that actor and action cease to be separate, a living dance from waking until sleep. And the many monks becoming, in essence, a single body in motion.

I can almost hear Koun now: "All of this formality. I want to be a *samu-e* and *rakusu* monk, not a *jikitotsu* and *kesa* monk. Bowing at the right time is not the point. Zazen is the point."

What kind of monk would I be? Formal? Casual? Would I embrace both versions of self—or neither?

Sunday, March 14

Sunday morning in Japan is early Saturday evening in Alaska, the previous day. A phone call, then, is a kind of travel through both space and time. I am thinking this while swiveling in my chair in my tiny bedroom-cum-office, trying to find a way into writing, when my mother calls, happy because she has had an epiphany about painting: "I just stopped worrying and started painting. I stopped being so attached to it coming out right."

She describes her still life: a small orange pumpkin, a potted ivy, two cloth-bound mystery books from her childhood, a glass block from a thrift shop in Anchorage, and an old bronze Buddha that used to sit on top of her Baptist mother's bookshelf and then, later, the family TV set. Behind this unlikely altar and to the side, the blue-tinged palette of winter in Alaska captured within big picture windows, the sky meeting the mountains and ocean as if all were frozen together into one great sheet of ice. (And, yes, my mother there, too—with features that are mine but also not mine—looking out over it all.) I am seeing/feeling this spacious landscape, even though I am also seeing/feeling a not-yet-put-away Japanese futon on a woven straw floor, delicate paper walls, the yellow palette of a wintry Japan outside, the condensed scale of rooms and houses and people and rice paddies and stores in the neighborhood around me.

While we talk, a huge blue-black crow swoops past my window screaming, *"Kaugh-kaugh! Kaugh-kaugh!"* Both my mother and I suck in our breath at the same time.

"My God," says my mother, "was that a bird?"

Thursday, March 18

This evening, I meet up at a restaurant with Jennifer, my Canadian coworker (who also happens to be my neighbor and the only other non-Japanese at the university), and two of the Shokei office ladies, Yuki and Tomomi, for a private going-away party. The two young Shokei graduates have greatly helped us in navigating our daily struggles at the school and beyond. Unfortunately, their three-year term is nearly finished, and they will have to take on new jobs elsewhere. This is the typical cycle for many workers in Japan.

"So," says Jennifer, after we have taken the customary photographs of the food on our table, "tell us all the stuff you couldn't tell us before but can now that you're leaving."

What follows is a rundown of various curious characters on campus. Neither I nor Jennifer is sure who is who, but what we do learn is this:

(1) At least one teacher and one staff member can't keep their mouths shut if you tell them something—anything (sometimes handy, sometimes not).

(2) Someone in the library will gleefully slice your car's tires if your vehicle registration has not been properly put on file in the office.

(3) Fifteen years or so ago, a then-young teacher married one of his students, and nobody talks about it openly even though everybody still holds it in the back of their minds as being a noteworthy scandal.

(4) One of the men in the office has a problem keeping his hands to himself but nobody can do much about it, because that's just how things are.

We also learn that

(1) Everybody hates the teacher we most like.

(2) Everybody adores the teacher who we think is kind of odd.

Sunday, March 21

I spend most of today driving around to various stores with Satomi, my long-time friend (and current Japanese teacher at the YMCA). As we drive, Satomi tells me that one of her British friends with whom she roomed in graduate school in England

and, later, Australia, came upon some cheap tickets at the last minute and plans to tour Japan over the next couple of weeks.

"She'll stay with me for a few days. But what should I show her? She says she's up for anything."

"It's such a shame that all of the usual places are so clichéd," I lament. What would capture the "real" Japan for a visitor? What captures it for me?

"I suppose she can clean house with me—in a real Japanese home with a real Japanese person," suggests Satomi. We laugh at the impossibility of this rudeness.

"Well, if you really want to show her something wild, take her shopping."

"Right!" says Satomi as we pull into the parking lot of one of the city's ubiquitous *denki* stores, which sell all manner of electronic goods.

My dear friend, a seasoned traveler with an uncanny mind for detail, knows what will appear surprising to those who are not from Japan. I have become a huge fan of our anthropological shopping excursions—after all, much of what we find, to me, resembles exhibits in a museum of a misaligned parallel universe. I am not the target of the products or the marketing, and so I rarely want to buy, but I am always fascinated.

Today, after a few hours of examining Hello Kitty–branded microwave/toaster ovens, dubious electronic facial dewrinklers, magical "diet" machines that shake the ankles back and forth vigorously while one lies prone and watches TV, and cell phones that appear to do everything, we arrive at the full-body massage chairs. These are lined up—no fewer than fifteen glorious models in all; each one is priced well over the value of my car. Nearly all of the chairs are full of weary shoppers, and the salespeople no longer bother to come over to this section to peddle their wares. This island of uninterrupted relaxation is a standard perk of visiting *denki* stores in Japan. I select a black leather model that boasts soothing stereo surround-sound *shaku-hachi* flute music and calf-muscle mashers, while Satomi moves on to check out the computer department. An hour later, with a fat envelope of informational fliers in her hands, Satomi wakes me from a deep and blissful nap.

On the way back home, Satomi tells me—in her ever-fluctuating British/Australian/American/Japanese accent—that her mother warned her before she left this morning: "You know, I've been hearing bad news about computers on the radio lately, so you be careful. You can even catch viruses from those things these days."

"What?! Doesn't your mother have one of those fancy cell phones that basically does dishes?"

"Sure, but that's just my mum."

Friday, March 26

In the late evening, I drive Satomi to the airport to pick up her friend, Claudine, who is surprisingly difficult to spot in the rush of airline passengers as they emerge from the gate. Finally, Satomi rushes toward a smartly dressed petite woman with shiny dark hair. *Chameleon*, I think. Definitely a foreigner, but you have to look twice to see it.

We stop by a *kaitenzushi* restaurant on the way back from the airport, and Satomi and I marvel at Claudine's unique ability to try absolutely anything that glides past us on the conveyor belt circling the interior of the restaurant. Glistening salmon roe that remind me too much of the jars of fish bait from my Alaskan childhood. Tiny raw octopi bearing an uncanny resemblance to severed, boiled, and peeled baby hands. Sushi of every kind. And when we remark on her bravery: "Oh, you know, 'When in Rome . . .'" One hour into her stay in Japan, and this woman is seemingly more at ease with local culture than I'll ever be.

"How odd," says Claudine as we zip through the dark and narrow streets to Satomi's place. "Except for the restaurant, I haven't seen much of anything in the light yet. It still feels as if I'm home."

Saturday, March 27

The much-awaited cherry blossoms are starting to reveal themselves—some trees earlier than others—and new life is springing up in the crevasses of that winter-yellow palette. Claudine has timed her trip brilliantly.

The three of us decide to begin our grand tour of the city with a visit to Kumamoto Castle, a towering, solemn structure overlooking downtown. As we enter the grounds, a woman in a flower-patterned kimono approaches us. "Try? Try?" She gestures toward a makeshift stage of portable tatami and red felt beneath new blossoms. Rows of fold-up chairs are set up off to one side for the meta-view. Bright, gaudy signage hangs from posts, advertising a tea ceremony demonstration in awkward English: "Please enjoy your happiness life with heart! We'll do my best!" Another woman in kimono beckons us to join her on the stage, while a third heats water on a low portable burner. I am determined to pass by the display, ignoring the gentle English invitations, but Claudine stops us. "Come on, let's do it!" The enthusiasm of a good guest—or simply of a curious mind. Maybe, in my more jaded moments as a foreigner living in Japan, I would do well to return to this state.

Claudine and I remove our shoes and arrange ourselves on the red felt as Satomi slips into one of the folding chairs nearby. A trio of Japanese boys, likely university students, settle into the remaining spaces next to us. All of us sit with our legs folded beneath our bodies and our backs straight. "This is *seiza*," I whisper to Claudine. "It's the formal posture. Foreigners and young Japanese struggle to stay in it for long. You can tuck your legs off to the side if it starts to get unbearable."

"So it's a contest, then?"

"That's right. An unspoken contest."

The women in kimono take their places, and we are instructed in how to accept and offer tea and sweets—a formal ceremony of guest and host. Nearly everything is done deliberately, with two hands. The women move in their prescribed motions—the *kata*—of tea, and despite my initial reluctance I am transported to the few times I have done this with Koun, how it moved me then as it does now. In this moment I see that it has always been the taking of the tea that I love most: bow low to accept what is offered, lift the ceramic tea bowl, observe the design by slowly turning it in the hands three times, drink, reverse the turns, set it back down. A complete experience of an object.

Thirty minutes later, when this abbreviated ceremony has come to a close, none of the guests on the red carpet can stand. The boys next to us laugh and massage their legs while Claudine and I struggle to put on our shoes.

"Does this mean that we all won—or lost?"

"Both," I say.

As the boys lean against each other, still laughing, and move off, a reporter approaches Claudine and me, and I translate the usual questions:

"Where are you two from?"

"How old are you?"

"How was your experience of Japanese culture?"

This all strikes me as amusing and a little sad. How many years do I have to live in this town to not be counted a tourist? The answer, of course, is that I am a tourist by birth—it's in the blood. We smile as he takes our photograph and then we find Satomi and move on to the castle itself, climb those dark stairs, contemplate the relics of ancient Japan behind the walls of glass on each floor: swords, samurai armor, scrolls, *shodo* writing implements, *bento* boxes of the better classes. At last, at the top, a panoramic view of the city and welcome gusts of fresh air.

"There!" announces Satomi. "Our next destination —Suizenji."

Off in the distance I can just make out the district where I lived when I arrived in 1999, during my first stay in Japan. Tucked between billboard advertisements and towering hotels is one of the "top three famous gardens in Japan," a replica in miniature of significant landscape features between the old capital, Kyoto, and the new, Tokyo. I explored the garden and the streets surrounding it for two years, and it is often in my thoughts as the scene of one of many life-changing moments for me: walking alone at 3 a.m., peering into a stream of overfed koi outside the gates of that famous garden, bawling like a two-year-old as I tried very hard to purge all my childhood misery. But from here, the area looks unfamiliar, impersonal.

"Cities all seem to look the same from above," remarks Claudine, as we turn from the view and begin the slow climb down the castle stairs.

Sunday, March 28

Satomi, Claudine, and I zoom along the highway in my little blue K-van. Our destination today is Aso, both an active volcano and the world's largest caldera. Nestled in the massive geographic bowl are a number of tiny villages, including Takamori, the town where Koun first met his teacher.

"He was placed there as an English-language instructor," I explain to Claudine, who wants to know how an American winds up as an ordained Zen monk in a Japanese monastery. "He knew he wanted to do traditional meditation, but he had no clue where to go. One morning he just got on his bike as soon as he heard the 6 a.m. bells and followed the direction of the sound. Luckily, it led him to the local Zen temple. Of course, they didn't expect him to come more than once or twice. You know, 'tourist Zen.' The priest made a big effort to create a ceremonial atmosphere, and his wife treated him like an honored guest, serving him tea and fancy meals on heirloom lacquerware. But after the first week, they stopped the formality and handed him a broom. For two years, he did zazen, cleaned the grounds, then had breakfast with everyone at the kitchen table, like one of the family."

Today the Hondas, Koun's other family, are out attending to a funeral, so we bypass Takamori and cut straight up the mountain to see the mouth of the volcano. When we reach the top, it is windy and cold and the various peddlers struggle to secure their hand-drawn signs and makeshift display tables. The three of us take hasty pictures in front of the steaming cauldron of noxious liquid and Satomi and Claudine race back to sit again in the shelter of the car, while I buy a bag of powdered sulphur.

Some years ago, one of the men there talked me into buying a bag of the stinky stuff to ward off large insects, and now it is a yearly ritual. Soon, I'll begin drawing a nightly circle around my futon against *mukade*, the giant poisonous centipedes that begin to emerge from the nooks and crannies of our aging town-house in spring. I don't know if it really works, but I haven't yet seen anything cross that yellow line.

On the way back to town, Satomi nods off in the back seat while Claudine continues to take in the passing landscape. As the blur of rice fields, trees, and mountains begins to give way to the concrete of the city once again, she asks, "Do you feel lonely? Living here in such a different culture and your husband away for a full year. . . ."

"Oh yes. Definitely. There is that constant and pervasive loneliness of being foreign, of being out of context. And then there is this new loneliness of missing him. There's a rawness there, a shock to the system. But it's only been a month. How will I feel, exactly, in six months? Or eleven? I just don't know. I do wonder how we'll have changed in that time."

"Or if he will change and you won't?"

"Yes, that's the fear, isn't it? Or worse—that he won't change at all. Twelve months apart for nothing."

Monday, March 29

Satomi and Claudine are on their own for the next few days. I find myself creating itineraries in my head and envying the adventures I have already had, that they will have.

At work, the Shokei office ladies Yuki and Tomomi give me going-away presents, bowing deeply and thanking me for help-ing them during our time together as coworkers—a standard custom for those leaving a work position in a Japanese insti-tution. In my office, I open the delicately wrapped packages, expecting the usual fare of *senbei* (Japanese rice crackers), *nori* (dried and salted sheets of seaweed), or some other local edible. Instead, a child's Minnie Mouse juice cup and a heart-shaped picture frame studded with pink sparkling glass beads. It's what they imagined I would like, this gaudy Americana. Such kindness. I will miss them very much.

Wednesday, March 31

Early this morning I drive Satomi and Claudine to Kumamoto City Train Station. Claudine's next stop is Kyoto. The three of us drink bad five-hundred-yen coffee while Satomi and I neurotically give Claudine rapid-fire instructions about how best to survive in this exotic Eastern land (Satomi, too, writing out detailed sentences in both Roman letters and Japanese script on page after page of notebook paper).

"I think I'll figure it out—don't worry," says Claudine, beaming at both of us. Clearly we are far more concerned about her travel plans than she is.

I offer my best advice, the thing that has gotten me around Japan many times, despite my faltering language skills: "Ask young people for help in simple English—they'll have studied it in school. Look very distressed. Say 'please' and 'thank you' a lot. Cry if necessary."

Satomi digs through her handbag and produces two envelopes, which she then hands to each of us. "I almost forgot." Inside, a copy of a newspaper article as memento: a black-and-white shot of Claudine and me kneeling beneath gray blossoms, sipping out of delicate gray cups. The Japanese on either side of us have been neatly cropped away. The caption reads, "Tourists experiencing tea ceremony at Kumamoto Castle."

"Typical," I sigh.

"It's perfect," says Claudine, and of course she is right.

When it is time for her to catch the train that will carry her away to other adventures, Satomi and I are not ready to let her go. We continue to wave frantically from behind the ticket stalls, even though we can no longer see her in the throng of dark-suited travelers moving in and out of trains. She has blended into landscape.

At last, we let our hands drop, and we turn toward the station exit. Satomi sighs. "Isn't it sad when your guests leave? They seem to have a wonderful destination ahead of them, but you are just here, as always, left behind and waiting for something."

~

After I drop off Satomi, I stand in the solitude of my kitchen seeing and not seeing as I pour tea into a cup that is overflowing. And when I do notice, finally, the puddle that is making its slow way across the table, all I can think about is the sound of Koun weeping in the shower downstairs on the afternoon of his leaving, how I cried because he was crying, how both of us composed ourselves, for the sake of the other, before that long drive to the sea.

APRIL

Unsui (Clouds and Water)

Thursday, April 1

"I feel like I'm going crazy. God, I *AM* going crazy. What's wrong with me?"

"Close your eyes."

"What?"

"Just—close your eyes."

"Okay."

"Now, imagine walking down a path in the woods. Can you see it?"

"No, there's nothing."

"Nothing?"

"Wait—yes. I can see it."

"Okay. Notice the details of the path, what it looks like, and also everything around you."

"Okay, I can see all of it now."

"Good. Now, you come upon some kind of vessel, a container—it's there on the path. Can you see it?"

"Yes—yes, I see it."

"Good. Describe the vessel and its contents."

"A rough earthenware bowl. Dark brown, mottled—imperfect. It fits comfortably in the palms of my hands, the weight of a stone. Inside, there's cold, clear water and . . . nothing else."

"All right, that is your ideal understanding of love."

~

This morning at 6:30 a.m. I am sitting zazen alone in a cool room with a sky-blue blanket wrapped around my shoulders and the cherry blossoms out back in full bloom and my husband only a month into his year at the monastery. Bits of conversation and images come up from somewhere in my mind, and I'm following them, feeling them viscerally, and thus not really sitting zazen at all but instead daydreaming—but with the appearance of an ancient religious practice. I am seeing a five-years-ago Koun, when he was just Garrett, my closest friend in graduate school, telling me a riddle there in his living room and me curled up on the couch, nursing a confused and volatile emotion that I never knew I had in me. I was angry at my ex-husband, at past friends and lovers, at those who contributed to a flawed childhood, at myself. I was terrified that I'd somehow married a younger version of one of my stepfathers—or a composite of all three of them—and that this was in fact a pattern with me, my only way to understand love, and that I would do it again and again until it destroyed me.

Sometime after that conversation, over coffee and pie at the dive diner in Spokane where we always met to discuss our writing—or What Comes Next—Garrett revealed that he had decided to move to Japan to study Zen. "I'll work as an English teacher until I can figure out how to enter a monastery."

I had been bracing myself for this for some time, this ending. It was not a surprise. "All right," I'd said, "but can I shave your head before you leave?"

"Yes, but not all the way to the skin—I'll do that when I'm ordained."

Late afternoon the following day, I showed up at Garrett's apartment, ready to cut away the trappings of desire and material life. I remember him kneeling on 70's-era kitchen linoleum, the sunlight coming in striped through the slats of half-opened blinds, and the feeble growl of clippers. Bits of fuzz floated up around us as my body bent over his, left hand pressing against scalp, right hand arcing through dark strands, forming one narrow path after another until all was revealed. Afterward, he swept up the hair while I let myself out.

Friday, April 2

The rain comes in soft sprinkles at first and then in fat, heavy drops that shred the newly opened cherry blossoms behind my townhouse in a few brief minutes. From my windows I watch the pink quiver and give way under the water's violence, revealing green-budded branches. Tomorrow will see gutters filled with bruised blossoms and children in the streets throwing handfuls of pink into blue sky.

The ladies in my pottery class have scheduled their annual *hanami* (flower-viewing party) for late this afternoon, and I've arranged to leave early from work to join them. But Nishida-sensei calls after the rain does its worst and says we'll have our meal at a restaurant instead of outdoors.

Yoko-san arrives just before noon to collect me in her massive white luxury sedan. Her current English teacher from one of the chain language schools, a tall American in his mid-twenties, sits in the seat beside her. He turns with a wide grin and thrusts his hand toward me as soon as I settle into the backseat.

"Dave," he says, "Japanesedriversarefuckin'awfularen'tthey." And then when he sees the look on my face: "Don't worry—if you talk fast she won't have a clue what you're saying."

"What?" blurts Yoko-san.

"The cherry blossoms," says Dave, now enunciating slowly and clearly, "they're really something." He looks back at me again and winks.

"*Neeeee,*" says Yoko-san, "so beautiful. It's heart of Japan."

Inside the restaurant, we tuck our shoes into cubbies and pad along the hallway in slippers to the formal tatami room the ladies have reserved for this event. Yoko-san insists that Dave and I sit together in the "seats of honor"—two opposite cushions at the farthest end of the long table, next to the alcove that holds the seasonal scroll and sprigs of fresh blossoms. Unfortunately, this placement isolates the two of us from most of the others.

Yoko-san sits on the cushion next to me. "Please, please— Tracy and Dave—speak English," she insists. "I just want to listen for study."

Dave obliges. "So you are all into making pottery, huh. I got into that for a long time. I had the hair, the clothes, everything."

"How long were you 'into it'?"

"Six months. I made a lot of cool stuff. This one vase, man, I wish I could show you. It was so good."

The servers rush in with our pre-ordered lunches, beautiful in ornate lacquered boxes. Grateful for the distraction, I chew slowly and stare intently into my food as Dave gives rapid-fire complaints about all things Japanese while simultaneously badly and loudly interpreting bits of discussion from the others. Volume and brevity as a second language. I don't bother to point out that my Japanese ability—though unimpressive—is considerably better than his. Yoko-san sighs her approval with each utterance, "*Saaaa*, such beautiful English. *Saaaa*, such good Japanese." The exotic food does a slow roll in my stomach, but I continue to chew so I won't have to speak.

The meal ends at last, and Dave is beckoned by the ladies to have his picture taken next to the *tokonoma* alcove. I turn to Yoko-san, who is discreetly preparing to pay the waitress. "Please, let me pay my share this time."

"No, no, you are guest in Japan. You cannot pay."

"But I've lived here four years, in total. Maybe I'll be here forever. You shouldn't always pay for me."

"Still, you are guest. We pay. This is how it is done. Please, take picture."

I turn and walk to the *tokonoma*, and one of the women instructs me to kneel beside Dave. Nishida-sensei slides in next to me on the other side, looping her arm through mine. And thus I am caught fast between two cultures.

Saturday, April 3

My mother calls very early this morning—a reasonable evening hour in Alaska—and the fog of sleep is still in my head as she tells me something about the weather and then her artist boyfriend and then a watercolor she's working on. It's not until that last part that I start to comprehend language again. "The colors. They aren't coming out right," she says.

"The colors—?"

"Yes, I guess I need to start over. Watercolor is not as forgiving as oil."

As she says this, I fully come out of the fog and realize that I can hear the crackle of distance and also another conversation, an enthusiastic young woman who keeps repeating, *"Uso! Uso!"* ("No way! No way!" Literally, "Lie! Lie!") in response to the less exuberant low-toned mumbles of a man.

"Wow—bad connection today. Can you hear that, too?"

"Sounds okay over here."

"I'm hearing voices. Probably losing my mind."

Sunday, April 4

I am in a foul, dark mood and am therefore grateful for the opportunity to take it all out in karate club today. The club was formed several years ago by Koun at the suggestion of Chinen-sensei, his teacher in Spokane, when the style he had practiced since high school appeared to be inaccessible in Takamori (or anywhere in Kumamoto, for that matter). To his surprise, several local people joined, and two young men—both announcing their desire "to become Bruce Lee"—drove two hours every Tuesday and Friday night to train with us in the Takamori Junior High School gymnasium. The "karate boys" as we came to call them—Mimaki-san, sly and fast, and Tsuda-san, a solid, blunt force—have returned to train with us, years after our first stay in Japan. Though now, as they are a little older and their families and jobs have become greater priorities, our schedules are harder to synchronize. Twice-a-month meetings in Kumamoto City are about all that we manage.

After knotting the belt of my *karate-gi*, I bow and then step into the sunlight filtering through the high windows of the huge dojo housed within Kumamoto City's expansive community Budokan sports complex. The boys are here already: Mimaki-san kicking over and over a thick pad braced firmly against Tsuda-san's stout, powerful frame. It is our first meeting without our sensei, Koun. When they spot me, we exchange bows and I enter their cycle of practice: twenty kicks for each leg, and then switch, repeat, and so on. We rotate through variations on this brutal repetition for two hours, replacing our bodies with the pad, and our feet and shins go pink and numb in the process. We don't speak much. I have no idea who among us decided that our only focus today will be kicking, but it's what we do and it feels so *right*. I think I am not the only one who is in a bad mood.

In the shower at home after practice, I really feel what we— the karate boys and I—have done to ourselves, and then I see the damage the violence has wrought growing brighter beneath the sting and rush of water: swollen lumps, weeping lacerations. After drying off, I search the freezer for some remedy. There is no ice, only a couple of bags of frozen edamame, which I take out and wrap with a thin towel around my feet and shins. Perhaps in America I would wrap frozen peas, and not soybean pods, around my wounds.

Sitting there on the wood floor of my kitchen as the pain throbs and subsides, I can't stop thinking about a moment in Alaska, in the final months of my first year at university, when I went running in darkness on a bitterly cold evening. I had been in love with someone who did not love me; it seemed nothing I did would extinguish that flame. Nothing I did. As I returned to campus, I slipped and fell on a steel grate, and for the first time in a very long time I felt some clarity, so I got up and kept running. There had been blood in the snow—dark droplets against all that white—I remember that clearly. That could have been the day I woke up just enough to leave Alaska for good. I can't be certain.

Monday, April 5

This evening at the Tatsuda Center, only Stephen and I show up for zazenkai, and nobody but the night watchman is in the building with us.

Midway through our meditation session, both candles go out so that we can't see much of anything, save for the pale glow of a streetlight coming in through the paper shoji covering the windows. We have to take slow and careful steps for *kinhin*, lest we trip over some unseen object.

"It was so quiet tonight," says Stephen as we pack up our things.

"It was."

"It's funny, though. The noises don't really bother me. I guess the sounds are just like the stick the monks use on the back of sleepy or daydreaming meditators. Whack! It makes you more present. Maybe a little distraction can be helpful."

"Since you're such a glutton for punishment, I'll remember to bring the *kyosaku* next time."

As we step out into night, the first cicadas of the season begin screaming in sudden unison. The sound is urgent, deafening—a swift and powerful blow to the body that does not stop. Then, the temperature shifts by a degree and there is silence.

"Hmmm . . ." says Stephen. "What do you think they are trying to say?"

Tuesday, April 6

Late this afternoon, the last of the *sakura* blossoms fall from the mostly green trees in spectacular puffs of swirling petals. Yayoi, the beautiful young wife of Mimaki-san in our karate club, and Iyori-chan, her two-year-old daughter, drop by for a visit.

Yayoi and I sit on the floor of my kitchen drinking green tea, talking, and watching from the open sliding-glass door as Iyori-chan joyfully chases after the falling petals in the back yard. Yayoi's speaking moves between Japanese and English without missing a beat, filling in words that she can't immediately define in one language or the other. "I wanted to name her 'Sakura,' 'cherry blossom.' But my parents . . . *Dame dame da to itta.* They said it's a very unlucky name—a beautiful thing falling out of life so quickly. But I don't think it's so bad. It seems that we're all sort of like that anyway."

We pause in our discussion to observe Iyori-chan running back and forth between us, distributing crushed bits of pink into our outstretched palms. Then she climbs up into the kitchen, kicks off her sandals, and runs past both of us, out into the hallway, leaving a distinct trail of crushed petals that have somehow stuck to her feet and then neatly released—little petal-colored footprints—onto the wood of the floor. "Clean it up," says Yayoi, and I hand Iyori-chan one of my many ceramic teacups to gather up the footprints, which she gleefully does before running outside again with her new collection container.

"Don't hurt it!" calls out Yayoi before turning back to our conversation. "Tracy, why did you come to Japan?"

I have been asked this so many times and usually I reply "for adventure" or "to experience Japanese culture." But this time I feel vulnerable and tell her the truth: "The first time I came here was in 1999, just after grad school. I followed a boy who was not mine across the ocean. I couldn't imagine a life without him."

"Did you speak Japanese?"

"Not a word. I didn't know anything about Japan. I got a job teaching English at a language school and moved into a tiny apartment near the Suizenji train station in Kumamoto City. Nearly every weekend I took the train out to Takamori to see Koun, or he drove to the city in his tiny blue K-car."

"Wow—that's very . . . *yuki ga aru.*"

"Maybe brave. Or maybe stupid!"

"When did you know that you would be together?"

"I think some part of me always knew, but our lives were complicated. Right before he left for Japan, I think he knew too. We both understood that he was going to be a monk someday so we resisted the attraction for a while. And then we both came here and stopped resisting it."

"What happened after that?"

"After those first two years, we went home to the U.S. for ten months or so and got married, and then came back to Japan—Yamanashi for a year and then Kumamoto again. I guess you could say that I'm always following Koun to Japan."

"Ah, I remember exactly when I fell in love with Hiroaki. He gave me a *gabera* daisy on our first meeting—like *sakura*, also the wrong flower. My mother told me this. But I have always loved this flower. How could he know that? It made me feel that it was meant to be. And he is a good husband—not like the other men. He watches our daughter and even cooks sometimes. I am very, very lucky."

Wednesday, April 7

This morning I squint into the resin-stained mirror above the sink in my office as I affix my hair into a neat ponytail, tuck in my white button-up shirt, and smooth the faint wrinkles from my skirt and jacket. Stepping back to take in the full effect, a small woman in a black business suit peers at me. I cover my face with my hands, view myself again through the space between my fingers. And there it is: save for the too-pale skin and brown hair, I could pass for a Japanese. As I turn, I see through my windows the imagined version of myself—one of the new office ladies with her long black hair pulled up, dashing across the front lawn toward the library in her stiff black "recruit suit," the exact cut and color as mine.

An hour later, I'm surrounded by the new Shokei students, all of us in near-matching clothing, and we file into the Kenritsugekijo Auditorium for Shokei's annual entrance ceremony. Some of the new students glance shyly at me, many others shout, *"Haro! Haro!"* above the cacophony. I make my way to one of the balcony seats in the huge concert hall and witness a déjà-vu moment echoing the graduation ceremony a month earlier: demurely seated figures lined up on stage, a bonsai on a pedestal, the Japanese flag prominent, the essential bowing to mark the beginnings and endings—but this time no bright kimono and traditional flowing skirt-like *hakama* trousers to draw the eye. These young women are the blank slates—those yet unformed by experience, by an education. They collectively hold a certain look in the eyes of being totally, utterly lost.

I must have felt this way as I entered adolescence, and then at the end of that first marriage—and then again when I came to Japan. It is how I feel now that Koun has stepped out of the comfort of our shared lives into a world that I cannot enter.

Friday, April 9

A familiar blue business envelope arrives in the mail while I'm home during the lunch hour. I've been getting this same blue envelope every few months for more than a year. Inside, a wildly scrawled letter on notebook paper in English from my friend, Masatoshi Yamada. Yamada-san was one of my private tutorials at the language school where I taught in Yamanashi, just west of Tokyo, two years ago. Once a week, this leather-skinned furniture dealer arrived in his turquoise jumpsuit for his English lesson. He had built his business from the ground up—working in design before moving on to public relations. He preferred design but was bound to do the upper-level work of his company as the years went by and the business profited. Even though he's long since stopped making furniture, his hands are the conduit for language. Our conversations followed a common pattern while he sketched out his craft on paper:

"What did you do today?" I'd ask.

"I delivered furniture to an old people's home."

"What kind of furniture?"

"Here, let me show you." He reached for the paper I always brought and pulled a knife-sharpened pencil from his jumpsuit pocket. "Here three shelf attached to a dresser, a shoji and a— *nan to iu?*—closet. It is used to divide the beds. Do you see? Can you understand?"

His drawings were elaborate and precise and so quickly executed, his words coming out almost as an afterthought.

One time I asked what he would do if he wasn't in the furniture business.

"Well, I collect guitars. I used to be a musician. I played country and blues with some guys from the American base. That's how I learned a little English. I would like to do that again, but I'm too old. And . . . no time."

"I would like to learn guitar, too. But I can only play a little. I've forgotten most of what I did know."

The next class session, he brought a guitar from his collection: a beautiful black Ovation. It must have been tremendously expensive. "I'm too old for this now. You take it. Learn to play and make me a recording. I want to hear 'Sakura.'"

~

In today's letter, Yamada-san tells me that he's turning sixty near the end of the month—a significant milestone in Japanese culture—and that he's tired of working so hard. He wishes he could turn over the furniture business to his son. But his son is not so good with people, and Yamada-san is afraid that he'll run the business into the ground within a few months. He writes, *I want to work with my hands again. I want to enjoy my life.*

When I return to work, I tell the office ladies that I'd like to get something for my friend, for his sixtieth birthday.

"Something red," they say. "Traditionally we give a cap and a Japanese vest. Like *akachan*, 'baby.' We say that old men and women become like babies again. They are *ojiichan* and *obaachan*. We give them our affection in this way. The red means that we are willing to care for them—like children."

I consider this gift. I like the idea. But all day I keep thinking, *hands, hands.* So this evening I break tradition and tuck wadded-up grocery bags into a box around my best handmade tea bowl, an accidental beauty.

Saturday, April 10

After I return home from Japanese class this morning, I call Yoko-san—there's something about Yamada-san's letter that's got me thinking. "Yoko-san, I really want to ask your opinion about something."

"Come to my house," she says. "I'll pick you up."

An hour later Yoko-san collects me in her huge white car and takes me to her home where she serves up Western-style tea and strawberries on dishes that she's made herself in pottery class. Her house is classic modern Japanese—*shodo* scrolls displayed in each *tokonoma*. *Wabi-sabi* pottery along one long, low bench of planed and lacquered natural slab. Numerous photos of her two tiny grandchildren in ballerina costumes filling one wall. A large and ornately carved *butsudan* altar. A Western-style kitchen set next to a gorgeous tatami room with an inset floor for the low dining table centered in the middle. I am taking all of this in from my seat at the table in the tatami room—the startling beauty of juxtaposition—while Yoko-san settles in across from me and pours me another cup of tea.

"You have the most beautiful house, Yoko-san. Like an art museum."

"Thank you. I made the *shodo*."

"Really? It's gorgeous."

"I would like to put it in a gallery or sell maybe, but my teacher will not give me license. She is a little . . . strict. But that is my problem. It does not matter." She waves her open palm in front of her face, as if brushing away her words. "What is on your mind, Tracy-san?"

"Well, I've been thinking about taking more *yakimono* lessons. Maybe on Wednesday nights as well. Do you think it would be appropriate to ask Sensei for this? Of course, I know I will have to pay more."

"*Eh*, you really like pottery?"

"Um, yes."

"Really?! Oh, this is so wonderful! I will call Sensei now. I can check."

When she calls, she speaks very quickly, but I can make out the word *deshi* several times. I know this word well from the Buddhist context—"disciple." Finally she hangs up. "Sensei is very excited, but she wants to make sure you are serious, that you will do your best."

"Of course." I have no clear idea of what has just transpired between the two women. "Ah, so is it okay to go on both Tuesdays and Wednesdays?"

"Maybe it is okay from next week. But—I'm so sorry to say this . . ."

"Yes?"

"Sensei says now you are paying a foreigner price. It is important to understand."

"Okay. How much should I pay?"

"*Saaaaaa* . . . I don't know."

"Okay. But will she let me go on Wednesdays?"

"I don't know."

"Okay. Should I call and ask Sensei myself?"

"No, no—I asked her already. Go on Wednesday next week."

"So I can go on Wednesdays?"

"*Saaaa*, I don't know. Just go and you will see."

Monday, April 12

Waking without breath always follows dreams of drowning. Push it out laboriously, the false water from my lungs, then inhale gasps of the life-giving air. I stumble to my dresser, slide open the top drawer, and claw through clothing until I find my emergency inhaler, take in that bitter grainy taste, and hold it until I'm nearly bursting with the outbreath. Another puff and I can breathe again. It has been a long while since I've had this sort of asthma, the stone lungs of my childhood.

Outside, it is a beautiful, warm day already. The wind agitates the leaves of the trees and moves through the house and all its open upstairs windows—left this way for the pleasure it lends to both sleeping and waking. I go downstairs to boil a pot of tea to soothe my lungs, and when I climb up again with the tray in my hands, the light from the window catches in such a way that I can see the cloud of pollen coming off the evergreen *sugi* tree out back in a neat, graceful puff into the upstairs living room. This is then carried to my bedroom by the periodic arc of an electric fan.

~

Today is the first day of classes, and there is a new fervor on campus. All of the freshmen—even those not enrolled in the English program—are trying out a "HellohowareyouIamfine" as we pass each other in the halls.

With a handful of students seated around me, I open my sophomore English conversation class with a brief review of a simple and culturally appropriate self-introduction, just to get them back into the swing of things. I mention my hometown, my hobbies, my husband.

"What? You're married?" interrupts Miki.

"Yes, haven't you seen my husband?"

"I don't think so."

"Aren't we neighbors? Where do you live?"

"In the dormitory."

"I live just across from you, next to Jennifer-sensei. Haven't you seen the tall foreigner with no hair?"

"Oh!" says Tomomi, "I know! I know! He is always wearing *wafuku*—Japanese clothing."

"Oh, that guy—sometimes he wears black *wafuku* with big sleeves like this." Miki gestures broadly at the wrist. "And sometimes *geta* shoes too."

"Right," I say. "He wears traditional Japanese clothing. Can you guess his job?"

"His job? No. . . ."

"Uh—skinhead?" offers Tomomi.

"No. . . ." I shake my head emphatically.

"English teacher?"

"No, well, sometimes. Usually, he's a priest."

"A priest? What's priest?"

"*Obosan.* He is doing his *shugyo* now."

"Eh? *Obosan?* Foreigner *obosan? Sugoi!*"

"Does he say '*itadakimasu*' before a meal?"

"Does he do '*nya-nya-nya*' and rubbing hands together?"

"Do you have *butsudan* in your house?"

"Can he read kanji sutra?"

"Is he Christian?"

Here everything is in the blood—even religion.

Tuesday, April 13

The rain starts gently in the afternoon, and by late evening all of us pottery ladies labor to the deafening roar of water pouring from the sky onto the roof overhead. I've been bracing myself for today's class, not knowing quite what to expect. Two things are immediately different: Sensei weighs and cites the cost of the clay (400 yen for 5 kilos), and then she instructs me to watch as she quickly kneads the clay into a spiraling blossom that morphs into a single fat cylinder. "Next time you do it just like that."

"*Hai*, Sensei."

As we settle into our workspaces, for the first time Sensei does not ask her customary question of me: *What would you like to make?* Instead, she pushes me out of my seat with a firm *"yoisho!"* and takes my place. "Watch," she says, as a single perfect cup forms beneath her fingers. She cuts it off at the hump and sets it on the table directly in front of my wheel.

"Here. Make teacups just like this. All the same size."

"*Hai*, Sensei."

As I lean into the work, I begin to realize that the ladies are engaging with me differently tonight as well—nearly everything I do seems to be punctuated by a cheerful and enthusiastic *"Ganbatte!"* (Do your best!). Obviously someone—Yoko-san, most likely—has announced that I have tentatively been accepted as a kind of *deshi* to Sensei. The ladies keep muttering as if they're watching me take a turn at bat in a local league: *"Ganbatte, Fight-o! Ganbatte, Fight-o! . . ."*

I manage three thick-walled cups, not at all the same size, even though I have used the *tanbo* (dragonfly tool) to measure depth and width, just like Sensei showed me. It seems my first efforts as "pottery disciple" are a complete failure.

After class, Sensei instructs me to take the clay scraps home in a plastic bag to dry and then knead again into a workable consistency. *"Risaikuru,"* she says, using the English loanword. Before, she always insisted that I leave my wet piles of scrap for her. Perhaps I am no longer a guest after all.

Wednesday, April 14

Between classes today, I mentally work through the basic creation process of pottery, noting how little I really know of any of it, aside from the sparest understanding of key steps:

Knead to soften and mix.
Form into the desired shape.
Dry to a semi-hard leather.
Trim away the outer excess.
Fire in the kiln to a porous, hard biscuit.
Glaze (simply—or add more elaborate decoration).
Fire again.

And then there is the life of the ceramic as it travels from hand to lip to sink to cupboard. And the eventuality, when it breaks, of returning to the earth from which it was born.

~

When I enter Sensei's receiving room this evening, I must have the look of someone who is about to learn some greater secret about the craft, and I get the feeling that the other ladies—the women I have yet to meet—are the protectors of that knowledge. It seems as if they have all been present in the room for quite some time. There is a distinct air of formality. "Please sit," says Sensei. I settle into a stiff *seiza*, as the others are seated. Sensei tells me to introduce myself, and I do, the standard mini-speech in formal Japanese that I have given so many times coming out faster than I intended: "It is our first meeting. I am Tracy Franz of Shokei University. I am from Alaska. Please favor me."

The other ladies introduce themselves in turn, bowing low after each introduction: Mikiko-san, the new young wife; Rie-san, the office worker; Yuko-san, also an office worker; Harada-san, the retired housewife. How the roles of women in Japan are so often of a type.

Sensei clears her throat and begins to speak as my proxy: "Tracy would like to humbly request to join our Wednesday night class. She says it is quite an inconvenience for all of you; she knows this will likely cause you all much trouble."

Harada-san, the eldest of the women bows and says, "We would be honored to have you join us."

Before I can respond, Sensei replies for me: "Tracy says 'please humbly favor me.'" I bow low to show the sincerity of the words that have been spoken for me.

"Sensei," I whisper as we rise to begin our work. "What do I do—in this class?"

"It's the same. Make pots."

Thursday, April 15

This evening is the annual Shokei welcome party—an event held in a Western-style chandeliered hall that overlooks Kumamoto Castle. After the higher-ups talk at length, the new hires are obliged to give short, modest speeches. Nearly all make some statement about the cherry blossoms (my coworker Jennifer kindly suggested that I mention the flowers in my own speech last year, resulting in the school president going on at length about my sincerity and unique understanding of Japanese culture).

After the speeches, a bounty of dainty French-Japanese fusion dishes is swiftly served and consumed, and the formal party ends in the traditional shout of "*Banzai!*" and three coordinated claps. People begin ambling off to the second party—which will be followed by the third, the fourth, and so on. The taxi drivers will do a brisk business in the wee hours of the morning, shuttling our drunken coworkers home to their sleeping families. Jennifer and I watch them weave away into the side streets, toward smoky karaoke and shared cups of *sake* poured for each other in the Kumamoto style—alcohol the oil that hones the wheels of all Japanese institutions. If we were more protective of our careers and positions at the university, we would participate; it is a dangerous business not drinking with the others. But instead Jennifer and I head to my car, which has been tucked into a monolithic vehicle-stacking machine. As we wait for the attendant to rotate my little van down to us, Jennifer remarks that she's gotten too old for long nights of alcohol and parties. "Maybe they'll forgive us because we're *gaijin*. We make everyone uncomfortable anyway."

"Yes, maybe. But they'll never forgive us for *being* foreigners," I add.

As we drive home through the darkness, Jennifer asks how things have been going, with Koun away in the monastery.

"I miss him a lot—but I guess that's natural."

"How does your family feel about all of this?"

"We haven't quite figured that out yet—I think Koun's parents especially just never believed that it would go this far, that he was actually serious about it all."

"They're Christian?"

"Yes—Catholic."

We'd revealed our plans to Koun's parents, Dick and Vivian, and my mother, Carol, during a visit to Montana this past Christmas holiday. My mother remained quiet, but the conversation was very tense with Koun's parents. *We're disappointed*, they'd said, and *How could you just abandon Tracy like that?* The force of the pushback taking us both by surprise, we explained again that we'd always known that this would be part of our path together.

"It's also difficult because Koun's mom has MS. She's lost much of her functioning in the past few years. To go more than six months without a visit is hard. Her condition may have changed considerably in a year. It's . . . a worry."

"We foreigners all struggle with this, don't we? Being away while change happens at home. There's just this occasional contact, but it's not the same as living in the same town, or even the same country."

"What's the solution?"

"There is no solution. Unless you go home, I guess."

"Will you ever move back to Canada?"

"No, my home is here now."

"I can't imagine that, staying here forever. But I also can't quite locate 'home' in my mind."

"Well," Jennifer sighs as we pull in to the dormitory parking lot, "maybe we're all a little lost."

Saturday, April 17

In Japanese class, I am writing notes as fast as I can, struggling with the impossible characters, when my fingers begin to cramp. I shake out the hand between each word, to the amusement of Okumura-sensei (aka my good friend Satomi). *"Ah . . .*

Nihongo ga muzukashii desu ne" (Japanese is difficult, isn't it?), she says, peering over my shoulder.

It seems that the extra day of pottery has affected my body. I want to explain this all clearly in Japanese, the constant and painful awakenings in the small muscles of my hands and arms and elsewhere, but all I can offer is this: *"Yakimono desu kara."* (It's because of pottery.) In this new language, I am always a simple and blunt object. I should have said "too much karate," because this at least provides plausible context.

After class, Satomi and I walk over to the discount rail ticket shop. "Kyoto during Golden Week—are you sure?" she asks.

"I've lived here too long without seeing 'the heart of Japan.'"

"It will be crowded. But I don't mind if you don't mind. Shall we buy some guidebooks?"

I laugh. "We are just like an old married couple, aren't we?"

"Yes—but without all the trouble," says Satomi, who, like me, has a complicated history.

Monday, April 19

"If Koun becomes a temple priest here in Japan, does this mean something will be expected of you?" asks Stephen as he navigates the narrow road to Tatsuda Center.

"Yes and no and it depends. But ultimately, I guess it's up to us."

Could I ever become like Mrs. Honda, the wife of Koun's teacher? I imagine attending to guests who arrive for a ceremony or funeral memorial service: boiling water for tea and arranging food into fine lacquer dishes in the kitchen, then carrying it all out to serve to the people in the outer receiving rooms. A bow and a greeting to each. Or managing the "dirty work" of the temple—the necessary handling of money for priestly services. Or, like other even more formal priests' wives I've seen, their bodies bound up in demure kimono, attending in near silence to the anticipated needs of others. They slip in and out through shoji drawn open and closed while in *seiza*, to a room filled with laughter or tears.

Tuesday, April 20

An earthquake strikes just before noon. Students stop talking in class, a collective tuning-in. I picture the housewives of Kumamoto poised in the act of striking their hanging futon, and the office workers with their official stamps in the air, heads cocked to the side, as if listening. When it is over, whispers of "That was a big one, wasn't it?" And then we all turn back to our work, this small interruption seemingly forgotten, but also noted as a tragic possibility. Uneasiness seeps into the fabric of the day. It is like this in Alaska, too. Another place with a dangerous character shifting and grumbling beneath the surface.

After school, I realize that I haven't kneaded the clay scraps Sensei sent home with me last week. They've been sitting, forgotten, in a covered bucket beneath my kitchen table. Luckily, I have some time before class. But when I dump it all out on the table and begin to knead, I create nothing more than a molten mess. With each push, clay squirts out like soft excrement between my fingers. It feels like some larger metaphor. I squeeze the excess clay from my hands, wash up at the sink, then slide the kitchen windows open completely—maybe the breeze will take up some of the water while I go out for a long, much-needed walk.

A couple of hours later, I return to knead the clay again and then gather it all up—a slightly firmer sticky mess—into one heap to take to class. It occurs to me that I should have gone at it with a hairdryer, but it's too late for that now.

In class, when I throw the lump down on the wheel and begin, the first cup comes out goopy—the edges simply won't hold. Sensei notes my struggles. "Recycled? Hmmm, it looks too wet. Also, your technique is not good."

I take a breath, begin again. But with each attempt, the pot folds into itself, and I have to cut it off at the hump and throw it in my scrap bucket, now growing full with half-formed misshapen clay bodies. "Next time you must completely mix the clay. Let it dry properly. This is important."

We are already in the final twenty minutes of class. I'm

focusing on my last bit of clay, determined to not fail this one time. Creasing my brow and biting my lower lip, I think, *Concentrate, concentrate. . . .* Suddenly, the ground begins to shake. I look up, my hands still spinning in clay. "Just a bus," says Sensei, laughing as my fingers destroy yet another hopeless form.

Wednesday, April 21

During tea this evening, the Wednesday pottery ladies drop their air of formality with me.

"All day I was so nervous, trying to think of how to say the thing I want to ask you in English," says Mikiko-san.

"You can ask me—don't worry."

"How did you meet your husband?—Is that correct English?"

"Yes, yes. I met him in graduate school, in America."

"In Alaska?"

"In Washington."

"Where did you get married? In a church? Was there big white dress?"

"No, we got married in a Japanese Zen temple in Hawaii. Koun wore his priest's robes and I wore a simple white Thai silk dress. The ceremony was in Japanese. Koun's teacher came all the way from Takamori to perform it."

"A Buddhist wedding! Even Japanese do not have Buddhist weddings so often. We say Shinto is for weddings and Buddhism is for funerals. But now Christian weddings are very popular, though we are not Christian."

"Ah, I see."

"I think," says Mikiko-san, "you and Koun must have been Japanese in a former life." Koun gets this all the time.

"Neee," adds Harada-san. "More Japanese than Japanese."

"If only I'd remembered the language a little better . . ."

"Eh?" asks Sensei, unable to follow our English.

"Zannen desu ne. Nihongo o wasuremashita." (It's too bad I forgot Japanese.)

Saturday, April 24

When I return home from karate practice at the Budokan today, there is a package from Yamada-san on my stoop. Inside, nestled in newspaper, are what look like huge, deceased rodents—but on closer inspection reveal themselves to be several fresh bamboo shoots coated in fine brown hairs. There is no note, only these oddly shaped edibles. A transmission beyond words.

When I ask Satomi later, she is not confident of the proper way to cook the shoots. "I think you'll need to soak them in water for a while to remove the bitter poison."

"The poison?"

"Yes—my mother will know how to cook them properly. I will ask her."

"But—is it safe?"

"Oh yes, and quite healthy. Good for the skin."

"It sounds as if you are describing the *onsen*. If we soak in the bath long enough do you think we will remove the bitter poison?"

"Maybe I will have to soak a very long time."

"Oh, me too."

Wednesday, April 28

At home after work, I receive a letter from Yamada-san in a blue envelope with his furniture store address on the pre-printed label. Perhaps it was meant to be delivered with the bamboo shoots. In his typical scrawl he writes that he likes the tea bowl I sent him for his sixtieth birthday and has given it a prominent space on his desk at work. *I am not sure which side is the front. But one edge has a long drip of glaze.* This he faces out for his guests to contemplate. I like the image of the tea bowl sitting there among his beautiful sketches of furniture, all those ideas that he dreams into being and then delivers, by himself, directly to his customers' doors.

He also writes that his good friend and gardener, the man

whom he asked to install fabulously huge trees from all over Japan into the garden he has been building for his father (who is "always caring for those troublesome bonsai"), was killed in a car accident. *I only found out because I read it in the paper a day later. It gave me a terrible lonely feeling.*

And then he tells me that one of his dogs died this past month too, his loyal Hana-chan. *My wife says Hana-chan died instead of my father, so I should be thankful.*

When I fold up the letter and attempt to return it to the envelope, I find two photos inside: one of a towering ginkgo in a sprawling Japanese-style garden labeled "the last tree the gardener planted" and the other of a small shrine, also in the garden, labeled "Hana-chan's grave."

Thursday, April 29

In the late afternoon, I take my usual long walk through twisting neighborhoods, rice fields, and community vegetable plots—pausing on my way back at the overspill area, a vast tree-lined basin filled with air or water, depending on the mood of the sky. On this day, the morning rain has filled it, and gray-white cranes fly low along the water's surface, creating bird and reflection, reflection and bird. For a moment, I don't understand what I'm seeing.

I remember, some years ago, trying to explain to Koun one of the reasons why I love being with him. *You're the only person I've ever been able to be properly alone with. That must sound terrible, but it's not. It is a comfortable thing, a beautiful thing.*

There is a certain pleasure in solitude, and yet I miss Koun in every moment of every day. These twin feelings reflect each other; I don't know what it means.

Friday, April 30

I'm dressing for work after morning zazen, that expansiveness still in me when the phone rings: it is Koun's mother, Viv.

There's an edge to her voice today. I try not to take it personally, but still this goading comment echoes in my mind: *Aren't you mad at him for leaving you?*

And later, as I'm packing up to return home, it hits me: "That's the wrong question." I say this out loud in my office, to no one.

Maybe the real question is this: *Why am I here?*

MAY
Authentic Experience

May begins in a crush of humanity pouring through the maze of hallways, entrances, and exits of Fukuoka City's Hakata Station, a bird's-eye view of which would surely fascinate any physics enthusiast. My stutter-stopping is the only apparent flaw in this grand design as I try to keep up with Satomi, who moves through the crowd with relative ease. My sight is fixed firmly on her yellow backpack—the one bright beacon in the jostle of uniformity. I am beginning to question my decision to travel to Kyoto, the cultural capital of Japan and favorite must-see tourist destination, during Golden Week, the single busiest in-country travel time of the year. This week contains a string of national holidays, and many Japanese embrace the rare opportunity of guilt-free time off, happily leaping into the flood of fellow travelers. As an Alaskan used to wide-open spaces, I've never navigated any crowd in Japan well; I've always felt lucky to live in the comparatively less populated outskirts of Kumamoto City.

Satomi turns, spots me, and mouths "this way," motioning with one hand and holding up her Shinkansen bullet train tickets with the other. And then she's off again, moving faster than before—and completely at ease.

I take in a quick breath and follow, running a little to catch up. And that's when I get it: when I stop concentrating and hesitating, when I stop examining people's faces and bodies in order to guess which way they'll turn, when I stop apologizing with

my face and body and speech, then I'm fine, winding and looping my way through, just another ball bearing in a great and
complex machine. Until, of course, a suited man neatly clips me
in the knee with the edge of his bag and I more fall than step
into the Shinkansen.

Satomi notices my limp and grimace. "Are you all right?"

"Yeah, thought I got the hang of it there for a minute, and
then—BANG!"

A few hours later, we are expelled from Kyoto Station in a
crowd, drift the streets in a crowd, are funneled onto a bus in
a crowd, and then enter our first destination, Sanjusangendo's
Buddha Hall, where we shuffle along in one great shifting
hug.

On display before us: seemingly endless, a thousand life-
sized and gilded Avalokiteshvara bodhisattva statues in *gassho*
prayer pose, stretching the length of the hall and disappearing into muted light. We move slowly in the presence of these
embodiments of compassion, these beings said to hear all the
cries of the world. Bodies brush against bodies, whispers in
every language. At intervals, hands emerge from the mass to
light incense and candles at stations that have been set up for
this purpose. I step forward, light a candle for Koun's mother,
gassho, step back into people. Faces around us glow in the flickering flames. We breathe in, we breathe out, as one crowd observes
the other.

Sunday, May 2

Waking this morning in the *ryokan*, our little Japanese inn,
I have no idea where I am. My not-yet-awake mind notes the
familiar: futon, tatami, fusuma, and light coming in the one
window, filtered by the shifting branches of a tree. Dust motes
circling above me. Familiar, yes, but not quite right—a flawed
memory, or an alternate universe. The sensation lifts away with
each blink.

"What adventure awaits us today?" I ask Satomi, who,
fully dressed and ready for the day, is silently studying her

guidebook. "I'm up for anything—famous sights or otherwise. It doesn't matter to me."

"If you don't mind," says Satomi, "I would like to learn *kodo*. It's something I've always been curious about. It is 'the way of incense.'"

"Scent and memory," I say. "I read somewhere how one is inherently linked to the other."

"Then maybe it is the best of the senses. Or the worst."

A few hours later, Satomi and I sit in formal *seiza* in an elegantly spare room tucked into the back of one of Kyoto's premier incense establishments. Six or seven Japanese tourists sit across and to the sides of us, while the sensei and his kimono-clad assistant sit at the head of the square, instructing us in a tourists' sampling of an incense ceremony.

"When we practice *kodo*," he tells us, "we do not use the verb 'to smell.' Instead, we use the verb 'to listen.'" He pauses, allowing us all to savor this unusual twist of language. "Here," he says, handing me the small ceramic container of burning incense. *"Yoku kiite kudasai."* (Please "listen" carefully.) When he beckons me to smell with this verb, I cannot help but hear/smell a synesthesia of the spiced friction of our collective bodies against tatami, muted sandalwood laughter from another room. I pass the container to Satomi, wondering if everyone is having the same mixed-up sensory experience.

"Incense has held both sacred and mundane functions since it first came from China," explains the sensei as the incense burner is passed around the room. "It was first burned as a religious offering, and as purification. Buddhist monks sprinkled powdered incense onto their hands before touching their *okesa*. In Heian times, court people often had their own signature smell. They scented their kimono, their hair. If the wrong smell was in a room—well, there could be trouble." The tourists chuckle in response to this last bit. "At court, people often amused themselves with incense contests . . . like the one we will try today."

The sensei presents a series of scents, and then gives us a blind challenge. My sense of smell and taste have always been quite good, and I am sure I know the answer when we are asked to write down the scent notes, wear it on my face in a self-satisfied grin when the sensei asks me. But when the key is revealed, I've guessed completely wrong. Satomi, in contrast, is merely a single note off.

As we exit out into the busy streets again, the aura of incense still on us, I ask Satomi what the smell of home is for her. *"Takana* rice," she replies. "It is something my mother makes very well. What is it for you?"

"I don't know. I need to think about it some more."

Monday, May 3

After fighting the crowds through two of Kyoto's more famous attractions—the massive cliffside Kiyomizudera temple complex and Kinkakuji, the Temple of the Golden Pavilion—Satomi and I find some relief in just sitting in the viewing area of the more modest temple Ryoanji, the visitors moving around us like water around two stones. "This is Kyoto's most famous rock garden," explains Satomi, who remembers coming here once on a high school trip.

The garden before us is relatively small and consists of just fifteen moss-covered boulders set haphazardly into a rectangular field of raked pebbles surrounded by a low, time-stained wall. "Not much to it, is there?"

"According to the pamphlet," says Satomi, "we're supposed to sit here and contemplate the meaning of the garden."

"Like a koan?" I ask.

"Yes," says Satomi. "This is our chance to get enlightened."

We sit and cycle through a few possibilities: Could it be ocean and islands—a geography of Japan? Or clouds in sky? Or—

"Well, 'Happy Clouds,' at least. For the characters in Koun's name," offers Satomi.

"How about 'nature of mind'? That's probably the Zen answer."

"Large rocks and small pebbles?"

"Okay, I think that is a better Zen answer!"

As we are on our way out, Satomi points to an object on

display in a dusty nook of the entranceway. The size of a tea tray, it is an exact replica of the garden. "You can touch this—they've put it here for the blind." We close our eyes, run our fingers over sculpted metal worn smooth by so many hands, fill up vast darkness with the idea of a garden.

Tuesday, May 4

Weaving along temple lanes on the outskirts of Kyoto after devouring a "traditional temple-style vegetarian meal" for lunch, we turn and amble down an unassuming dirt path lined with tall, cooling bamboo. Multi-colored ceramic shards embedded in the dirt beneath our feet glisten in the sun. We pause to take in what must be a potter's spacious backyard. Huge open-bottomed crockery accommodate the thick bamboo stalks that shoot up from the earth, through the pots, and into sky—houseplants that can't be contained.

"This has to mean something, don't you think?" I ask. "A failure or a triumph?"

"Maybe it depends on the perspective."

"Of the pot or the bamboo?"

"American or Japanese."

"Good point." I take out my camera and snap a couple photos before we move on. "Satomi, is Kyoto different to you? Aside from the various landmarks, can you tell that it is not your home?"

"Well, the dialect is somewhat different—that is obvious. But there is a curtness, a distance here, and that doesn't feel like Kumamoto. When people offer tea at the end of a meal or conversation, here it means that it is time for you to leave. It is a very *direct* indirect communication."

"I always feel a distance here—I mean, anywhere in Japan."

"Of course. That's because you are not Japanese."

Wednesday, May 5

The day begins with rain, more crowds, and the imminent danger of wet umbrella spokes gouging out our eyes as we move on and off Kyoto's buses and trams and along walkways. We decide to escape the main thoroughfares, working our way instead through the neighborhoods. We spot lush miniature gardens tucked into the two-foot spaces between houses, talk with well-fed cats peering at us from the dry promise of open doorways, marvel at all the traditional family specialty shops nestled among homes: sellers of *manju* sweets, *shakuhachi* bamboo flutes, formal tea ceremony paraphernalia, kimono and other textiles.

Eventually we happen upon a small, discreet sign that points the way to a destination on our list: Kanjiro Kawai's house. We enter the late eminent potter's home—now a museum—through a low sliding door and pay a fee that gives us free reign to wander through the past. Despite (or because of) the rain falling outside, very few tourists are here and the rooms are nearly silent as we move through them. Everywhere, there are natural wood surfaces and patterned shadows. Windows and walls open to an interior courtyard. Though large and labyrinthine, there are distinct similarities between this place and the house where Koun first lived in Takamori some years ago, and to the many temples and old houses we have visited.

"It almost feels too intimate, doesn't it? Like stepping into another person's dreams," says Satomi in a whisper as we crawl through a "humble door" into the tea room overlooking the garden. "I feel that I am a spy or an intruder."

After we move on and inspect the great wood-fired kiln, old-style potter's wheels, and various artifacts displayed behind glass, I stop in the lobby to buy a postcard photo of one of Kawai's angular, thick-walled pots—a humble blue ash-speckled vase. Like all of his pots, the postcard explains, it is unsigned. The artist rejecting ego.

"I love this," I say to Satomi as I show her the postcard. "It reminds me of something, a visceral, homey feeling."

"Oh yes, you can almost feel it in your hands."

"Satomi, why don't you join my pottery class? I think it would suit you."

"The *yakimono*, yes. But I know about those groups, so nosy—not that they're bad people. It's just the way of Japanese women. I don't want anyone picking at my personal life." Satomi, a child of divorce like myself, has a complicated family—made more complicated by the local habit of directly or indirectly shaming those outside the so-called norm. The dark side of a collectivist culture.

"Here, I always lie about my family," I say. "Or I just let people make assumptions. I learned early on that it makes things easier. I remember trying to explain divorce and step-parents and half-siblings to students who kept asking—what a nightmare."

"It is more difficult for me to lie about such things. They would be *very* nosy with me. They would feel sorry for me. I couldn't stand it."

"The cultural barrier protects me, doesn't it? Maybe sometimes it is better to not understand."

"Yes."

~

In the evening, the rain continues on and off, and we stroll the famed Philosopher's Walk lined with temples. I picture the monks inside making their nightly preparations. We wander off the path a bit as the light begins to give way and find ourselves walking the grounds of a tiny temple that is seemingly uninteresting to the other tourists. In one of the buildings, the doors are propped open and we discover an art exhibit of soft pastel nudes. The colors run over and through the bodies, the feeling permeating our own damp skins, as if we are meant to be part of the art. And then stepping out again, we are surrounded by the soft wet blur of green moss and endless bamboo dissolving into near-total darkness. The lit stone pathway shows us the way to busy city streets, but Satomi touches my arm, motioning to another dimly lit side street. "Let's not just yet. It's so peaceful here away from all that artificial light and noise."

I nod and follow her lead. "You know, my first two years in

Japan I spent most nights walking the streets of Kumamoto at odd hours. It felt a little like this."

"Why? Maybe that's . . . a little dangerous."

"Yes, well, it's difficult to explain. I had a lot going on in my head. A lot of anger at first, and then mostly this terrible feeling, like shame. I wanted to find a way out of that bad place in my mind. It seemed important for my relationship with Koun. So I walked every night until I couldn't walk any more."

"Did you find the way out?"

"Maybe. It got better after a while."

"And did you keep your habit of walking at night?"

"Not so much now."

"That's good. After dark, a city changes."

"True." I saw many things in the night. A couple making love against the shadow of an office building. Teenagers drinking alcohol and laughing in the tall reeds near Lake Ezu, their disembodied voices rising out of the darkness. Solitary drunken salarymen in black suits weaving more horizontal than vertical. An old man practicing kendo *kata* in a parking lot. A mother, framed in the light from an open window, disrobing for her evening bath with her children. A man thrown from a slow-moving car by *yakuza* gangsters, a bag of groceries tossed after him, like an afterthought, and him on his hands and knees weeping and collecting the cans and packages of food into his arms.

Once, I was attacked by a groper, a *chikan*, as I walked beneath an overpass. He bloodied my face and tore at my clothes as cars flew past—the people in the cars perhaps seeing nothing, or seeing nothing in that way that is Japanese, or misunderstanding what was seen: just lovers drunk and quarreling, stumbling over each other in the flash of headlights.

As I made my way home that night, a woman gave me wide berth, crossing the street when she saw the blood, the intensity in my foreign eyes.

Thursday, May 6

On the final morning of our Kyoto mini-vacation, we fold

up our bedding into tall piles and move the low table back into the center of the tatami, where we take breakfast each day: homemade *onigiri* rice balls and miso soup and dishes of pickled vegetables. When the lady of the *ryokan*, a demure woman in her fifties, comes down to collect our trays, we ask if we can hear about her father's *obi*-weaving business, something we've learned about by reading the guest log in our room. The wide, often ornate belts can be as treasured as the kimono they hold in place.

"I'm very sorry but he's out today," she explains in formal Japanese, "but I'd be happy to give you a look around the shop."

We slip into our shoes in the *genkan*—that traditional space marking the transition from inside to out in nearly every building—and cross the narrow street to a row of dilapidated wooden structures. Sliding open one of the low doors, the woman beckons us to follow her into a history. Inside, our eyes adjust to low light that reveals a maze of tatami rooms stacked high with papers, scrolls, books, shelving, boxes, bound cloth. An ancient computer is tucked into one corner. At a low table she offers us *zabuton* cushions and pulls down dusty boxes from tall dusty shelves, unrolling each of the family's designs with great care. We pass swatches of *obi* around the table—there are elaborate cranes, chrysanthemums, other famous symbols of Japan.

"We used to design them all by hand—now we use the computer. Still, it takes a very long time to create each design. And the detailing is very fine. Most of the fabric is silk. Here is an exception—see this gold-colored thread? It is *washi*—fine Japanese paper."

I see now that her body—somehow much smaller than mine—is bent: the flat feet and bowed legs of constant *seiza*, the deeply arched spine of a laborer. I imagine her working the loom as a girl—straight-backed and fresh as a reed, her body defying the angles of her craft. But now, surely it is difficult to distinguish the mechanisms of her body from those of the tools of her trade.

"I will bring tea," she says, and Satomi smiles at me knowingly. This is the Kyoto farewell.

"Thank you very much," I say, "but we must go now."

~

The taxi delivers us to the train station, and we rush about searching for the necessary *omiyage* souvenirs for our respective coworkers and associates. I buy beautiful flower-shaped sweets for the pottery ladies and thin sheets of *mochi* filled with *anko* bean paste for the office, and then another set with chocolate for Satomi and me to eat on the train.

"I must be becoming Japanese after all—I can't go anywhere without getting nervous about *omiyage*. What if I forget someone? I need a list whenever I travel!"

"Don't worry, you can always buy famous cities' goods at the train station when you arrive."

"That seems like cheating."

"Not authentic?"

"Something like that."

Outside our window, the urban/rural/urban/rural landscape begins to slide by and when I briefly close my eyes I see a shifting rainbow of religion and culture: great arced eaves, gilded statuary, a woman in the shape of a loom.

"Satomi," I say, "when you close your eyes, what do you see?"

Satomi closes and opens her eyes several times. "Hmmm . . . I see my bed." She unzips her bag, produces two bottles of green tea purchased earlier from a vending machine, and hands me one. "Well, did you find what you were looking for? In Kyoto?"

"It was beautiful. Perfect in every way. I feel more lost than ever."

"What were you expecting?"

"I don't know exactly."

"Well, I travel to escape my boring life. When I go home, I always find myself there—just as I left me."

Looking out over endless fields of rice, I can almost see the tall mountains of Alaska in the distance. I think of a school friend telling me once, as we drove the Seward Highway on the way back from a high school ski trip, *You see those mountains? Most of us don't see them, not really. But someday, if we leave, I bet that's all we'll think about.* When I got home that evening, I drew a ridge of mountains on the interior wall of my closet. A secret drawing in permanent ink. I was compelled to do this. I don't know why. Perhaps even in chaotic youth there can be moments of pure, unfettered clarity.

Friday, May 7

The house feels cloying today—too intimate. Perhaps it is just that odd feeling of arriving home after a trip, a momentum lost, a returning to reality while the dreams of elsewhere dissipate. At least I have a few days to recover before work begins.

As I unpack from my travels, I hear a metallic clang at the mail slot in the door downstairs. In the *genkan*, I find a plain white postcard from Koun, this small unexpected communication slipped into the usual pile of afternoon mail. *I'm allowed to write to you early only because I will be transferred from Zuioji to Shogoji, in Kikuchi, to assist with the international ango. If you could send some things soon, that would be good.* A short list of necessities and, *I'm OK. I love you. I miss you. I'll write more when I'm able.*

I wonder how many monks of rank will have read and scrutinized (or understood) this brief missive before it made its way to me? The pages of a thick dog-eared dictionary turning under suspicious hands. I know Koun would have wanted to write more. Still, I am grateful. Kikuchi, very much unlike the far-off island of Shikoku, is in Kyushu and within reasonable driving distance of the townhouse. Two hours, tops. I may have a chance to see him during our year apart after all. The possibility sits inside of me strangely, a new flavor of loneliness.

Monday, May 10

A beautiful warm day. Entering my office, I note that my plants have become lush and overgrown, an interior jungle in the making. Revived from a long winter sleep, it would seem. And perhaps I am, too. The thought of Koun being nearby is a comfort, though who knows when I will have a chance to see him, or what our visits will entail. Most likely these will be highly formal encounters. I think, suddenly, of the old woman I pass by on my walks nearly every day. She sits in her house in a cloth-covered chair behind a long wall of sliding glass doors, looking out blankly. I always want to lift my hand and wave at her, but I always stop myself. I am seeing something that I am not supposed to see. In Japan, there are many invisible boundaries, and they must be kept.

~

Kyoko brings a guest to sit with us this evening at Tatsuda Center: her tea ceremony teacher, Saito-sensei, a dignified-looking woman in her seventies. She wears a dark suit, her graying hair tightly bound up in a bun. She bows to us all in the formal way—in *seiza*, fingertips angled in and head nearly grazing the tatami—and asks in ultra-polite Japanese if she may join us. Kyoko had been mentioning this possible guest for weeks, but we weren't quite sure what to make of it. Now, we fidget uncomfortably, perhaps feeling collectively for the first time how very odd our little group must appear to others.

During zazen, Saito-sensei sits beside me like a stone—completely fixed in her posture. When we finish the session, she bows low to us all again and thanks us profusely for showing her "true zazen," before gracefully slipping from the room just ahead of Kyoko.

As I gather my things, Stephen says, "I think I've been holding my breath the whole evening."

"Yes, I feel as if I just failed a test."

Sakamoto-san, rising from a deep stretch, lets out a loud exhale.

Tuesday, May 11

In pottery class this evening I carve a set of cups one by one that, to my eye and hand, seem nearly identical. But once I take a good look at them side by side, I see they are not at all the same. Here, a small circumference but a thick body. There, a thin body and a wide circumference. Not one cup appears identical to another. *"Onaji ja nai,"* I groan.

"*Un*," says Sensei. She takes up a ruler and reveals the obvious: "Next time, use the dragonfly tool to measure from the inside lip to the inside lip, and also the depth—NOT just the outside edges. Remember: It is the nothingness in the middle that determines the true size of the vessel."

Thursday, May 13

All last night, wind and rain raging against everything. I somehow manage to leave my window open and sleep through much of it—my dreams storm-colored. When I wake, a wide swath of tatami beneath the bedroom window is damp, and continued bursts of wind and rain slam against the townhouse. On the way to school my jacket whips around me as I struggle with a flimsy umbrella that turns itself inside out again and again, and I step gingerly around lakes of water. By the time I arrive, tributaries have slipped down the back of my neck and along my collarbone, soaking patches of my shirt. My knees to my feet are damp and muddy. My hair is a mess of humidity-induced frizz and my umbrella hangs, destroyed, from my wrist.

When I enter the building, Hiroe-sensei, whose office is opposite mine, is there, too, looking tidy and dry in his pinstriped teacher's suit. He puts on slippers, tucks his shoes into a cubby, and sets out a pair for me at the edge of the *genkan*, while I swipe water and muck from my clothes. "Ahhh—a lotus blooms from the mud," he says.

"Was that supposed to be a compliment?"

"Yes."

"Thanks a lot. Is there some reason why you are not wet?"

"Of course. I used my umbrella."

~

The storm abruptly stops just after the first bell, and the frogs begin to sing. I'm warming up my students with easy questions-and-answers in English, but the frogs keep starting up their collective song midway through each exchange—a great wave of sound, drowning us out.

"Kanae, how many—"

"*Yayayayayayayayaya . . .*"

My class erupts in laughter after the third or fourth attempt to make ourselves heard.

Frustrated, I ask, "Does anyone here speak frog Japanese?" (I pause for another bout of frog song.) "I only know frog English." My students look out the window, considering the problem with a seriousness that surprises me.

Suddenly, the usually reserved Kanae shouts, "*Yayayayaya . . .*"

The class becomes a multitude of questions and comments: "What did you say to them?" and "Your noise is too big!" and "Did you tell them they are so rude frogs?" And then, finally, everyone is laughing and trying to speak frog while Kanae, who is from the countryside and knows the mysterious and special language of frogs, translates.

Friday, May 14

The "poodlers" are out in the morning sun—I watch them from my office as they cut away the rogue angles of trees and form sphere after sphere, an exercise in conformity. The men all wear wide yellow straw hats and blousy sky-blue jumpsuits and black rubber boots. They seem to float in the air at varying heights around the Shokei grounds, their tall three-legged bamboo ladders keeping them aloft. My windows are open; the cutting machines whir and click. The smell of tree blood is carried on the warm wind into my office. *Exquisite violence*, I think.

There is a knock at my door. It is Midori, one of my more shy and gentle students, nervously laughing in hiccup-like bursts and wanting to tell me something, but it won't come out in any language. Tears flow from her eyes. She pauses to look up a word in her electronic dictionary and shows me: "molester." Finally, in Japanese, she explains that on her walk to school today there was a boy who put a cell phone under her skirt and took a picture. "Let's go report it together," I offer, but she shakes her head *no no no*. "But maybe the people in the office can warn others."

"Please don't tell anyone. Please." She shows me another word in her dictionary: "shame."

"Come find me before you go today. I will walk home with you."

"No, Tracy-sensei—I just needed to tell you this secret."

After she leaves, I stand in the middle of my office for a long time, not knowing what to do.

Saturday, May 15

I am walking downtown after Japanese class, contemplating how I should spend the rest of my day, when monks in *takuhatsu* (formal begging) gear run past, and I hear the chant: *"Kan ji zai bo satsu . . ."* (Avalokiteshvara bodhisattva . . .). They are very likely monks from Shogoji in Kikuchi, where Koun is now cloistered. I have been told that this old begging practice of the monastics has become a rare sight in Kumamoto. Perhaps Jisen-san, the tiny yet powerful Japanese Argentinian nun who now currently runs Shogoji, is compelled to set them back on this old route. I met Jisen-san last year, during an international ango—a rigorous ninety-day training session—that Koun attended. Her strictness and harsh ways, from what I remember, had become legendary with the monks—and were perhaps necessary. A woman, a foreign woman, put in a place of rank in a primarily Japanese male context. I do not envy her.

It is difficult to see the monks' faces beneath their straw hats, so I follow their movement along the Shimotori Arcade through the many shoppers, trying to look casual in my search for a tall foreign monk among them before finally fishing a coin out of my purse and approaching one of the men at the end of the line. I see that his legs are scabbed and pale, and his robes appear to be hitched up a bit too high—not Koun, but not Japanese, either. I put the coin in the bowl and he thanks me with a chant in a distinctly Spanish accent.

Rising from the last bow, he exclaims in emphatic Spanish-tinged English, "Ah! Tracy-san, do you remember me?"

I squint at the face hidden in the shadow of the wide hat. It is Aigo-san, from Spain. He also had been part of the international ango last year. "Yes, of course! I'm happy to see you again, Aigo-san. And Koun?"

"Koun-san is doing well. But he is not here with us today. He is *tenzo*—head cook."

"Please tell him . . . 'hello.' Take care, Aigo-san."

"Yes," he says, and is off again, running to catch up with the other monks and match their rhythm as they weave in calculated intervals through the crowd. I am left, breathless, watching as he disappears.

Monday, May 17

All night, a gentle but constant rain, and now quiet this morning—though the clouds are still heavy and dark. I washed clothing and towels yesterday, draping each drenched item on the backs of chairs, on the tops of doors, along bamboo poles balanced haphazardly across rooms. Nothing is dry yet. The smell of damp cloth permeates the house. Opening windows to the flaccid motion of damp outside air is only a slight reprieve from damp and unmoving *inside* air—but it is something. How I miss such conveniences that I once took for granted. A clothes dryer. A dishwasher. A temperature-controlled home. In so many ways, living here feels like living with one foot always in the past.

After breakfast, I put on my too-warm suit and wade through thick air to the hot balloon that is my office. A short while later, one of my energetic freshmen comes in because she needs help on a report for one of her other classes—she wants to write an explanation of Japanese temples and monasteries in English but doesn't know where to begin. I take out some paper to jot down ideas, and her eyes grow wide when I offer possibilities: the special food, the sacred clothing, the grounds and buildings, all the daily activities of a monk.

"Have you ever been to a temple?" she asks. So I explain, and she giggles uncontrollably. "Really? Really? Your husband? A foreigner? *Shugyo?*" Though I adore my student, today this annoys me and I feel my patience growing thin. Perhaps it is the heat, the terrible humidity.

Tuesday, May 18

At Nishida-sensei's table, Yoko-san is speaking to the other pottery ladies in a low, serious tone. She is telling the story of a man who slipped and fell nearly ten years ago, hitting the back of his head against a rock in such a way as to cause him to lose nearly all functioning in his limbs.

"He can't use his legs at all anymore. He can't use his fingers. His hands have curled into fists like this. He can only lift his right hand and arm a little."

The women lean over two six-by-ten-inch framed pictures while she talks, considering each before passing them on. The pictures are silhouettes: one of *nori* farmers standing on little boats in the ocean, stirring seaweed with long poles; the other depicting several houses in the old style with thick rice-bale roofs. The images—both printed from a computer from the dot-matrix era—are simple yet moving.

"He always wanted to draw, so in those ten years he taught himself how. His wife tapes his hand to the computer mouse so he can make his art. It takes him a long time to make each one— but he loves it."

After class, Sensei gives me a shopping bag filled with some of my pots wrapped in newspaper—free of the usual "firing" charge—as well as a small bushel of carrots and an onion. "Make soup," she says.

Yoko-san also tucks the picture of the *nori* farmers into my hands as a gift. "We are worried about you," she says. "You look thin and lonely."

Friday, May 21

Fierce rain all day—the edge of a typhoon passing from

Okinawa up to Shikoku. When I get home from work, a small pile of damp mail greets me in the *genkan*. I am surprised to find two items addressed from Koun.

The first, a postcard, details a drunken fistfight between two monks over "the nature of enlightenment"—the only pointed discussion of Buddhism he'd heard from any of them yet. *And, he writes, I've mostly stopped hitting my head against the doorframes. Mostly.*

The second, a long letter written in the brief lulls between daily duties, points to even more fascinating happenings: A monk passed out from lack of sleep during an important ceremony. Everyone watched his half-lidded eyes open and close, him swaying in and out of proper posture, and then his body hit the tatami hard, like a felled tree. And once at night, while dreaming about me and trying to "spoon," Koun crossed the edge of his four-by-six tatami into another monk's space, apparently touching the monk somehow (Koun not really remembering in his sleepy state), eliciting this firm warning shouted in darkness, the monk hovering inches from his face: "NEVER . . . AGAIN, KOUN-SAN . . . NEVER . . . AGAIN!" And also, during one morning meal, Jisen-san disowned one of her most promising *deshi*, the handsome and gentle Kodo-san. It was the morning Kodo-san was to complete his training, and he still needed money to return to his home country, Argentina. He wanted to see his daughter, who was having some trouble. So he had asked Jisen-san earlier if he could borrow some items from the monastery in order to do *takuhatsu* to raise money for the journey. She was not happy about his idea. All of this was expressed in angry Spanish over the formal morning tea, and then explained later, in English, to Koun by Aigo-san in hushed tones. *Probably there was another argument going on here—one that we observers couldn't really understand.* And then Kodo-san, a short while later, was sent down the mountain in his rough rope sandals while the monks sang "Stand by Me" at the tops of their lungs until he surely could no longer hear them. And then they all turned to their daily chores again, because what more could they do? *When a person leaves, it is like they were never here.*

Sunday, May 23

There's a sports event at the Budokan this weekend, and I have to wait in a line to park so long that I'm thirty minutes late for karate practice. Still, Mimaki-san and Tsuda-san don't show up for another half hour, so I practice *kata* alone in one corner of the dojo while a tiny woman and her tinier student do the same nearby. The girl belts out fierce *kiai* that put my shy shouts to shame. She's obviously being coached for a competition—her *kata* are heartbreakingly beautiful: powerful, bird-like moves.

I, on the other hand, have not been practicing my *kata* much these past couple of months, and it shows. I tried going over each set form in my kitchen when it became obvious that I was not going to drive out each weekend to train properly, but the dimensions of the room cut into each routine to the point that I could feel my muscles learning a new habit: a kind of hopping back (from a wall or cupboard), stunting the flow. Better to save it for the proper place and time, I thought (yes, an excuse), and instead embraced my yoga practice—one kinesthetic memory replacing another. Today, my body is screaming "downward-facing dog" with each punch and kick.

When the boys finally join me, we take turns leading the *kata* and exercises, and when it's my turn Tsuda-san says, *"Yoka?"*

"Eh, Yoga?? Yoga shimashoka?" (Shall we do yoga?) It's almost as if he's reading my mind.

He laughs for a long time at my bizarre misunderstanding and explains that *yoka* means "yes/no/ready" in Kumamoto dialect. How is it that I never noticed this before? I am a complete linguistic failure.

Monday, May 24

As I'm walking through the dorm courtyard, a movement behind the window of one of the guest houses flashes in the corner of my eye. A tiny brown bird is throwing itself at the glass again and again, trying to escape the dark interior. Without thinking, I open the door to a place that I have no right to enter, and the bird tumbles up into blue sky and disappears—as if it were never there at all.

~

At Tatsuda Center this evening, we say our farewells to the elegant Kyoko, who will be transferred to another office for three years. She hopes that she'll be able to return to Kumamoto in the next transfer, or the next. As a going-away present, I give her a small bundle wrapped up in a *furoshiki* cloth—some incense from Kyoto and an incense holder in the shape of a lucky owl. *Fuku*—the Japanese homonym for "owl" and "luck." I made the piece with the help of Nishida-sensei before being relegated to only simple cups and bowls.

"I hope to find you all sitting here when I return," she tells us. I do not want to let her go.

Tuesday, May 25

In pottery class, it is becoming clear that whatever boundaries existed between the Tuesday and Wednesday cohorts are blurring, perhaps because of my presence, perhaps not. Some of the ladies occasionally appear in both classes, some switch days. There are always just enough seats to go around.

This time, Yuko-san joins us with her bubbly, youthful energy and constant laughter. I'm deep into trimming my third cup—really one of Sensei's creations, as I destroyed all of mine during last class—when Yuko-san screams, breaking our collective concentration: her bowl had come unbound, flying off the wheel entirely. She lifts it from the floor and begins talking to it and stroking the surface tenderly, as if it were alive: *"Daijobu? Daijobu?"* (Are you okay? Are you okay?)

Her scream is not unlike the *kiai* that one produces in karate, so I try a joke in Japanese: *"Ano, sore wa yakimono no kiai desu ka?"* (Was that a pottery *kiai*?)

Everyone giggles while Sensei stands behind my shoulder, eyeing my work with a frown. She reaches over to the table and lifts a pot.

"Omoi" (Heavy), she scolds. *"Mo chotto. Kihon, kihon."*

Kihon is a word I also know well from karate: "basics."

I carve the next cup with great care. "Too slow and careful." Sensei scolds me again, then steps in and finishes my work in about one minute flat as the other potters watch and gasp *"Sugoi!"* (Wow!) in unison. When she returns the cup to me, it is as light as a sparrow.

Friday, May 28

I've been avoiding visiting the new mall that's on the other side of Kikuyo town. Over the past year or so, we've all watched it rise out of dirt: a giant, gleaming two-part monstrosity that— according to the signage—houses all the usual chain stores, Toho cinemas, and at least two American coffee chains. My students can't stop talking about it.

Today I decide to see what I've been missing. As I walk, the urbanization of this sleepy suburb of Kumamoto City overwhelms the senses. When Koun and I arrived at the end of March last year, everything between Highway 57 and the outskirts of this town was primarily rice fields and lush overgrowth. Now, all of that has been erased with block-like houses, tall apartment buildings, convenience stores, parking lots, clothing outlets, resale shops, a huge new central post office, chain restaurants, cell phone outlets, fast food (some American chains), and at the center, the massive new mall. The rural, open feel is a fast-fading memory. The only thing missing is a new highway to sustain all the traffic these new attractions bring in. The roads in this area have become choked with cars during rush hours, on weekends—all the time, really. Will this touch the not-so-far-away countryside of Aso, I wonder? And would it be appreciated there? Probably, I think. In Japan, convenience and modernity seem to win out over natural views. A seeming paradox in this culture steeped in heritage and tradition.

The parking for the mall starts a half mile away. I gawk at how full the lot is and also at the many big red "Youme Town" signs—the words a pun on the Japanese word *yume* for "dream" and the English "you" and "me."

The outside of the mall is beautiful and gaudy at the same

time—brightly lit signs are affixed to the upper levels. Identical landscaped little trees and flowers line the walkways. And the blue-gray mountains of Aso in the distance make for a gorgeous, almost serene backdrop to the whole complex. But when I step inside, I am swallowed by pandemonium. A crush of well-dressed shoppers. Shrill-voiced women in blue uniforms and little hats rushing up to offer floor guides and gift packs. Men in red tracksuits pressing sale leaflets into my hands. Everything is so shiny—the tile floors, the walls, the fixtures—nothing has yet been marred by the passage of time, and so the light reflects perfectly; I am blinded by brilliance. The sounds, too, overwhelming because unlike American malls, different stores are not always separated into distinct, walled compartments, and every retailer blasts its own theme song.

I loop through the hallways in the first building, getting lost. And then at the Swiss Kanditori stall, I spot one of my students, Aya, grinning sweetly and waving at me. She's wearing an adorable (and fetishy) black-and-white French maid's uniform, as are the other four girls standing alongside her in a rigid line behind the counter. They look vaguely embarrassed, but shout, *"Irasshaimasse!"* (Welcome!) in high-pitched voices on cue. A young man stands with them, but off to the side (no French maid outfit for him—a dignified white chef's uniform instead). He steps forward and offers me a piece of madeleine on a toothpick. I accept it, take a nibble, and nod at Aya.

"Is it good, Tracy-sensei?"

"Oh yes, very good. *Oishii.*"

"You like Youme Town?"

"It is a big place," I say.

"Yes, yes, very wide! Many stores! So great!"

"Well, *ganbatte ne.*"

"Yes, do my best!"

I don't want to linger too long and get her in trouble.

As I cross the glass-encased walkway on the way back out, I stop to watch the sunset. Purple-blue clouds hang in the vast sky and the dark mountains of distant Aso slip into night. A woman and her toddler pause briefly and watch with me before moving on. Below, I see crowds of people disappearing into the dark maws of cars with armloads of shopping bags. All those fleeting desires. Standing here, at the edge of a river of people, drinking my Starbucks latte while the sun goes down on us all, thinking, *This is true loneliness.*

Saturday, May 29

There's a letter from Koun today when I return from my Japanese lesson in the city. He writes, *Everyone seems to think it would be great for us to take up residence in one of the temples in Hawaii.* How wonderful it would be to live on, say, Maui, at the temple where we were married—that fusion of exotic tropical beaches and Japanese structures. The temple grounds were so Japan-like, in fact, that we pulled out onto the wrong side of the (luckily) empty road as soon as we left the parking lot on the day before our wedding, the two of us thinking nothing of it while Bryan, Koun's brother, shouted, "Hey! Hey! What are you doing?!"

Koun also writes that he has come upon a clue as to why he got so sick last year when he stayed at Shogoji for the annual international ango. It seems the Japanese monks never drink anything from the taps unless it's boiled into tea first, as the water comes directly from the river. The other foreign monks at that time drank the tap water but didn't get sick—many of them happened to have traveled to Japan from developing countries, and they may have been less affected by common pathogens. Perhaps the amount of salt was an issue as well. It's used heavily in the monks' food as a preservative, because there is no electricity for a refrigerator. The consumption of salt, in turn, only encourages the drinking of more water. Last year Koun lost forty pounds in six weeks.

Sunday, May 30

It's a cloudless and warm sunny day—perfect for drying futons, and the students are doing just that in the dorm this morning. The thin, brightly colored mattresses hang from long poles along the length of the roof, on top of the main building across from my townhouse. The young women move among the bedding, smacking each hard with pieces of bamboo, the *thwack thwack thwack* echoing throughout the neighborhood. A rhythm passed down through generations.

In the afternoon I go out to buy a convenience-store *bento* and pass by the house where the old lady always sits in her chair by the window. But today she is absent, and her driveway is filled with newly cleaned cars, and men and women in black suits move around the poorly tended courtyard. A lump rises in my throat—surely this is a funeral.

On the way back, I note that the cars remain while the people must have disappeared into the sprawling old house. Then I see her at the window: standing naked, shoulders sloped, breasts bared to the neighborhood that will not see while two women in black pull a thin white under-kimono around her body. Long gray hair bound up in a knot. I imagine a third woman—she must be there—carefully lifting the black silk kimono from its protective paper. This one last beautiful thing for her husband.

Monday, May 31

In the evening, finally the endless rain of a too-long day stops. While I'm boiling water for tea, Koun calls from the Shogoji cell phone—I know it is him—but the connection is lost before he can finish saying my name. When I return the call, it is busy—no doubt due to the whims of clouds passing over mountains.

There is a gathering at the neighbor's tonight. Laughter, the smell of Italian food carried through open windows while I sit at the kitchen table with a warm cup in my hands, waiting for my ride to Tatsuda Center for evening zazen.

I am thinking about Kyoto, about the meaning of authenticity, about whatever it is that I hope to find during this year. I am thinking about Satomi's words, too: *I travel to escape my boring life. When I go home, I always find myself there—just as I left me.*

Summer

JUNE
Being Here

Tuesday, June 1

During the solitude of a rice-and-miso-soup breakfast taken in my kitchen, I am thinking about my first year in Japan, how Koun—then Garrett—and I spent weekends together and, because of distance, how we led completely separate lives on the weekdays, me in Kumamoto City and he in the Aso countryside. But still we were partners and best friends; we were boyfriend-and-girlfriend; and for a long time—much longer than normal, perhaps—we never once admitted it to others, or to ourselves.

It was some time later, then, when we had settled into this new country, that we fully arrived to each other. Garrett and I had been driving through the narrow, winding side roads of the Aso countryside, when we burst out of a bamboo grove into an expansive view: rice fields sown with new seedlings, brimming with water and fanning out and down the mountain, like a mirror shattered on a staircase. We pulled over and got out, stood there together for a while in that vast and fragmented reflection. *This all feels significant somehow, doesn't it?* I'd said.

That night, stretched out on futon, in the semi-darkness of moonlight filtering through paper shoji, we were listening to the murmur of insects and frogs percolating through the thin walls of the house around us when he said, *I love you.* The words rang out startling and clear—a bell strike—in the room.

~

Outside, it begins to rain—violently. Perhaps *tsuyu*, the monsoon, has begun. That fifth, secret season to wash away the sweet memory of spring before the harsh heat of summer.

I rise from the table to rinse my bowl.

Wednesday, June 2

It is a warm and breezy day, a wonderful day. But unfortunately I am inside, standing in Shokei's sweltering gymnasium with the entire population of the school. Both students and staff stretch rhythmically to a narrated calisthenics routine set to scratchy piano music squawking from ancient loudspeakers, the audio a nostalgic relic of the prewar era. It is the very same program that plays at 8 o'clock every morning on the radio stations of Japan—for the benefit of schoolchildren, housewives, company employees, and anyone else who chooses or is required to tune in and participate. From what I'm witnessing, everyone has long since memorized the moves. This is our warm-up for Shokei's annual Sports Day. The activities generally include all manner of sports pomp played out on a track field, but our organizers have opted for a single day-long "soft volleyball" tournament instead.

Now semi-limber, we fan out across the floor in search of our designated team members. I find mine, and we begin tossing an oversized volleyball across one of the six nets set up in the room. We on the all-staff team are a scruffy lot—especially compared to the spry young women in semi-matching exercise wear. The students must have been practicing for this event for weeks or months, the way they handle the ball with such ease. And I gain some clarity on an odd happening after school last week: when I returned to a classroom in search of a misplaced textbook, I walked in on a group of sophomores writing out in chalk what looked like football plays. The girls screamed, *"Dame, dame, Sensei!"* and covered the chalkboard with their bodies and waving, outstretched arms.

"Hey, I'm just here for the book," I said, dramatically shielding my eyes.

After the initial warm-up, the tournament begins. It's to be a full-day event, as it turns out, the speakers now pumping out too-loud J-Pop and—eerily—American music from my high school days ("We will we will ROCK YOU!"). We play until arms and hands are an angry red from being smacked so many times by the ball. At least two significant leg injuries take girls out for good. "It's better than at elementary school," explains one teacher semi-proudly. "A few kids die each year from heat exhaustion."

During the final matches, I lean against the wall next to Santoki-sensei, exhausted. Both of our teams are out. "I am so tired," she says, "but they are all still *genki*—look at that energy."

She gestures toward the students, winces, and lets her arms flop to her sides. Then we discover that neither of us can make a fist. "It's as if I'm made of solid rubber from my elbows to my hands," I say.

"Me, too. Must be old age," she says with an air of sincerity. Santoki-sensei, the only teacher younger than me at the university, could easily pass for one of the students.

We rub our arms and look out over the court. "You know," I say, "these girls are amazing in so many ways. I was a mess when I was their age."

"Yes—they are very strong. Kumamoto strong."

"I do always wonder if it is hard for women here."

"Oh yes, very hard. Very terrible."

"So it's a bad place to raise girls?"

"No, it is a wonderful place for that. It is wonderful for girls here." A referee whistles and Santoki-sensei is called back to the game, to fill in for yet another injured student despite her own wounds, so I have no chance to ask about the apparent contradiction of her words. How, if I am honest, might I answer these questions about my home, Alaska? And are the ways in which we are haunted by the past, or suffer in the present, nothing more than a cultural habit? Is an experience good or bad, depending on how the question is asked? Can two realities be true at the same time?

~

At home, I stumble into my bedroom and fall asleep flat on my face until I jolt awake, just before pottery class. Driving is painful; turning the wheel takes significant effort. I explain my freak injury to Sensei, telling her that perhaps it would be best if I just watched today. *"Eh?"* she grabs one of my arms, inspects it, and begins to knead it with her powerful hands. It hurts like hell, and I gasp—repeatedly. She holds her ear close to my arm, listening while she kneads, ignoring the pained expressions and whimpering. Then, she releases me and arrives at her verdict: *"Pikapika, ne."*

"Um—*Pikapika?*"

"Eh. Pikapika pikapika pikapika."

Japanese is famous for its frequent use of onomatopoeia, but this new word I've never heard. Maybe it's the terrible sound a body makes while being forcefully massaged.

Taking some pity on me, Sensei rolls out a thin slab of clay and sets on the table a little statuette of Jizo—a character often recognized in Japan as the bodhisattva for women and children. The tiny figure clutches a bowl against its robed chest. "You can make one of these today. It's good for putting outside, next to your front door. You fill the basket with salt to keep out bad spirits."

Saturday, June 5

Walking past the rice fields today with twenty kanji flash-cards in my hands, I am concentrating so rigidly, tracing each character against paper, that I almost miss seeing a group of people—maybe seven or eight on a side street—taking pictures of the sky with their cell phones. All of them hold up the gadgets and stand perfectly still, as if capturing an alien invasion. I stop walking and glance up in the direction of their photo-taking, almost expecting to see a flying saucer. Instead, a bright double rainbow arcs across the complex jigsaw of buildings and rice fields. Could Koun be seeing this too? The monks stepping away from the midday cleaning of their mountain monastery, taking tea outdoors just to watch this prismatic echo for a few brief minutes before it all fades away? As I move on, the words from the day's flashcards rise back up into my consciousness: *bowl, vermillion, revelation, texture, cultivate.*

Sunday, June 6

Last night, the community loudspeakers announced over and over something that, as usual, I could not quite catch because of the scratchy too-loud reverberation of the ancient equipment. A typhoon? An emergency town meeting? A *chikan* in our neighborhood stalking my girls yet again? This morning, the mystery is solved as I walk down the street: everyone is outside sweeping, picking weeds, and gathering litter into big plastic bags. Right—the announcement had been a reminder to clean up the neighborhood on Sunday. Guiltily, I greet my neighbors and hurry past to the parking lot where I've agreed to meet with Yoko-san from pottery class. Today is one of Kyushu's premier pottery exhibitions, to be held at Grandmesse. Sensei will be selling her wares, and all of us students will drop by to offer support.

When we arrive, there are crowds of people moving through the labyrinth of makeshift pottery stalls, filling the great hall that is really more airplane hangar than showroom.

"Wow—*yakimono* must be incredibly popular in Japan," I say, feeling overwhelmed already.

"Oh yes, very popular," says Yoko-san. "You can get very famous names here for so cheap price."

Everywhere, people encircle stalls in bird-like flocks, then lift away with big bags of carefully wrapped treasures.

A map on the wall helps us to locate Sensei's stall, where she has arranged fragrant white lilies in some of her taller vases. "The smell draws in customers," she explains. Indeed it does— several women stop along the aisle, exclaiming about a familiar smell that they can almost but not quite name. They swivel their heads, looking around for the source, and then approach Sensei's booth to touch, lift, and consider.

After checking in with Sensei, Yoko-san and I spend the next couple of hours moving from vendor to vendor, she pointing out the more famous family kilns. "This is good," she says, motioning to one small corner stall, one of the more humble affairs. "*Hagi-yaki*. Very traditional style. Not like Western ceramic at all. Very . . . *wabi-sabi*."

I lift a mottled brown bowl. *Ideal for a monk, or for the wife of a monk*, I think, and pass it to the vendor, an older man with a kind smile.

"This foreigner is a *yakimono deshi*," Yoko-san announces loudly—not for the first time today. For Yoko-san, I suspect that her foreign friends are always a bit of a fashion accessory.

"Ah, is that so?" He smiles as he wraps the bowl.

"Yes. Her husband is a Zen monk—an American from Montana."

"Ah, is that so?" he says again, indulging Yoko-san's bragging as he also tucks a handful of ceramic chopstick rests into my bag as a "service."

Exhausted by the beauty of it all, we stop for tea and cake at a central food booth, where we can eat and drink from pottery made by the artist of our choice. I select a hand-pinched tea bowl and palm-sized oval tray in coordinated texture and color.

"It is even better when you can use it, *ne?*" says Yoko-san. I have to agree. The art is in the experience—glazed clay against the lip, a certain weight and texture in the hands, earthy taste of grass-green *matcha* against the tongue. Warmth as it enters, and then becomes, the body.

Monday, June 7

This afternoon I am assisting with Taguchi-sensei's Local Culture course—my role is to give feedback on drafts of the students' hometown reports. As I move from group to group, I learn that every town—no matter how tiny (or how indistinguishable from the surrounding towns)—has something for which it is purported to be extremely well known. Watermelon. Sweet potatoes. Oranges. *Dango.* Dried persimmon. Shellfish marinated in soy sauce. Altogether, a veritable feast of fame.

"How about Kikuyo—this area. What is produced here?" I ask one of the groups of girls.

"Carrots." Of course. How many times has a bag of carrots been pressed into my arms by a neighbor or one of the pottery ladies? Yet another obvious miss on my part.

I continue to survey the room, making note of all the edibles, when one of my students answers, "Goldfish."

"Goldfish?"

"Yes. Very famous."

"Are they . . . delicious?"

She giggles uncontrollably in reply. "Not for eating!" she at last manages. "Pet! Pet!"

"Tracy-sensei, what is your town famous for?" asks her partner.

"Nothing special." I pause. This answer isn't quite right. "Oh, well, come to think of it, in the town where I went to high school there are giant vegetables—pumpkins, zucchini, cabbage. They grow very big in Alaska—bigger than a big American man, even—because of the very long sunlight hours and a special way of growing them."

"Giant vegetables bigger than an American man? That is strange," she says. "We have never heard of such a thing."

Tuesday, June 8

On the way to school this morning, I meander through the neighborhood and really notice those temple darlings, the great pompoms of color-changing hydrangea, tucked against the sides of several houses. Was it only yesterday that I was walking past the very same flowers and they were a brilliant blue? Could they really be the same flowers? And now I admire them in green and white. Fickle, like my moods.

At noon, I opt for a long lunch hour to work old clay and attempt to free the dark cloud that has lodged in my mind. Unfortunately, I have yet to truly understand the process of recycling clay—it seems a koan given by Sensei to torture me. I've figured out that I need to dry it considerably beforehand.

But there's also the difficulty of getting it to blend. My new plan is to tear it all up into smaller pieces and knead these into workable chunks before pushing them once again into one big lump to pummel and massage. And so I do this, really putting my weight into it. The worry, though—I begin to understand this as I push and pound the final product—is that I'm just creating a more thorough set of faults for the clay to break against later, when I'm forming it on the wheel.

Finally, I've been at it for too long. The muscles in my arms are cramping, and I sigh, step back, and lean into the wall with my clay-stained hands outstretched before me. What am I doing? What can I possibly hope to accomplish with this constant reworking of dirt and water?

The sound of the mail coming through the slot in the front door startles me. I walk to the sink, rinse my hands, and wipe them on a towel—though not well enough. In the entryway, I find a single letter addressed from Koun and tear it open eagerly, covering the paper with damp gray fingerprints, little kisses.

Koun writes that Shogoji's *nichiyo sanzenkai*, the monthly day of meditation for laypeople, will be this Sunday—and I've been given permission to attend. He also writes that Jisen-san has said that it will be "too hard for him to see me," that she will allow it but doesn't encourage it. All in all, it is good news—something to look forward to. Still, the cloud lifts away only momentarily.

~

I falter this evening in pottery class. I can't seem to get the cups to stay put for trimming, as my heavy-handed, clumsy scraping yanks them clean off the wheel again and again. This frustration is punctuated by Yoko-san asking me question after question about Alaska—*Snow in summer? Famous sights? Famous food?*—she's wrongly got it in her head somehow that I aim to return there over the summer holiday. But no simple clarifying comment seems to stop her, so I just answer each question as it comes. *Usually there is no snow in summer, unless you are at a very high altitude. Denali is the tallest mountain in North America. The king crab is very good, as are the many varieties of salmon.*

What I've given up on explaining—mostly because she

won't understand, culturally or linguistically—is that I very rarely return to Alaska; there have been only a few brief visits in the past eleven years or so. Because Koun's mother can no longer travel, all of us, including my mother and brother-in-law, go to Montana over the winter or summer holidays.

Suddenly, Yoko-san exclaims, "*Yosh!* I decided. I will go to Alaska with you. Your parents live in a big house there?"

"Wait—what?"

"Your parents have a big house?"

"No—my mother. . . it's just a small condo."

"Okay. I will book hotel. Maybe my granddaughter will come too. You tell me the dates."

I collapse the bottom of the cup I've been working on, ruining it.

"Pay attention!" says Sensei, shaking her head.

Giving up on trying to explain to Yoko-san, I rise to clean up all that I have destroyed.

Saturday, June 12

In downtown Kumamoto City I sit in a café, adjacent to a wall of window, scribbling in a notebook and watching people pass by beyond the glass. Every few minutes, someone seems to startle and notice me, an exotic fish in captivity—while I, looking out at them, witness a similar effect, but in the plural.

In Japanese class earlier this morning, a baby-faced American boy in his twenties had learned my age during a practice discussion and lapsed into English, "Whoa—you're thirty? I guess I've got some years to learn Japanese then."

I'd laughed. "I feel that I was twenty yesterday." And that's true. But now that I really think about it, I also feel that twenty was a million years ago—I was not yet, but nearly, twenty when I moved away from my home in Alaska.

Opening to a new page in my notebook, I draw a line down the middle and label two possibilities: *Go home* and *Don't go.* Though it is unlikely that Yoko-san really intends to go to Alaska, her comments have sparked this idea in me—an idea that I have been circling around for some time now. But my pen hovers over the page. I don't know what to write. There is just the felt-sense of Alaska—a single, inexplicable knot of emotion. Is it possible to long for a place and hate it at the same time?

I put down my pen and look up just as two of my students, Risa and Kanae, appear behind the glass. They pause, seem briefly shell-shocked with recognition before exchanging emphatic waves with me.

A minute later, the girls enter the café and find my table. "Tracy-sensei! Surprise to see you in natural life setting."

"I'm surprised to see you, too!"

"You are writing something?"

"Just thinking mostly. What are you two doing?"

"Shopping!"

"Where are your bags?"

"Oh, few money. Looking only."

"Window shopping?"

"Yes, yes."

"Does it make you feel bad, looking and wanting all those things that you can't have?"

"Yes, but—we enjoy."

After they sit with me for a bit and chat about their many fashion desires, the girls wander off to more shopping adventures. I finish my tea in a swift gulp, tuck my notebook into my bag, and consider my needs for the journey to Shogoji on Sunday: a modest dark long-sleeved shirt, cookies or something else to offer for the monks' tea time, and simple comfort foods for Koun—most likely snacks from the foreign-food section of the big department store.

As for Alaska, the question can wait. Tomorrow I will see my husband for the first time in over three months. There is enough to obsess about already. And seeing Koun—it might be a little like window shopping.

Sunday, June 13

I wake much too early and, after a frantic bout of zazen, sit out on the steps of my townhouse for a long while, drinking a can of cold and too-sweet bitter coffee purchased from a nearby vending machine, as the neighbor's cat passes through and around my legs—an infinity loop of furry affection. When it is time to go, I toss the can in the recycle bin and get into the car.

I've driven the route to Shogoji several times before, as I dropped off and picked up Koun for the international ango, as well as other events, the previous year. It's about an hour-and-a-half drive out of the city and into the smaller town of Kikuchi and then another twenty minutes or so through a tiny village and up into the mountains. Driving this last bit, up the one-lane, shoulderless road that clings precariously to a steep cliff, I am thankful that our car is so compact. The drop-off is terrifyingly sheer. Below, small rice paddies staircase down to the river. When I pull up, at last, to the parking lot that overlooks the valley below, Koun is there waiting for me in *gassho*, a twig broom on the ground next to him and a wide grin across his face. For three months, I've been longing for that familiar smile.

"Wow—you look thin!" I say as I get out of the car, and he does, the *samu-e* falling loosely around his body and his cheeks hollow.

"You should see me naked!"

"Not for another eight and a half months, Sweetie." I want to embrace him, but cannot. As I know from his previous ango stay, this is a potentially delicate situation. Somewhere lurking in the shadows of the monastery could be Jisen-san, or perhaps some other monk, eager to spot some small indiscretion (real or imagined) that will be used as evidence to keep me away. Instead, Koun helps me with my things and we ascend the stone stairs to the main cluster of buildings, both of us walking slowly and grinning like idiots, just happy to be in each other's company.

From the top of the stairs we follow a stone path across a field of pale rocks, at the center of which is the huge temple bell. I scan the complex, this centuries-old monastery that has fallen and risen again and again from the dirt. The *kuin* (reception, kitchen, and informal dining hall) is to our left. The main building, the *hatto* (Dharma Hall), sits directly before us, and to our right is the *sodo*, where monks and laypeople do zazen. Beyond that is the bathhouse and monk's quarters. The *koki-an* (abbot's quarters), though I cannot see it, is behind the *kuin*. All of the buildings are joined by open-air walkways, and many of the thin walls of the buildings slide open so that the monks spend much of their days outdoors—even when they are inside. Surrounding the complex is the pulsing, vibrant life of the mountain, always threatening to swallow it whole.

"It must be hard to keep the forest at bay, especially in summer," I say.

"True—it occupies a lot of our time." We stop together at the open front veranda of the *kuin*. "I need to get ready, but I'll see you again soon. Oh—we're doing formal *oryoki* lunch today."

"That complicated thing with all the bowls and whatnot?"

"Don't worry—just follow along with the others." As Koun moves off to finish his duties, I remove my shoes and bow into the receiving room, where one of the Japanese monks greets me formally and indicates where to sign my name on the temple ledger. "Please follow," he says, and leads me past the ornate *hatto*—where the gilded Buddha looks down on us from a high altar—to an adjacent vestibule, where I drink tea alone, contemplate the serene face of a large Medicine Buddha, and wait for the others to arrive.

Several people amble in at the same time, talking among themselves, and then almost immediately we are all beckoned out onto the walkway, where we slide our feet into slippers and shuffle along the smooth wood to the *sodo* for zazen. I choose a seat near the entrance, pull my body up onto the platform while tucking the slippers beneath, and then face the wall and settle into meditation posture. Koun and I are now sitting together— under the same roof at least—and it is a comforting feeling tinged with longing. I feel I could stay here, in this rigid posture, forever.

My body jerks when the drum sounds, signaling the end of the morning session. I gracelessly follow the monks and laypeople through a series of bows and prostrations. The ceremony begins after this, and I pretend to chant while the others recite the lineage from Shogoji's founder to the Buddha. Through these small failures, I can feel myself growing more and more nervous about *oryoki*. Koun explained it to me once, when we were preparing for his entrance to the monastery. But I don't remember much about this ritualized way of formal monastic dining. All I can recall, I think, is that I must eat a bit of the rice first, and then move from bowl to bowl in a circle, until all has been consumed. The drums sound and the server monks begin to rush around, delivering lacquerware *oryoki* bowl sets wrapped in *furoshiki* cloth to all the guests. Jisen-san looks on from the teacher's seat at the center of the room, orchestrating everything with her eyes. We untie the stack of bowls and place them on the cloth, and I can see that I am not the only one who is nervous. Some of the monks' hands shake as they rush from person to person, delivering rice, miso soup, and vegetables. A couple laypeople, too, are muttering under their breath, asking each other what to do. We eat fast and as efficiently as we can after a monk announces second helpings, and then we are delivered water and then tea to wash out the last bits of food from our bowls. Finally, we restack the dishes and tie them up into neat packages with the *furoshiki* cloth. We laypeople shuffle slowly out of the *sodo* afterward, as if defeated.

As I'm putting on my shoes at the exit, Koun appears next to me. "I'll walk you to the car." He lifts my bag and I follow him.

"What did you think about *oryoki*?" asks Koun.

"It's a lot like tea ceremony . . . but on steroids."

He laughs. "It *is* like that."

"You don't eat that way all the time, do you?"

"Not exactly, but even the informal way is ritualized."

"Right—everything is sacred for you guys."

"Well, or the opposite. You know, 'If you meet the Buddha, kill the Buddha.' . . . Oh, look at this," he says as we descend the long stone staircase from the temple grounds to the parking area below. "The leaves have covered the stones again. I'm always noticing things like this now—all these little details."

"Remind me to save plenty of housework for your return."

"Nothing would make me happier than to sweep floors for you."

As we stand before the view of the valley, for a moment I can't speak. I want desperately to hold his hand, to hug him.

"Are you okay?" he asks.

"I'm okay. It's just—I don't know—surreal. Like moving through a memory or a dream."

"I wish we could have had some time together today."

"I know—me too. I'm just glad you're closer now. That's something." I open the back of the van and Koun sets my bag inside. "I've been thinking about going to Alaska over the summer break."

"Well, that's new. Do you feel good about it?"

"I'm not sure how I feel about it."

"Maybe that's okay, you know."

"Maybe."

~

In my rearview mirror, I see that he stays in *gassho*—the good manners of a monk—as I drive down the mountain.

Monday, June 14

Such storms and gloom in my mind. Sitting zazen at Tatsuda Center this evening, stories from my childhood float up from somewhere—little devastating clouds. I've gotten better at not following those ugly emotions. But I follow today, really really follow, because I can't quite figure out my simultaneous need for—and trepidation about—returning to Alaska. What I'm seeing is my stepfather driving our red Chevy Blazer on the way home, him talking, a long riff that won't stop—teasing me in that way that isn't teasing and looking in the rearview mirror again and again to see how badly I am taking it. My mother beside him, laughing nervously, and me in the back turning away, finally, to stare out my window at the passing landscape. And then the moose coming fast out of the trees and down from the embankment next to the road. The impact sound and sensation all in one: a rush of cold as the window bursts to the left of my face and my body thrown forward, instantly bruised by the seatbelt across my hips. I must have closed my eyes. When I open them, I see that my hands are shaking and covered in glass. My breath low and shallow while my stepfather swears and gets out of the car, moving around it to take in the damage. "Must have rolled right over us," he says when he gets to my side of the car. "Looks like it took out your window with a hoof." He opens my door and slams it shut. "Door's fine." I look beyond my destroyed window, see blood, the dark flank of the animal, my stepfather's boots kicking gravel. "Fucker shit himself." He kneels and I see that the animal is still breathing. I become aware of my mother then, her getting out of the car. I stare down at my hands. I don't look up again until we get home.

With his friends—the various people he entertained at our house (and elsewhere) on the weekends—my stepfather told his version of this story and it always got a big round of laughter. "That moose jumped out of nowhere—from the sky," he'd say. And then there was the punchline: "When I opened Tracy's door, she was covered in shit. Completely covered. It was disgusting."

Once, I spoke up. "That's not really what happened."

"What?"

"That's not what happened." He stared down at me. I lowered my eyes and retreated to my room, closing the door behind me.

Days after my small act of defiance, a humor piece appeared in the local paper detailing the escapade of our family car versus a flying moose and a girl inexplicably covered in excrement. The article was written by a family friend, a journalist, and my stepfather had it framed. It hung in the hallway next to my room so I would not forget his power to shape reality and to make others see exactly what he wanted them to see.

My mother, now divorced from this husband of many years, who knows the depths of his cruelty, still repeats his version of this and other stories. Her memory, too, rewritten.

Wednesday, June 16

I am walking my usual route this evening, lost in my thoughts, when an old man looks up from his work in his garden and calls out to me, waving his hand to get my attention. "Hey there!" I'm pretty sure I've seen this gentleman before, walking the streets dressed in nothing more than long underwear and an undershirt. "Hey!" he calls again. "Don't I often see you walking past here?"

I explain that yes—it's my daily exercise, "for the health."

"Please," he says, "you must come inside and meet my wife. Just for a moment."

I protest—after all, I haven't got that much time to finish my walk, eat dinner, and get to pottery. But he keeps pushing, this lonely man who just wants to be kind to a stranger, so why not? We stroll the length of the narrow driveway to his house, and he names each tree that he's planted himself along the way. It occurs to me that he might actually be a little drunk, and this could be a funny situation I've gotten myself into.

Inside, I slip off my shoes in the *genkan*. It is a typical old-style Japanese home—elegant and also cluttered. I'm led to a sitting room, where his wife joins us shortly with a tray of expensive fresh-cut melon and steaming cups of coffee. "I used to be a painter," says the man, pointing to the many paintings hung along one wall of the room and filling an adjoining room entirely. "But I can't do it anymore," he says, tapping his head and grinning.

He reaches beneath the coffee table and pulls out a thick photo album, and we begin to flip through scenes of Europe. "They're beautiful—have you really been to all of these places?" I ask.

"Oh yes," he replies, pointing to the albums that nearly fill two tall bookshelves. "There's more, too—those are just some of them."

His wife looks agitated, twisting her hands in her lap. "Come on now, she doesn't want to see all your pictures. Tell us, what do you do?"

"I teach at Shokei."

"How about your husband? Or—you are single?"

"I'm married—he's at a monastery this year for *shugyo*."

"I see. Excuse me, there is something I would like to tell you. Do you have time?"

"She's always doing this," says the old man, chuckling.

"Stop that," she says.

"Well, I don't have much time. I have a class this evening."

"Really, it won't take any time at all. And I'm afraid it is very, very important." She returns with a worn leather-bound book and sets it on the table before me. "Have you ever heard of *The Holy Bible?*"

"Oh yes—Christianity is very common in my country."

"I see. Well, let me explain. There is a God, you see, and He lives in the sky, in Heaven. Can you understand my Japanese well? Can you understand 'Heaven?'"

"Woo—there she goes now!" The old man begins to chuckle again.

"Stop that!" She shouts back at him while he lifts himself up out of his chair. Then she continues, "You can go to Heaven only if you believe in God. Otherwise, you will go to Hell. That is the place where the Devil lives. It is very, very bad there."

"*Hora.* Do you see that beautiful woman in this painting?" The old man is standing now, unsteadily, and pointing at a painting on the wall of a woman wearing an elegant dress slit high up the thigh. "Do you see her?" His voice becomes high and shrill. "Do you see that woman?! That's MY WIFE!"

"Stop it, will you! Sit down."

He sits back down, looks at his hands, and pouts.

"Not so young any more though." He snorts and chuckles again.

"I'm so sorry—I really should go," I say. It appears that I have indeed gotten myself into something interesting. "I'm late for my pottery class already. . . . "

"Wait!" the old man stands up again. "You like *yakimono?* My daughter used to do *yakimono.* She is in Tokyo now. No time for her old parents." He limps off to another room and then puts something into his wife's hands, and they both disappear, and for a moment I wonder if I should just go but they both come out again as I finish tying my shoelaces.

He presses a bag into my hands. "Please," he says, "won't you come visit us again? Please? Please?"

Later, I try to explain to Sensei why I'm so late to class. "Did you all catch that?" She says, "Tracy-san was kidnapped by an *ojiichan*. He gave her this little vase with *sakura* petals etched on it."

They pass around the fragile vase of my lonely kidnappers. "Beautiful . . . beautiful . . ."

Saturday, June 19

Satomi and I sit in a dark theater in downtown Kumamoto, the sound of fast food being unwrapped around us, while on the screen mostly Japanese actors in a Japanese-produced movie speak Korean in a vaguely European setting. For Satomi and me, it has become a habit to watch foreign films together—that is, films that are in a language unknown to both of us—followed afterward by our question-and-answer sessions at a local coffee shop. Maybe being immersed in a lack of cultural/linguistic understanding has become a source of pleasure for me—I seek out confusion as entertainment.

Today's film is in black and white, what appears to be a love-lost-and-gained story. The subtitles are quickly appearing and disappearing lines of Japanese—always much too fast to even begin to make sense of what little I can read. Thus for me, this is a film of visuals only. I am following the cinematographer's obsession with images of shoes and feet intensely, trying to make meaning out of it against the relationships of the unlikely ménage of characters living in an apparent hotel. Each time we see a character, we are introduced to their feet in a flash, and later we see their feet again during times of discordance. What can it mean? Feet traveling along the path of life? Walk a while in his or her shoes? I look down at my own feet—dusty, sockless, calloused from my obsession with long daily walks, and bound up in a pair of worn, un-pretty hiking sandals. What depth of my character is revealed here? What metaphor?

Later in a coffee shop, Satomi and I sip cool drinks, fanning away the cigarette smoke around us while I drill her with my questions, but the answers this time just leave me feeling more confused.

"Why did the young woman who worked in the flower shop move out of the hotel?"

"I don't know."

"Why did the angry men take away the little girl's father, and why didn't anyone stop them?"

"Well . . . that wasn't the girl's father, and anyway he killed the little girl's mother."

"Wow. Okay. But what was with all the feet?"

"Feet? I'm not sure what you're talking about."

"Let's back up here. It's a love story, right?"

"I think so. Maybe. I'm not sure."

Monday, June 21

Amazingly, a typhoon just missed Kyushu again—the edge grazed us while the full storm went straight up to Shikoku. All that weather-report drama for nothing much. So far, Koun is lucky that he's on this island for the summer.

This evening there is a welcome party for a few delegates from College of Saint Mary, one of our sister schools in the U.S., and it's turning out to be more lively than usual: Hiroe-sensei is very drunk and keeps making passes in the form of marriage proposals to one of the visitors, a beautiful Japanese expat (now forty, Hiroe-sensei seems desperate for a wife lately—I have been jokingly proposed to by him on more than one occasion). The woman coyly replies over and over that she already has too many boyfriends in America. And the usually stoic Takahashi-sensei teaches me Japanese drinking idioms: "We Japanese have two stomachs—one for food, one for beer" and also *"Ashi-kun"* which means "Mr. Legs," essentially "designated driver."

In all of this drunken chaos, Cynthia, our honored and wonderfully big-personalitied foreign guest, asks the inevitable, "Married? And so what does YOUR husband do?" And when I reply, she stares at me hard. "Well, isn't THAT interesting," letting me know, in her tone and stare, that it is not interesting in a positive sort of way. The handsome and reserved Takeshita-sensei—sitting at an angle to me and slightly out of earshot of Cynthia—unwittingly saves me from a religious challenge that I have never found all that compelling. He leans in and asks about my experience with Zen in Japan. "My teacher does zazen, too," he says. "I also am learning the way."

Wednesday, June 23

"What's Koun's blood type?" Sensei asks as I am turning cups in pottery class this evening.

"I'm not sure."

"How can you not know his blood type? That's important information."

"Is it? Americans don't think about it so much."

"How about you? What's your blood type, Tracy-san?"

"I'm an O."

"Ahhh . . . so you are an O."

"Does that mean something?"

"A is very active. B is lazy. AB is crazy. O is pretty good— good balance."

"How about this teacup, Sensei?" I show her how I've snuck an American-style mug handle onto one of my cups. "Good balance?"

"No, it is AB—crazy."

Friday, June 25

It is that hour between light and dark and I decide to drive out to the *onsen* because I need to do something to boil out the tension that has been rising in me all week. I enter the complex, buy a ticket from the machine, and put my shoes in the rack while ignoring, as always, the big sign in English that reads "No Tattooed People"—a sign meant, perhaps, to ward away *yakuza* but for some reason is only printed in English. When I hand my ticket to the attendant, he warmly bids me good evening—I am a regular here, after all. I'm careful to select the character indicating the women's entrance, as the designation changes every few days (I've nearly made a mistake more than once!).

In the changing room I remove my clothes and tuck them into a cubby. An old woman stands next to me, also naked and clutching a tiny white towel. "Excuse me. I lost my cubby before I took the key out. It's 34, but I can't see the numbers well."

I locate the cubby for her, but her clothes are not inside. I check the whole wall, and then the next. Then we move to a different area and find her things.

"Oh!" She says after thanking me and really seeing me for the first time. "Where are you from?"

"Alaska. In America."

"Ah," she says, "that's good isn't it." Then she thanks me and bows deeply—such formality between two naked strangers—before moving off.

I slide open a glass door and enter the steam-filled bathing area. As is necessary and customary, I spend a long time at the seated showers, washing my hair and body and taking care not to spray those seated next to me. Little boys and girls wander past—all of them stopping to stare at my foreign skin growing pink beneath hot water, before being called away by their mothers.

And then I slip into the indoor baths one by one—the delicious-smelling *yuzu* (citron) bath, the jacuzzi, the ionized bath. I step outdoors to cooler air and test the sauna, the cold pool, the waterfall falling hard against aching shoulders.

I am sitting on the ledge next to the newly-installed *denki* (electric) bath, letting my skin cool, when two chatting young women swiftly step down into the water, not seeing the warning signs. They scream, *"Nani? Nani?!"* (What? What?) and then laugh when they realize what they've done, subjecting their bodies to the sensation of electricity as it contracts their muscles into relaxed submission.

In one of his recent letters, Koun wrote that whenever the monks go to the *onsen*—a treat after *takuhatsu*—they shave each others' heads. After that, he likes to sit full lotus in the water, the heat helping his body to settle into the posture.

I have been wanting to try this special zazen. Slipping back into the water, I tuck each foot over the opposite thigh and sit for a few minutes before the heat compels me to get up and move on to the walking bath that is in the shape of a great circle. Water *kinhin*, I think: this slow tide of women flowing in silence, the water at the ribs below our breasts, our hands trailing rippling wakes, our legs and torsos pushing powerfully forward forward forward.

Alaska. That's good, isn't it.

Saturday, June 26

"Everyone keeps asking me if I have a gun," says Chad, a fellow language student, during our morning break at the YMCA. The animated twenty-something from California continues, "So the other day I started pointing to my pocket or a drawer at work or whatever. This guy—you should have seen his eyes—'Really? In . . . your . . . pocket?'"

I offer my own story of the delightful and ever-joking American Ed, who took to practicing his possessives in Japanese by inquiring if all precious items around him were *"boku-no?"* (mine?). This was good fun, as it caused the Japanese a considerable amount of discomfort. "But one day, one of his coworkers insisted that he take the very expensive pair of binoculars that Ed had been declaring 'mine' all day."

"Awesome," laughs Chad as he gathers his things to return to class. "I'm trying that one tomorrow."

"So . . . um, that was meant as a cautionary tale," I add, too late, as I follow him into the classroom. I've missed a beat and he's already well into a jovial conversation with someone else.

After class, Satomi and I go to lunch. "I know I don't understand Japanese culture very well. But I also feel like some kind of anthropologist around the younger Westerners who are new to Japan," I tell her over bowls of steaming ramen. "Sometimes I feel they don't understand me, and when I listen to their stories, or the details of their lives, I know I'm not understanding them in the way they intended. It's as if I'm constantly looking through these layers, or maybe accessing a myriad of meanings. And then my rhythm is permanently off because I'm always thinking in prism form, *That means this and this and this and this and this. . . .*"

"Something like that happens to Japanese who leave Japan for a while. They come back, and they are still Japanese, but they are also changed forever. We are of a group culture, so everyone senses a difference. Sometimes those people become ostracized because they can't quite fit back into the group."

"How can a foreigner ever hope to fit in?"

"It's impossible. That difference will always be noticed. But at least they are foreigners, so it is expected." She brings up a recent argument among the teachers: Should Japanese teachers correct the manner of student speech if it is impolite—if it is not culturally appropriate in the classroom context? Or is it taking away the students' personal choices? "We don't want to take away their autonomy in expression, but the behavior or way of speaking is inappropriate for Japanese people."

"It's an interesting question. I've met many foreigners who speak Japanese so much better than I do, but for some reason appear to have no sense of what cultural significance their words and actions have on others."

"Or maybe they do know, but they choose to behave that way anyway."

"So I guess we're back to the original challenge—but with a new twist!"

"Yes, we're all outsiders. None of us fit in."

Monday, June 28

At Tatsuda Center after zazen, Stephen and I look on as Richard, ever the dashing academic, climbs astride his motorcycle and zooms away into the night.

"I get the feeling that Richard is frustrated with us," says Stephen as he unlocks the truck door for me. "Maybe he wants us to talk about Buddhism more, to make our meetings more intellectually stimulating."

"Yes, I can see that. He's a smart guy. Super smart. And I don't mind if he has something to offer up—that would be great. But honestly I don't know what to say about Zen or Buddhism or any of it. And what could I say about my own experience, even? It might just become therapy. I have an ugly mind."

"What do you mean?"

"Lately I keep circling around some fragment of memory or other. I think, with Koun gone, it's gotten worse lately. There's that fear of change, I guess. Or a fear of the past. Maybe it's just too much alone time."

"Good memories or bad?"

"Some bad, some good."

"Try more of the good."

"Easier said than done. And also—I'd be doing it wrong, right? I'm pretty sure that I'm not supposed to be focusing on anything."

"You could give up zazen for a while."

"Sure, but it doesn't only happen in zazen. My mind is always ugly."

Tuesday, June 29

"Tracy-sensei, do you know *hanakotoba?*" Naoko asks me this as I circle around the classroom in a long, flowing skirt.

"'Flower words'? What does it mean?"

"It's uh . . . ," she consults her dictionary briefly, "'the language of flowers.' I don't know well, but my mother knows. She always tell me I should be careful when choose flower for person—it must express good meaning."

"We have something like that in our culture—red roses for love, white lilies for funerals, daisies for innocence—but I don't know much about that either. It seems that flowers are very important in Japanese culture."

"Yes, our other foreigner teacher said flowers are only for women, but flowers are for men *and* women in Japan."

"Oh, yes," Yukari pipes in beside her. "Flowers are powerful for man. Samurai power!"

Naoko whispers to her seatmates, then asks, "Tracy-sensei, why do you have red rose tattoo?"

"What?!" shouts Yukari. "You have tattoo? Only *yakuza* have tattoo!"

"Well, now you know my secret, Yukari." I smile knowingly. "Do you all want to see the mark of the *yakuza*?" The girls lean forward, eyes wide, as I lift the bottom edge of my skirt to reveal a clichéd metaphor of love and pain, the bright red rose thick with thorns, that I have worn since I turned eighteen.

Wednesday, June 30

During tea with the pottery ladies, Yuko-san, who is clumsy and beautiful and always laughing, reveals that she is pregnant with her first child. As the women congratulate her and rub their hands over the slight rise of her belly, I envy her. I often wonder if I will be a mother someday, if Koun and I will take that leap.

Afterward, as we enter the studio, one of the ladies asks, "What are you all making tonight?" and this is met by a mantra of indecision:

"I don't know—what are you making?"

"I can't decide."

"I don't know."

"Maybe another vase."

"Maybe a teapot."

"Maybe . . . "

"Sensei, what should we make?"

"I don't know—make bowls and cups with Tracy-san again. That's good practice."

After the initial kneading is finished, the five of us begin to draw clay up from our wheels, up into tall gray and brown phalluses, and then fold the tips over and down again with the force of our bodies. Down and up, down and up, down and up. I always expect a dirty joke about this ritual, from these women who make me laugh so unexpectedly. But then someone says the obvious, and it is taken and given only as a statement of fact:

"*Chin-chin mitai.*" (It looks like a penis.)

"*So ne.*" (So it does.)

And then powerful as gods, each of us trades one sex for another as smooth, open vessels form beneath our fingers.

JULY
Homecoming

Thursday, July 1

All day, I think about a thing that Koun wrote in one of his letters, puzzling over it, because it makes sense and also because I don't completely understand it: *In every moment*, he writes, *I keep coming back to a sense of wonder about how closely linked this formal practice is to a sense of place.*

This singular thought inspires me to linger in each of my frequently inhabited spaces, noticing how the placement and functionality of objects and architecture determine the flow of movement, like boulders jutting from a river. In the bedroom, the fragile tatami encouraging a light and shoeless step as I dress for the day. In my office, the wall of windows and vast view of green and blue pulling my gaze, and then my body, up again and again, away from work at my desk. In a classroom, the inexplicably permanent wood lectern around which I am constantly maneuvering in order to deliver my lessons.

And in entering or exiting all of these spaces, a heavy sliding door requiring one to *pause. open. enter. turn. pause. close. turn.*

Friday, July 2

I have a visitor to my office during an afternoon break— Kiyoe (aka the *Totoro* character "Nekobus"—affectionately called this by her classmates due to her overly broad grin and perfect row of shiny white teeth). She recently returned from her year-long homestay with the College of Saint Mary in the States. Something in her manner is different and recognizable all at once. "I didn't understand what you said about eye contact and smiles," she tells me, "until I went to the U.S. Now I understand completely. Everybody smiles and looks you in the eyes—even strangers."

I relate to her my story of being stalked through the side streets of Kumamoto. I was headed home on the tram and I happened to be sitting across from a man about my age. When I looked in his direction, our eyes briefly locked. "I just smiled once before turning away—that's what we're likely to do in America. Maybe especially in small-town America." But when I got off the tram, he followed me everywhere I went. I couldn't shake him, and I certainly didn't want to lead him to my home. At one point I started yelling at him in English to go away. After a little while, he did. Later, a somewhat older man did the same thing, him going on and on about my breasts looking like some kind of fruit. By that time, I knew exactly what to do. When I started walking toward the nearest police box, he veered off.

"After that, I got better about not making prolonged eye contact and smiling so much at people here. But I still do it sometimes. It's a habit, you know." I tell her, "You be careful—even more boys will be following you around now." I imagine all the CSM girls locking eyes and flashing brilliant smiles at unsuspecting boys—dangerous, or a dangerous skill.

What I don't tell her is that I once walked down Shimotori Arcade during the crowded daylight hours, casually looking into the eyes of those who passed by to see what would happen. Everyone looked away quickly on that day—except the old women. *Obaachan* (old lady) power. They stared me into the ground and I always looked away first. Why does this remind me of Sensei?

Sunday, July 4

We're in the dojo—Tsuda-san, Mimaki-san, and I—and all of us are sweating rivulets, though we've barely begun to stretch. "Motivation goes down in heat," says Tsuda-san. "Let's do our best!" Our practice quickly evolves into a fever dream of pushing our bodies through thick air while Tsuda-san barks orders at us. There is something said about breathing—apparently I'm not doing it right—and then, I think, a long riff on my inability to move in anything but a straight line when I attack and receive punches and kicks. All of the advice sounds somewhat like the buzzing of an insect in the ear when one just wants, desperately, to lie down and sleep it all away. By the end of practice, I'm pretty sure I'm missing time.

Though the shower afterward is delicious, it is only a brief reprieve. Clean clothes on, and already damp through to the skin. This season of *mushiatsui* may most literally mean "hot and humid," but a better translation would be "a hell realm; a constant state of discomfort."

Monday, July 5

It's the last week of school before the mid-year summer break, and I'm playing Pictionary with my students for fun—though it's an abbreviated and improvised version in which I filter out English words that are likely beyond their understanding. This game often fascinates me because fluent native speakers of English such as myself are rarely assets on an all-Japanese team. The girls create sketches that I would not necessarily associate with the given word—but the images work well enough for their Japanese teammates.

Today, the one additional quirk is that the good-natured and sweetly naive Risa keeps shouting "Over easy!" as the possible answer or perhaps as words of encouragement to her teammates. (I guess it is a phrase recalled from one of her other English classes; I'm not at all convinced that she has any idea what it means.)

One of the girls draws a card, hands it to me, and I point to a word that looks doable: "pie."

She immediately draws a circle, which surprises me. I would have sketched a slice on a plate.

"Over easy!" shouts Risa.

"Circle!" shouts another student.

I begin to offer advice: "Maybe you should give more detail, or draw another . . ."

"Pie!" shout three team members simultaneously.

Meanwhile, Risa peeks at one of the spent cards on the table. "*Ano*, Sensei—what is . . . 'stupid'?"

"*Baka*," I explain. Her eyes grow wide and confused, and her neighbor starts to laugh. "Sensei, she thinks you called her '*baka*'—hahahahaha!"

"Oh, no no no—that's not what I meant. 'Stupid' is '*baka*.'" Risa remains a deer in the headlights. I'm getting nowhere on this one.

"Ah, Sensei, Japanese okay?" I nod and they huddle around Risa, explaining and laughing, and I think how much the five of them are often like borderless slices of pie in a dish, and how this image, when set against my single slice on a lonely plate, is also a rather useful representation of Eastern versus Western cultural habits.

Tuesday, July 6

This afternoon I stand beneath the ginkgo trees on campus, waiting to meet up with Akihara-sensei. He has volunteered for the task of delivering me to a couple of local high schools, where I'm to give sample lessons as a kind of advertisement, and he will present about our university programs.

My partner last year, a *shodo* professor from the Art department, had seemed both terrified and resentful of my presence as we drove around together. Hopefully, Akihara-sensei, a teacher from the Japanese department whom I have not yet met, will be less so. He promptly pulls up in his immaculate white sedan and steps out of the car to greet me—a true gentleman. He has, I note, a kind face and a shock of neatly combed white hair. "Furanzu-sensei, it is nice to meet you," he says. "I heard you are a big fan of pottery. I want to show you a very famous shop today." This is indeed encouraging!

On the way to our first school, we turn down a side street and pull over next to what looks to be a quaint showroom attached to a large old house. As we enter, my first thought is that the matte wood-lined walls are the perfect backdrop to the rough folk pottery inside. And then it hits me: I am not standing among the usual bowls and cups and vases. Instead there are thousands of statues of various sizes—mostly fertility monkeys with huge, erect phalluses protruding, as well as a few sets of the slightly less pornographic (but still perky) "three wise monkeys" covering eyes, ears, and mouth. An old woman follows us as we move from display to display, commenting on the efficacy of her talismans. My escort chuckles but doesn't say much— maybe he's waiting for something. As we turn to leave, a huge penis/monkey statue (more penis than monkey, that is) provides the opportunity for comment. "You know what this is?" he says, slapping a hand on the top, as if on a buddy's shoulder.

"Hai—yoku wakarimasu." (Yes, I know very well.)—probably a truly hilarious response. Both he and the old woman laugh wickedly.

After I teach my sample classes at the schools, we drive toward home and Akihara-sensei begins to tell me all about what's wrong with youth and education today in Japan—but the rhetoric flies by too fast for me to follow. He sighs, "I wish you could understand me better—I really want to tell you all this stuff. I want to know your opinion as a foreigner. . . . By the way, do you like *onsen*? Do you use shampoo? Conditioner?" These seem very personal and unusual questions, but then he adds, "Is it okay if we're a little late getting back? Maybe thirty minutes at the *onsen*? It is a very good one."

I'm thinking now that he might play another sexual joke of some sort on me and deliver us to one of those rare Kyushu *onsen* that allow both men and women to bathe together. "You must remember to go outside—try the outside baths because they are the best." Right—a clue. Perhaps the outside baths are shared, then?

We arrive at the *onsen*, and I stare desperately at all the signage as we enter, trying to locate some scrap of information. But, as always, there is so much that I cannot understand.

Akihara-sensei procures towels and tiny bottles of shampoo and conditioner at the front desk. He offers the lot to me in a neat pile, and so I tentatively enter the "Women's" area. It is early, and I am the only patron this afternoon. I quickly undress, shower, and enter a bath, which is indeed wonderfully soothing. As far as I can tell, behind the steamed windows there is nobody in the outside bath—and though I'm worried that a man will show up out there, I think I had better give it a try in case Akihara-sensei asks me some specific question about it afterward. With the too-tiny bathing towel clutched to my front (which shameful bit is most important to cover?), I step outside and nearly tumble into a gorgeous little bath nook surrounded by natural rocks and foliage. I enter the water, but I can't relax. My eyes remain fixed on the unmarked door opposite the one from which I just entered, semi-expecting a naked man to come strolling through at any minute. Having dutifully experienced the outside bath, I exit quickly and return to the "safe" zone.

Just before we leave the *onsen*, Akihara-sensei asks me to pose for a photograph in front of the building. "Very nice," he says. "I hope you could enjoy Japanese culture today."

"It was . . . a very interesting experience," I assure him.

I am duly delivered to my townhouse, and I immediately change clothes and rush off to pottery with my bag of too-wet recycled clay. I am late, but also just in time to produce one big watery, wavy bowl. Wiping my hands, I notice that the *onsen*-saturated skin of my fingertips is still deeply wrinkled. "Too much water in the clay again," chides Sensei.

"Or maybe too much water in my skin?" I offer, showing her my fingertips.

She nods, and instead of insisting that I toss my work in the recycle bucket as usual, she helps me cut the bowl off the hump and sets it gently down on the board to dry.

"Oh—it's pretty," says Yoko-san, leaning back from her spinning wheel, "like lotus petals opening."

Thursday, July 8

In my mailbox at work, there is a clean white envelope in which Akihara-sensei has tucked some pictures of our journey together—me standing in front of the high school where I delivered the sample English lesson, squinting into the sun; me standing in front of the pornographic pottery hut; and me in front of the *onsen* sign with disheveled, damp hair and a relieved smile—as well as three stunning photos of white cranes lifting off from a lake's surface.

At the end of the work day, I walk down the stairs and along the hall to the English Speaking Society lounge for a chat with my students. *"Ojamashimasu,"* I announce as I enter, noting the vibration and weight of the sliding door as it moves with my touch. Inside, several ESS members are sitting on *zabuton*, huddled around *bento* at a low table, and intently discussing the contents of the little lunch boxes.

"What is this—*mama bento?*" I ask, knowing that many of them still receive elaborately packed meals from their mothers each morning.

"No, Sanae brought it from the store for us—we couldn't eat our lunch today because we had to take a test. Try?" Yukari reaches for the jar of spare restaurant chopsticks and pulls out one set from a popular sushi chain, and I accept her offer, settling in next to her on one of the cushions.

"Oh! Do you know? Can you read this?" Sanae points to the *kana* text on the chopsticks wrapper.

"Ah . . . *'ichi-go ichi-e.'* What does it mean?"

"Hiroe-sensei taught us. 'Each meeting is unique and never to be repeated.' It is very famous words in Japan. It comes from *sado*—tea ceremony. That is very special times and place."

Naoko giggles and says, "Or very special times like here, now, in ESS room!"

Just then, the door slides open. It is Hiroe-sensei. "What's going on? You are talking about me?"

The girls laugh and make space for him at the table. Having lived a number of years in England to work on his Ph.D., Akira Hiroe is one of the few teachers who always has an easy, almost Western-friendly relationship with the students.

"They were explaining this Japanese phrase." I hold up the chopsticks wrapper as he settles in next to me. "It's 'seize the day' in English, right?"

"Maybe. But . . . it is a little sadder in Japanese. There is a kind of melancholy or a nostalgia. In this, we understand impermanence."

"So, 'this moment too will pass.'"

"Yes."

Friday, July 9

Today is the last day of classes before the summer break. Everyone on campus seems distracted and happy—chatting excitedly with each other. In composition class, my students tell me about their plans: part-time jobs, trips with friends, visits with family. When I say I have decided to go to Alaska, they ask if they can come too: *"Ii na!* Will there be snow? Can you see aurora?" Always the same questions, the same fascinations. It is strange to see my home through their eyes—an exotic, magical place. To me, it is mundane reality. A mottled and too-ordinary bruise on the psyche.

Later as I am locking up my office to leave for the day, a group of my students pass by in the hallway. "Tracy-sensei, tonight, TV, 6 p.m. It is Shokei promotion. Please watch us!"

Indeed the Shokei girls are on the television tonight, though I can't quite see them through the poor reception of that one elusive channel, only hearing something about "Enjoy English!" and "Do our best!". . . In a way, it is perfect though. I think this is how we always see each other—through a heavy static fuzz that will never clear for more than a second or two.

Saturday, July 10

For the first time in a long time I talk with Koun's parents—they've decided to have Viv go ahead with the permanent catheter surgery they've apparently been discussing as an option for some months. "We know there's no turning back once we do this, so we've held off for a while. But it's time. Hopefully it will make it easier to get around." Dick's voice sounds resolved and tired at the same time. I feel for them. And I feel guilty, too. From here in Japan, it's impossible to offer much more than a distant phone call. I know Koun will be worried when I pass along this information. At least it will be in person, as I have permission to visit Shogoji again tomorrow.

Sunday, July 11

The last time I drove out to the monastery in the mountains of Kikuchi, the rice fields were filled with fresh water reflecting sky; now they resemble a lush spread of emerald carpet. As I drive, the van clings to the thin strip of gravel and weeds that is the "road," and I dodge several mushroom farmers carrying pails and bamboo poles.

When I arrive, Koun asks Jisen-san if I can assist in the dimly lit kitchen where he is serving as *tenzo* (head cook). She grants permission for this slight impropriety, so I spend the first half of the day working with my husband, cutting vegetables, washing dishes, and preparing the noon meal over portable gas stoves: a simple vegetarian fare of *wakame*-and-cucumber salad with red pepper bits for color; miso soup with cabbage; carrots and potatoes in a thick, sugared soy sauce; brown rice; and, of course, the necessary pickled *daikon* to clean the bowls afterward. There is also a special treat today: a small canned fruit-and-nata-de-coco salad with slices of ripe *mikan* on top. All of the recipes have been written out by hand on slips of stained and tattered paper.

Though Koun and I can't relax and just talk (we are, as always, surrounded by thin walls and keen ears), I find that I truly enjoy sharing space with him in this new way. We work quickly and efficiently, with minimal speaking—Koun pointing to the tools he needs or succinctly explaining a heating technique or the proper way to cut food so that it can be easily held with chopsticks. He tells me that we've got to be swift and accurate with the recipes, getting it all out on time and arranged just so. "The food matters so much," he says. "It's one of few great comforts in the day."

As per Jisen-san's instructions, we heat the ceramic dishes with boiling water before placing the hot food on them. "It's really too bad we didn't add a little bit of onion and garlic," I lament.

"Onions and garlic are strictly forbidden—'incites the passions.'" I smile at an image of him sweeping away all of the little dishes of fruit salad, a struggle with the ties of our *samu-e*. Impure thoughts from the very mention of onion and garlic. Koun grins at me broadly—he must be thinking the same thing—and hands me a lacquerware tray of food to deliver to the informal serving hall.

During the free period that follows lunch, Koun and the monks are busy with various duties. I ascend the stone staircase with the aim of making a rice-paper rubbing of the Buddha's feet that are carved into a boulder at the entrance to the main grounds, but it won't take—the surface is too rough and uneven. *Nature and art conspiring against a frame*, I think. It's a shame, as this was to be my special gift for Koun's older brother, Bryan. I know that he especially would find something poignant in this small memento from his brother's current daily life.

As I'm putting the paper and charcoal back in the car, Koun finds me and we walk the trail that loops above the complex. "It's okay—as long as we don't wander too far off," he assures me.

"And we will be watched?"

"Someone is always watching."

As we walk, we talk about his mother's upcoming surgery, about that edge of worry in his father's voice.

"They must really be hurting. I know they've been trying to avoid that step for a while now. Once it's done, you can't go back. Still, if it means more mobility for Mom—that's great."

When we return to the parking area, it is time for me to leave but I've left an interior car light on and the engine won't start. We jump it using the Shogoji car, and I'm grateful for the excuse to stay just a little longer.

Tuesday, July 13

The phone rings early this morning—Koun's voice so casual and familiar, as if he were standing next to me in the kitchen. "I just spoke with Jisen-san—she told me to remind you that you can call if there is a problem with my mom's surgery. Just leave a message."

"Got it."

"Oh, and . . . I thought I should tell you that I had an odd chat with a visitor the other day. She knows one of the women who visited the Monday zazenkai at Tatsuda Center. Supposedly, it's known far and wide as 'the zazenkai that does not serve tea.' She seemed very annoyed about it."

"What? You've got to be kidding!"

"Yes, she was going on and on about how 'zazenkai is not zazenkai without tea'—I believe she said 'zazenkai without tea is pointless.' She was as direct as I've ever seen a Japanese person be. It was really weird."

"Okay—but, do I own the zazenkai? Who's responsible for providing tea? And how does said tea get prepared while we are all sitting? Is zazenkai zazenkai without sitting?"

"I really don't know."

At pottery in the evening, Sensei passes out a selection of her beautiful handmade cups to each of us. The tea is lightly astringent and shimmery grass-green. I have never been to pottery class without this ritual happening first. The tea, the pleasantries, and then it's down to business. Is pottery not pottery without tea? What else am I missing every day and in every way here?

Friday, July 16

It's been two days now since Viv's surgery, and there is still no answer when I call, so I talk to Bryan again. "I think something's definitely up," he says. I call Shogoji and leave a message for Koun. A short while later he calls my cell: "I couldn't get hold of my parents so I left a message. Jisen-san said you can come visit this Sunday—I think she must feel sorry for me."

Saturday, July 17

A lot of helplessness and worry today mixed with something like a residual angst. I take the bus into town for my Japanese lesson as usual, hopping off at my stop in front of the towering downtown department stores, but instead of heading directly to the YMCA, I turn and walk in the opposite direction, toward my home of some years ago. When I arrive thirty or so minutes later to that old Suizenji neighborhood, it takes me a few more minutes to orient myself away from the main thoroughfare toward the little four-story building tucked against the claustrophobic crush of taller, newer constructions and the dilapidated holdouts of past eras. When I find it, that place where I used to live, there is a surge of emotion. I stand beneath this dirty wedge-shaped building, looking up at the new inhabitant's brightly colored futon stretched out across the balcony railing. There are moments—like this—when it strikes me how odd it is that I am still in Japan, a place to which I gave little, if any, thought in all the years prior to my arrival.

As my gaze falls away from that third-story apartment, something catches my eye. Beneath the building, taking up half of what would be the first floor, is a small open parking lot for bicycles, two-wheeled vehicles, and various building maintenance items. There also, tucked into the shadows, is a modest wood-and-metal computer desk—constructed so that the user can type while sitting in *seiza*. It is *my* desk, the very same one I abandoned out of desperation because it would not fit into the car on the day I moved in with Koun in Aso, in the months before our wedding. This relic was my first piece of real furniture in Japan. The desk at which I began to put words to the experience of being out of context. The writing—I threw it all away, into the electronic ether, or into the garbage, on the day I left. But the desk, it seems, has been waiting here for me for over five years. I walk under the awning, run my hand over the dusty piece of furniture before becoming aware that probably everyone in the neighborhood knows that an unauthorized foreigner is standing beneath a building that is not (no longer) her home.

And so I move on, following the slender line of water that

flows past my old building along a concrete streambed and beneath the tiny urban bridges before opening out into the river that feeds Lake Ezu. As I enter the trail into the park surrounding the lake, I see that in the widening river next to me colorful koi swim lazily, sunlight catching along the gold and white of their scales. I know if I trail my hand along the water's surface, the fish will nip at my fingertips. On several occasions while out on my daily walks, I found all manner of fascinating and idyllic scenes here: an old man playing *shinobue*, the mournful tune of the flute carrying all the way across the lake to my ears; fat, drowsy cats leashed to the open doorways of dilapidated houses; men fishing with long bamboo poles; brilliant white blooms of lotus flowers; children with their trousers rolled up to the knees, catching frogs in a creek. And at the furthest point of my daily walk—if I was lucky—a view of Kumamoto Zoo's Indian elephant standing forlornly in his pen.

Yes, I walked here a lot. Sometimes I wept here, too, as I grappled with the strangeness of a new and immediate country juxtaposed against the memories of a distant home.

But mostly, I spent long hours staring into water reflecting sky, a stone slowly turning over and over in the hand as I turned all those old stories over and over in my mind, trying to understand and let go.

Sunday, July 18

Koun and I stand in the dirt-and-gravel parking lot of Shogoji, trying to get phone reception beneath the fickle clouds. Finally, the call connects, and I'm standing close enough to Koun that I can hear his dad answer on the other end. "The doctors don't know what's going on—she's been talking to her twin sister as if she were still alive. She's saying 'help me' over and over. It's just terrible. I don't know how much more I can take." His voice sounds gravelly, raw.

"Dad, you need to tell me if I need to go home. Call Tracy. She can call the monastery. I'll just do what I have to do. But you have to tell me if it's time."

After he hangs up, the phone rings again immediately, and I move away to kick at stones while Koun listens and responds again and again in the affirmative in Japanese. "What now?" I ask, as he tucks the phone into his sleeve.

"That was Ganzoji. The head of the temple board has just passed away. The wake is this evening. They're coming here to pick me up now, to take me to Aso."

"I could take you."

"No—it's bad form. They're already on their way. And they'll need to explain the situation to Jisen-san. It should be okay for you to follow along, though, if you're up for it."

A couple hours later, we arrive at the house in Aso. Koun and his teacher are led to one room to dress while I am waved toward another room full of mourners in black suits, kneeling on tatami.

The priest's wife pats me on the arm, and I hesitate. "Are you sure it's okay?" I whisper.

"Of course. You are from Ganzoji."

I nod and enter the tatami room, choosing a spot near the back. Incense burner, candles, and flowers have been carefully placed on a low table in front of the body, which lies in an open casket beneath an opaque white lace cloth. Black-suited people continue to file in and, at some point, the priest's wife decides that I'm sitting in the wrong spot, so she waves me to the other side of the tatami. "Family side," she whispers. Koun and the priest enter, and the wife of the deceased begins to sing—an anguished, wailing refrain. Afterward, the priest offers a short eulogy that is difficult for me to follow in his countryside accent, but for this one unmistakable, heart-rending statement: "We were the same age—we were growing old together. He helped me to be a better man all the time."

As he begins to cycle through the *Heart Sutra*, Koun serves as *doan*, hitting the bells and wooden fish block on cue, his voice layered in with the priest's. One after the other, mourners step forward to offer incense and to bow. *Makizushi* and green tea are passed around, the guests nodding as they accept the trays. There is also the stillness of the deceased, the stillness of his wife as she sits in seiza.

The wake is still in progress when I excuse myself, and Koun walks me to my car. "It's the first time I've seen the priest really choked up at one of these things," he says.

"It was a hard day, wasn't it?"

"Yes, and the funeral will be harder. But maybe I'll have a chance to check in with my folks on a decent phone connection before going back to Shogoji."

The priest's wife strides toward us to collect Koun, nodding at him that it is time, and he clutches my hand for a moment before turning to leave.

Monday, July 19

Koun calls in the afternoon, and it is frustration tinged with a wrenching feeling: "Jisen-san let me use the phone to check in with my folks. But, you know, the connection here is so bad. Dad says my mom's lost most of her motor skills since that surgery. She still can't feed herself. I didn't realize—[*click-click*]."

And when he calls back: "Sorry, oh, this connection. Anyway, this is the hell she's been imagining herself in her whole life. A lifetime of worry leading to the exact thing she's worried about. Now it's here—right now. Trapped in her own body. It's just—[*click-click*]."

And again: "This is so irritating. Well, I just don't know what to do. Mom doesn't want a rumination on the nature of life. What [*click-click*]."

And again: "Oh, T, someone's hitting the bell. I should say good-bye before it cuts [*click-click*]."

~

It's just Stephen and me again at zazenkai this evening. It is quiet but for the usual passage of trains and the cough of the night watchman, who seems to have developed a summer cold. This is becoming normal, this falling away of attendees. I wonder how long our group will continue, especially given my upcoming absence. (And then, of course, there is the matter of the tea for the visiting Japanese. I have yet to address this issue.)

On the drive back, Stephen assures me that the waning zazen group is not a failure. "It's just how it is—people get busy with things that feel more important."

"Yes well, I guess it doesn't help that I'm just sitting with this general guilty feeling lately. I feel that I'm letting Koun down, and at the same time I'm worried about his mom, about being so far away. I'm terrified that she's going to die, honestly. I feel that I should be doing something for her."

"What can you do? I lost my sister some years ago. I was here at the time, but I went back for the funeral."

"That must have been hard for you, being so far away."

He shrugs. "Yes and no. Everybody dies. That's just reality."

Tuesday, July 20

In pottery class—our last before the summer holiday— Yoko-san announces, "I got the tickets!"

"What tickets?"

"To Alaska! I will bring my granddaughter, Satsuki-chan!"

Oh—right. "Yoko-san, my mom's condo is very small. . . ."

"Don't worry! It's package. We have a hotel in Anchorage."

Yoko-san has an amazing ability to delight and annoy and make one feel guilty all at the same time. Mostly, in this moment, I feel annoyed. Meanwhile, the cups I'm trimming simply won't hold their form—the edges fray up and smudge where I carve. Sensei points out that I'm not using the correct finger, the middle one, or enough *chikara* (power) when pressing at the center of the pot. The muscles in my hands tense up and lock while I try to maintain this posture, and when I pause to massage the pain away, I note that the pottery ladies seem to be now discussing fortunetelling while peering into one another's palms—much too complex a topic for me to engage with. Starting my wheel up again, I concentrate on the pressure of my fingers against the pot.

"*Te o kudasai!*" (Give me your hand!), says Sensei.

"*Hai, ganbarimasu*" (Yes, I'm working at it), I say automatically.

"*Iie, te o kudasai.*" (No, give me your hand.) I look up, see that she's holding out her hand expectantly. I stop the wheel and hold out my right hand. She squints at the lines in my clay-wet palm for a long moment before sucking air between her teeth and cocking her head.

"Is it okay?" I ask.

"Hmm. I don't know. It's difficult. Hmmm."

This cryptic pronouncement about my fate, and then she is back into fast banter with the ladies. I am about to push on about the meaning of the lines, but already they're on a different topic so I go back to my work. I wonder what is missing from the geography of my skin, what secrets are revealed. Surely it is imprinted here somewhere in the clay turning beneath my fingers, in all of my failed creations.

As I drive home, I note that my mood is decidedly dark. A line from one of Koun's letters comes to me: *Today it's sunny; I feel good. Yesterday was rainy; I felt bad. Following the same schedule every day makes these kinds of variables really obvious.*

Saturday, July 24

Bryan calls in the morning from Helena. "I got in yesterday. Mom's basically doing okay now, but still there's a dramatic difference. Hard stuff. You'll see when you get here."

Today is Shokei's Open Campus Day—Jennifer and I have been slated to team-teach a sample class. We are doing our best to be as super *genki* (happy/healthy/energetic) as possible, though my heart is not in it at first. But once we get going, I'm back in the flow. After we introduce a short film about how to greet an American host family, we practice introductions, shaking hands and giving hugs. The girls in their high school uniforms giggle and scream playfully through the whole thing. Will I see their sweet, open faces in my classes next year?

"How's your mother-in-law doing?" Jennifer asks after the last student has left.

"Not so great—we're all really worried."

"Yet you smiled all day. What we do is amazing, isn't it? We're always putting on this other persona."

Tuesday, July 27

It's my wedding anniversary, and it seems particularly melancholic that I will spend the day—two days, actually, thanks to the curvature of the Earth—in transit to the U.S., rushing away from the love of my life.

Satomi, driving her mother's car nervously but with great care, delivers me to the highway bus stop for the airport early in the morning. She hugs me and then continues to wave as I slip beyond the gate, my rolling suitcase in tow. This farewell is her gift to me, and I am grateful to not be driven by an impersonal taxi at this hour.

Once on the bus, I phase in and out of consciousness, the announcement waking me just as we pull into the international airport in Fukuoka. I shuffle from check-in to terminal to airplane, arrive in Taipei at a reasonable morning hour, and then spend the following five hours wandering the seemingly endless, (mostly) empty personality-free terminal wings, trying to get my exercise before the much longer flight ahead to Seattle, where I will stay for a few days before moving on to Montana and then Alaska.

At one point, I find myself in an especially shabby dead-end corridor. Hung along the length of the hallway is a surprise of art: ten ink paintings, many ox-themed. As I am looking at the images, wondering at their beauty and simplicity, an older Taiwanese man approaches me (we've passed each other a few times now, walking laps in these sparse hallways). He says in English, "Do you know about these?"

"I know I read about them some time ago, but I don't remember the meanings well."

"The horned cow is your mind," he says, tapping his head. "You have to tame. That is all you need to know." Looking again at the paintings, I see that they reveal in stages the process of finding the ox, bringing it to submission, and then, perhaps, moving on to some kind of final transcendence.

I arrive in Seattle at nearly the exact date and time as when I left Fukuoka. As I exit customs, Bryan and his girlfriend, Kathy, greet me. Though they have been dating nearly two years, seeing them together shocks me. Their relationship blossomed entirely outside of my spatial proximity—it has been a romance for me viewed through spoken word, not image (as if the mind needed the image as proof of reality). So I accidentally see him—the brother-in-law whom I love as my older brother—still as a kind of permanent bachelor, while also recognizing him as he is now.

As we wait for my bags to appear on the conveyor, Bryan presents me with an earth-colored ceramic pitcher he picked up with Kathy while on vacation in Mexico. "Happy Anniversary," he says. "We thought you would appreciate this."

"It's perfect," I say, and it is, the weight of it in my hands.

Wednesday, July 28

Bryan has already left for his job at Microsoft by the time I wake this morning. So I dress and head out for a walk around Green Lake in a jet-lag daze, dressed like a middle-aged Japanese woman, with my skin dutifully covered with hat, long-sleeved blouse, and pants. I long for a parasol, but know that's a little too much. Most people look pale, under-dressed, thick, tall. In Japan I always feel ten pounds overweight and rather average in height, but here I feel tiny and delicate. As I walk, I catch snippets of conversation in English that I assume are about TV shows that I have never heard of, and acronyms for business and new technologies that I don't know about. There is one familiar face: the old man with his sandwich board advertising Spanish lessons walks past, speaking to a young man who nods, listens intently, and then responds slowly. That gentle volley of language. A comfortable feeling comes over me. Their speech is pleasant background music, whereas the English makes me tune in and feel exhausted, as if I'm being constantly addressed.

I ride the bus out to the mall with the intention of buying several things on my list, but when I actually get there, I have to leave after twenty minutes. Everything is big, abundant, overwhelming. And the advertising is definitely talking to me, but it's just too much desire. So I get back on the bus and stop at a high-end grocery store near Bryan's house to pick up a few essentials—tofu, rice, fruit. When I check out, I present my rarely used debit card to the cashier.

"Slide it in the machine," she drawls lazily.

"What? Sorry, I don't use a card very often." In Japan, it's cash only.

"You know, the MACHINE." She points to a gadget on the counter that I have never seen before in my life.

"Okay, what do I do?"

The woman behind me in line, nearly naked in her sexy yoga gear, mutters "What the fuck?!," rolls her eyes, and storms away (to another line—and then on to Nirvana—I presume). *Namaste to you, too,* I think.

I return to Bryan's home and sleep, sleep, sleep.

Thursday, July 29

Today I wake late again and don't leave the house for the better part of the afternoon. Instead, I sit in the small enclosed backyard and read with the smell of roses and sun-heated wood and the sound of distant traffic around me. A fat fluffy gray cat wanders in, climbing a neighbor's tree and leaping from a branch over the fence to get here. She sniffs my ankle and then curls up in a ball next to me. There must be something to how I attract cats, my greatest allergenic nemeses, in whatever country I happen to be.

In the evening, I go contra dancing with one of my dear friends, the soulful Brinda, who has worn the same velvet-short haircut since she shaved it all off in 2002 after her divorce (inspiring me, a few months after, to cut off my own long locks for the first time ever). She has a new beau in her repertoire, an undeniably sexy, bald, and not terribly kind ex-marine in a "utili-kilt," a manly new Seattle fashion trend, apparently.

"You have lead feet," he tells me as I am passed to him during the dancing. "Slide!"

"Are you kidding? I'm wearing hiking sandals—they don't slide!"

"You could if you were graceful."

And then, gratefully, I'm passed to another man with sad eyes and another who introduces himself far too formally and another who acts like an old lover, the way he tenderly grips me—until I've met all of the men and a few of the women at the dance. When, finally, it is time for a break, we take plastic cups of cold water and step outside to cool air. A man about fifteen years my senior sits down next to me on the curb, asks me where I'm from. While we talk, a woman his age looks over at us with pain in her eyes. I excuse myself when I see that look, taking a slow lap around the outside of the building. I get the feeling that many of these men and women are carrying out unspoken and spoken romantic mini-dramas. Reading between the lines is devastatingly easy, and it's all too intimate.

Afterward, Brinda drives while Bill sits in the seat beside her. They talk animatedly while I lean back, exhausted, ready to be nestled in bed. I sit up when we are nearly to Bryan's, making my best effort to participate—after all, Brinda really likes this guy. They're basically talking about the battle of the sexes now, about men and women and annoying lovers past.

"You're lucky—you've got a great one now," I offer, when Bill laments yet another horrible relationship.

"What?" There is a hint of irritation in his voice.

I lean forward, speak louder, "You're lucky—" Brinda catches my eye in the rearview mirror, says "no" with her eyes. "Oh nothing, I'm just so tired." I slump back into my seat. Nobody speaks for the rest of the trip.

"How was the dancing?" asks Bryan after Brinda drops me back at his place.

"I don't know. Fun and athletic, but weirdly emotionally draining. I have this feeling that it's really a place for those who desperately need to be touched. Oh and—I don't think I understand what 'dating' means."

Friday, July 30

Brinda and I sit in the steam room of a neighborhood gym, rubbing handfuls of sea salt across our bodies, flaking away the old skin to reveal the new. "I'm sorry about that thing with Bill in the car yesterday," says Brinda. "He's got boundaries. He says I bring out the worst in him."

"'The worst in him'—what does that mean?"

"I don't know. He's a complicated guy."

You deserve better, I think. And then, *We're all complicated*. But I don't trust my ability to evaluate anything right now, so I say nothing.

"You know, in relationships there are cycles. In my marriage, we went around and around. And then we got to the bottom of a cycle and just didn't come back up."

"I've never experienced that. I had a bad marriage before, and now I have a good one."

"You will experience it someday. Maybe."

"How are things, now that you are separated from your husband?"

"When we were first together, he painted. He was very artistic. And then he stopped. Now that we're apart, he is painting again. We are both happier now. So much happier."

After the steam, I sit in Brinda's apartment drinking tea while she moves around the kitchen, gathering dried herbs for me into brown paper bags. "This will nourish your lungs," she says, "and this one's for your heart." Brinda, the wise woman/ Microsoft professional/mother of three who knows the intricacies of healing plants, who walks the earth barefoot on every solstice—I'm always touched by her inclination to nurture. Having finished gathering a pile of remedies for me (some of which may or may not get me stopped in the airport), she sits down with a deck of cards in her hands. "Okay, are you ready for a tarot reading?"

Cards are placed. Complex symbols are interpreted. The herbal teas flow freely. I have no idea what any of it really means. Yet another foreign language.

I sigh, rub my forehead. "So, I'm on the verge of a breakthrough?"

"Something like that."

~

In the evening, I trust the old bus route to take me to the karate dojo where Koun and I train with our Seattle sensei, Steve, whenever we're in town. I am duly delivered to a recognizable neighborhood. In the studio, I find myself among a few familiar, but mostly new, faces. After a warm-up bout of *randori* sparring, Steve points out the obvious, "You haven't been training enough, have you?"

"Jet lag," I reply, but we both know he's right.

Saturday, July 31

Bryan, Kathy, and I hike a mountain trail some hours from the city. Clear skies, warm sun, and just enough breeze to keep the bugs off as we wend our way up and around and through the ever-evolving terrain. At last, we traverse the final ridge and emerge at the peak. All that effort and then there is nothing to do but take in the sun and breeze and the brilliant blueness of sky and distant lake.

"It's like standing on top of the world," says Kathy, and it is, the illusion of it. Why is it, I wonder, that a certain landscape inspires us? Why one and not the other? Or why one in a certain way, and another in a different way entirely? I realize that I associate broad, natural vistas with the U.S. and cultivated close-ups with Japan, but that may not be an entirely fair assessment of the aesthetics of two complex nations—the cultures may in fact be in direct opposition to this view. What I do know is that the landscapes of both countries move me, and whenever I pay attention, the familiar becomes foreign; the foreign becomes familiar.

As Bryan and Kathy explore the mountaintop from every angle, I settle onto a broad, flat rock, pick up a stick, and etch and re-etch a phrase into soft dirt that the wind or a hiker's boot will sweep away by the end of the day:

> *ichi-go*
> *ichi-e*
> *ichi-go*
> *ichi-e*

When it is nearly time to descend the mountain, I think I

must look as pensive as I feel, and Bryan asks, "Is it weird to be back in the U.S.?"

"Yes, maybe. It always feels so unreal at first, this re-entry period. I'm an outsider in the place that I know to be my home. Of course, the feeling will pass soon enough. It always does eventually."

"Do you feel this way in Japan, whenever you return?"

"Yes, but—it's different. I expect it to be weird."

"And the first time you arrived there?"

"I knew immediately that it would change me."

How could I ever forget my first day in Japan after an ill-advised forty-eight-hour journey via a bargain airplane ticket, purchased for the selling price of my car, the only thing of value I owned? I stepped off the plane wearing a simple blue dress, wrinkled from travel and humidity. There were buttons along the front of the dress—this detail strangely clear. Feeling tired, drugged almost, and the surroundings assaulting the senses in such a way that I felt I had arrived in the *idea* of a country. I slept most of the way in Garrett's car as he drove us to that old house in Takamori, me waking at brief intervals to a cacophony of complicated architecture and signage in an unknown language, to massive gray apartment buildings that seemed to echo each other, to a rise of mountains and greenery, to a village of rice paddies and ornate tile roofs, and finally to that old house nestled against a bamboo forest. And then, standing in the bedroom for the first time, noticing the squares repeating again and again and again throughout the angles of the interior—the large silk-edged squares of the tatami flooring, the dark wood slats crisscrossing the white putty walls, the smaller squares of paper shoji, the ceiling patterned, too, in square wood tiles. An angled mandala, this recursive architecture. There was just the roundness of the buttons coming undone beneath Garrett's fingers, and of his head beneath my hands.

AUGUST
Legacies

Sunday, August 1

Today Bryan and I opt to explore Seattle's Chinatown. At first, we are in a classic Seattle city district of tall brickwork buildings, endless concrete and glass. And then the landscape transforms: kanji looping across sidewalk art signs, storefront windows filled with Asian artifacts, passersby looking up at us with eerily familiar faces. "It's so weird—I feel as if I'm recognizing people, their names on the tip of my tongue. It happens in Japan, too. I see a foreigner and I think, hey—didn't we go to high school together? Aren't we old friends? It's an unexpected empathy."

We duck into Uwajimaya, peruse the aisles of goods that are identical to those available in my neighborhood store in Kikuyo, save for the sheer quantity and also the exotic additions from Korea, Thailand, China. And then into the adjacent Kinokuniya, the bookstore that bears the same name as my favorite bookseller in Japan. "But this is even better than the one in Tokyo!" I exclaim, rushing from aisle to aisle like a kid in a candy shop. I am vaguely aware of Bryan trailing after me, amused, and then my focus shifts entirely to the books. The English section is exceptionally well stocked—and the theme is all things Japanese. It seems that I am the ideal consumer of this particular complex of consumables, and oh how badly I want to buy, buy, buy.

Some while later, Bryan's voice pulls me from my frantic seeking.

"Lost you there."

"Oh—I'm definitely lost."

"Hey, are you hungry?"

"Starving. Lost and starving."

From the stack in my arms, I select just one tome to purchase for now—a basic how-to on Japanese ceramics in English, complete with illustrations. "Is this really all you want?" asks Bryan as we leave the store and move toward the food court.

"No, I want it all. But it's too much. I'll start with the pottery."

After we make our purchases at the food counter and seat ourselves at the one unoccupied table, we lean eagerly into our meals. I pop tuna *makizushi* and bean-paste-filled *mochi* into my mouth. Bryan twirls a fork through spicy pad thai. At the neighboring table, two twenty-something Japanese boys—I imagine them to be local university students—slurp udon loudly and complain about the windy-wet Seattle weather in fast, rough Japanese. I want to embrace them, but I know they are as inaccessible to me as whatever it is I am searching for now. I think of Koun, then, how he should be here with us, experiencing this out-of-context abundance. I chew my final *makizushi* while a familiar bright sting grows wider and wider in my nostrils and pressure builds behind the eyes.

"Are you okay?"

"Very authentic *wasabi*," I explain, laughing and weeping at the same time.

Monday, August 2

The University of Washington campus is, at noon, nearly free of students. But soon, I imagine, they will move in and out of the buildings in little tributaries of humanity, their backpacks slung over one shoulder, casually, as they arrive and arrive and arrive into their bright futures.

As if on cue, a young woman with a backpack and dark, purple-tinged hair exits the building I am about to enter. I recognize something in her downturned eyes, that countenance of being heavy with one's own thoughts. I turn as she passes me and feign the look of having possibly forgotten something important while I observe her quick, deft insertion of earplugs and her entrance into a personal reality that now comes with its own soundtrack.

As I turn back to my destination, I fish out of my pocket a slip of folded paper with an office number written on it. My aim today is to meet up with an old friend, Lisa, during her lunch hour. I met Lisa through Bryan some years ago, and she has become a mainstay in my repertoire of Seattle people—those I try to check in with when passing through. I am always struck by Lisa's humble steadfastness in her ever-evolving practice. She has, I think, lived in every Buddhist residence in the city, and I am hoping that today she will offer some insight into my own floundering attempts along the path.

When I find her, a small and radiant African American woman, she is poring over a stack of paperwork, her expression serious and focused.

"Lisa?"

She looks up, smiles, and it transforms her instantly into the friend I have not seen in a long while.

I gesture to her office, the vague-but-official title beneath her name on the door. "What exactly is it that you do anyhow?"

"Oh, you don't want to know about that. Let's go to lunch."

As we make our way to a restaurant overlooking the nearby river, Lisa tells me that she's been taking classes in preparation for converting to Catholicism.

"What?" I stop walking and turn to her.

"I like the singing," she explains. "That's always been a strong spiritual practice for me. The first time I went to this church and sang—I could just feel it. It was *right*."

"But—I mean—you're Buddhist, aren't you?"

"Well, I don't know—I've never decided that I am this or that. Buddhism appealed to me, so I guess I've done Buddhist practice. But I'm not so worried about what to call myself."

"I envy your sureness. I guess this is my year of waiting for Zen—or maybe waiting for me. I keep thinking, *If I just pay attention, surely I'll get it.*"

"So what did you pay attention to today?"

We arrive at the restaurant, but stop short of entering so I can consider this question. Before us, we watch as river water flows toward the ocean. "Your words, just now. And a girl, probably a student, as I was coming into your building. I don't know why I noticed her. Maybe it was how different-yet-the-same she seemed in comparison to the young women in my classes in Japan. The posture and movement and fashion was all wrong, but there was some other unnameable feature there that was the same. Or maybe it was just her youth, the fact that she was female."

"What was she doing?"

I smile. "Nothing, really. Just listening to music."

Tuesday, August 3

Brinda picks me up at the end of her work day and delivers both of us to her weekly yoga class. Together we sit in a circle, a mandala of women. Roz, our instructor, leads us through slow stretches. "Remember to breathe," she says. "Don't hold it in—let it go. Out. In. Out. In. Not breathing is not doing the pose correctly." The women around me are all shapes, sizes, colors, ages. Some are limber as cloth, others only water-soaked wood, bending just a little, and a little more, and a little more. Roz rises and begins to move among us, guiding our bodies into impossible postures. "Breathe," she urges each of us, "breathe." A sculptor, I think, or maybe a goddess.

"It's funny," I tell Brinda as she drives me home, "most Tuesday nights I spend with a bunch of women, making pottery. I'm not sure that it is so different from what we were doing tonight."

"Yoga is a wonderful spiritual practice—is your class like that too?"

"Oh no—that's not what I meant. It's difficult. I'm always failing." Brinda looks at me, smiles. "So, okay, yes. It's exactly like a spiritual practice in *that* way."

"Have you made anything interesting?"

"No. I just make the same things over and over again."

"Well, that's definitely spiritual practice."

Wednesday, August 4

This morning, Bryan and I pack the car and stock up on snacks and coffee before heading off to Montana to visit Viv and Dick, his and Koun's parents. As we drive inland, the moisture is slowly sucked from the air, and the temperature rises. We roll down the windows, and I put my hand in the wind. I imagine water droplets lifting off everything around us, pulled by the slipstream of the car as it glides down the highway.

"Is everything going okay with you and Kathy?" I ask as I roll up my window.

"Yes . . . and no. Sometimes we're really great. And I have to say that I'm learning more in this relationship than in any I've ever had before. We clash a lot though—we have very different styles. But I guess it's all just process."

"Process. That's good. It sounds so mature. I don't understand love."

"What do you mean?"

"All of my other relationships were terrible—embarrassingly terrible, like I was actually trying to damage myself—and I don't think I learned all that much. Then I fell for Koun and had this kind of epiphany, and we're great. I think I must be tremendously lucky."

"It has to be more than luck."

"Maybe. Koun once mentioned this theory about two versions of love relationships: endothermic versus exothermic. One takes energy; the other creates it. For some reason we are the latter."

"I think Kathy and I are both sometimes—but maybe mostly endothermic, if I'm really honest. There's a lot of work involved."

We stop for a rest at an old Catholic church in Idaho that is now a kind of monument. As we enter, there is an immediate sense of recognition. "The iconography," I say, "I've never noticed it before, but it looks like Tibetan Buddhism, or maybe Hinduism. All these bright colors, the deities."

"Yeah, I wish I'd noticed all that when I was growing up in the Church," says Bryan. "I think I would have appreciated it a lot more. And there's ceremony too. It's actually really nice stuff."

"One of the residents at Shogoji, Jisen-san's son, is thinking about getting ordained under his mother. He's Catholic, and I believe in some sense she may be, too. Koun tells me that every day he prays to the statue of Avalokiteshvara in the temple. To him, she is the Virgin Mary, and Mary is the Goddess of Compassion. Sometimes I think it must be only the Americans who are hung up on labels—me included. We see everything in black and white—you are either this or that. But the Japanese, they ask Koun if he's Christian all the time. They'll ask him while he's wearing his full monk's robes, after he's just done prostrations in their living room. It was one of the first questions the reporters asked just after he got ordained."

"Japanese tend to also be Shinto, don't they?"

"Most are both Shinto and Buddhist, married together into one complex cultural aesthetic. Maybe Shinto is like the religions of the Native Americans—there is spirit in all things, the stone, the river, the mountains, even things created by people, like furniture or *washi* paper. Everything is sacred."

As we turn to leave, we find a book of pictures and descriptions of local Native Americans being converted to Catholicism in this church. What is immediately striking is the mix of traditional clothing and Western attire that each Native American wears, one culture obscuring another in dark shades of cotton. That devastating history.

As we pull out of the parking lot, we roll slowly past a younger and an older priest walking together in full robes. How similar their dress is in comparison to formal Buddhist monks' garb. If Koun were walking beside them, he would look as if he belonged.

As we continue on to Montana, we drive a bit out of the way in order to visit a petrified forest. Walking along the trail, we stop frequently to touch the wood transformed to rock. Out here in this sparse high desert, the sun is so hot against skin and stone. And quiet, so quiet—the only sounds are a few insects moving around us, and I hear each one distinctly as it passes by. "I miss that—the clarity of no-sound. Like an Alaskan winter.

It's easy to forget, living where I do." The skin on my hands feels dry and tight, as if I've just cleaned them after working clay.

It is dark when Bryan and I finally pull into his parents' driveway in Helena. "Are we missing time?" I ask.

"I don't know how that happened. I guess we should have done more driving and less exploring."

Dick greets us at the door and hugs us both, and I am reminded of just how much bigger he is than either of his very tall sons. A gentle giant. "I already put Viv to bed," he says. "Guess I'll probably do the same. Sure am glad you guys are here."

Thursday, August 5

Bryan and I are already up, sitting on the couch talking, when Dick wheels Viv out to the living room. He sets the brake on the wheelchair, bends toward her in a kind of embrace, leans back, and pulls her stiff body forward into him, pivots thirty degrees, and then leans forward and lowers her slowly into the plush recliner. This activity—performed several times a day— must take considerable strength on his part.

"Hi guys," says Viv weakly, as we each lean over the chair for a hug, taking in the smell of roses, the primary note in her favorite perfume. As Bryan warned earlier, her condition has changed considerably since I last saw her. She is not nearly as mobile, nor is her face as animated during our casual catch-ing-up discussions; there is a slackness, a distance. And a more pronounced smoothing of the features, a side-effect of MS. I get the sense that she's having a hard time keeping up with even the easy narratives.

"When do you go home to Canada?" she asks.

"Alaska? In a few days."

"How is your mom?"

"She's okay."

"Is she in Texas for the whole summer?"

"No. In Alaska. I'll visit her there."

"Oh."

We speak in simple, measured sentences, and I can see that Viv is grasping for words, translating from the language within the mind to the language of the voice. And then there are the cognitive hiccups—little flaws in thinking that occur during that process of concentration and translation, a misfiring of the synapses.

"Could I have a glass of water?" she asks, and when I rise to get it Dick turns on the big television, something that has become Viv's constant, comforting companion these past years. When I return, glass and straw in hand, Viv is asleep, despite the volley of sound coming from the television—some kind of impassioned courtroom argument—and Dick and Bryan are out on the deck, watching deer tumble across green lawn.

In the late afternoon, Bryan and I go to the nursing home to pick up his grandmother Eve—Viv's mother—who is now in her nineties. She, too, has become much less responsive since the last time I saw her. Still, she smiles when she sees us, and we remind her who we are and where we're taking her. "Let's go home and have dinner together."

"Well, that sounds nice," she says. "How was your trip?"

"Great! We took our time and made a few fun stops along the way."

"Well good," she says, settling into a silent stillness that will not end for the remainder of the evening.

While Bryan sweetly carries on a one-sided conversation with his grandmother as we drive, I think about Dick's years-long idealization of how he might like to live in an island light-house someday, and how one relative or family friend—I forget who—pointed out the raw truth that he'd gotten his desire at last. His life now almost monastic, cloistered.

Friday, August 6

Kathy shows up at the airport on a last-minute whim— she had called Bryan with this news last night, after I'd gone to bed. We all pick her up and drive out together to eat lunch at Jade Garden, Viv's favorite Chinese restaurant. Bryan and I are talking animatedly and laughing as we take our chairs, using the language of brother and sister. "Watch it, or I'll break out the buzzybee!" I say.

"Excuse me," snaps Kathy. "Nobody understands what you're talking about." I stop talking, look at Bryan. "Well— what's so funny?"

"Oh, it's um. . . It's just this story about when the boys were kids. I guess Garrett used to jab Bryan with this little buzzy-bee-on-a-stick thing when the family went on cross-country road trips together. Bryan was always trying to read, so that bee drove him nuts. Garrett could never entertain himself by reading or drawing because he got carsick. Harassing Bryan was his only entertainment. I—"

Kathy looks at me unsmilingly, blinks slowly. Dick leans over to set the brake on Viv's wheelchair. Bryan appears to be listening to something intently. It occurs to me that I have no idea what's really going on.

"I guess it's not that funny. Never mind."

Bryan and Kathy decide to drive out to the hotsprings after lunch, and I decline Bryan's invitation to join them, sensing their need to discuss some urgent lovers' business. Instead, I sit in the living room with Viv, placing pictures of Garrett/Koun in her good hand and removing each after I finish explaining: Here, Koun grinning in a group shot in front of Shogoji, so much taller than the other monks; Koun chanting sutra; Koun in his begging clothes, affixing the hat strap beneath his chin; Koun in his robes carrying a tray full of delicate tea cups down an open-air hallway, intention revealed through that upright posture.

"Oh," says Viv weakly after each photo is explained.

In the evening before going to bed, I look over the collage of family pictures downstairs. Bryan, the kind and sensitive intellectual bookworm with a penchant for science and the subtle realms. Koun, the baby brother, always the ham, constantly vying for his big brother's attention. Koun explained once, "I was the look-at-me kid, the crowd pleaser. I think Bryan just wanted to be left alone. It's ironic that I wound up the monk." And Viv and Dick there, too, standing behind their sons, smiling down at them, this legacy of children.

I remember a hard conversation, on a visit a few years ago, with Koun and Bryan and their father in the living room after Viv had gone to bed.

"How are you holding up, Dad?" Bryan asked.

"I got to tell you, it's been getting harder and harder." He had recently started putting up big red STOP signs all over the house, reminders to just pause and reorient himself to a more positive state of mind. "I'm angry all the time. I catch myself swearing—saying really bad stuff. I never used to do that kind of thing."

Gin, Viv's identical twin sister, and Jim, her husband, had already gone through a version of what Viv and Dick are experiencing now. Even after Gin became blind and completely bedridden from MS, Jim refused to accept help. He died a few months before her from his six-packs-a-day smoking habit. The addiction had been his way of coping. This story—this history—colors the family discussion about Dick's situation.

Garrett leaned forward on the sofa, wringing his hands together, in pain at the sight of his father's pain. "Dad, if it comes to a nursing home, nobody will blame you."

"You don't understand, she's my sweetie. It's like you and Tracy. Imagine that. Imagine that."

Saturday, August 7

While wandering out of Dick and Viv's neighborhood and down into Helena proper for my daily walk, I happen past an iron buffalo skull the size of a car. Two young children—a boy and a girl—attempt to climb on the sun-heated metal as their parents look on. I think, *Perhaps this is the true end—or start—to the ox herding pictures.* The building just beyond the skull is the Montana Historical Society Museum, a place Dick has mentioned that I might find interesting. Turning up the path, I enter the museum and buy a ticket to view the art gallery, which boasts an extensive Charlie Russell collection. "It's one of the best collections of his stuff around," says the man at the counter.

"That's wonderful," I say. I don't have the heart to tell him that I have never heard of Charlie Russell. Inside I find classic paintings of cowboys and Indians—that complicated and tragic history idealized—and cattle ambling across the hot, dry landscape of Montana. It's not the kind of art or narrative that I am usually drawn to; looking at it now makes me feel like a foreigner. But there's also something intimate there. Something that tugs at memory and old desires.

Koun told me once that he used to want to be a cowboy, like his grandfather. When his grandfather found out, he started making all of their outings more and more difficult. "He was worried that I'd actually grow up and choose such a hard life, but I was just a kid who thought my grandfather was cool. And the more difficult he made it for me, the more I loved it." I imagine him riding for hours on horseback, an eight- or maybe ten-year-old boy floating through a stream of cattle. Brown leather gloves too big for him. A rough rope held tightly in one hand.

When I return to the house, the television is on as usual so I settle into the overstuffed couch next to Viv and try to be present in some small meaningful way as she falls into and out of consciousness. I feel sad and useless; I can't begin to imagine how Dick feels every day. Viv—the center of his life—and the two of them held fast in a love story of what should be, not what is, not reality. The TV drones on, the hands of the clock make their circles, the sun drags shadows across the carpet. A few days ago Viv had been hallucinating horses galloping through the living room—something to do with a change in her medication or her condition. The doctors did not know which.

Horses. Now I'm starting to remember. Sometimes I think our lives—all our lives—are variations on a theme. I close my eyes and see the art gallery from earlier, all of the images there. I always thought I'd be a girl who rode horses. After all, before I was from Alaska, I was from Texas. I remember visiting my grandfather's ranch—over a child's handful of summers—with my father. There are photographs of me smiling, high up in a saddle. The one time I rode alone, at thirteen, the animal ran fast and angry. She feinted crashing into trees and then a barn. When we at last returned to the farmhouse, the both of us

panting and sweating like we'd returned from a vicious struggle, my grandfather exclaimed that he'd never seen her act in
such a way. Perhaps, he'd said, the horse sensed some weakness
or lack in the rider. This was how I came to feel about my awkward adjacency to family in Texas—a child of divorce in a culture of tradition, I was the thing that did not belong. By that
time my father had another family. I never rode a horse again.

Sunday, August 8

Bryan and I slip out of the house early to see Eve in the nursing home one last time before heading back to Seattle. On this
trip we have witnessed flashes of lucidity from her, and now she
is back to total non-lucidity: perhaps just a magnified version of
how our minds are always working, this switching back-and-
forth. But as always, there is a ground of sweetness to her. "Her
essential nature," as Bryan puts it. Today Eve gives up trying to
talk at all, and just squeezes our hands and smiles brightly to
each of us in turn—taking in our faces slowly as if savoring a
delicious flavor—until it is time to go.

"Do you remember Eve's koan—that thing she said about
cookies?" I ask Bryan as we step out of the nursing home.

"Oh yes—that was great."

A few years ago, on a similar visit, we all ate sugar cookies together after a meal, each person passing the plate like
communion.

"What's this?" Eve had asked as she touched the cookie on
her plate.

"It's a cookie," replied Viv.

"I know that. What is it?"

"It's butter, sugar, white flour, baking soda...."

"Oh, I know how to make it. But what IS it?"

"I don't understand your question, Mom," said Viv.

Eve tried again: "What's—a cookie?"

"That's an excellent question," said Bryan, holding up one
of the cookies and really looking at it. "I honestly have no idea."

When we return to the house, Kathy is talking animatedly

with Dick in the living room and Viv is watching on from her chair. There is a sort of frantic good-naturedness to her speaking, an injection of sunlight into a dark room. *She is kind*, I think, *a kind person who wants to do right by others but who also struggles—just as I do, just as we all do.*

That cheerful sunlight stays in the room as we say our farewells and I am grateful.

"Your Dad seems to be dealing with Viv's condition pretty well, considering," says Kathy as we pull out of the driveway.

"Yeah, he's doing a lot better now than he was even last week," says Bryan. "Still, he's having a hard time. He just doesn't always show it."

Yellow-green landscape slips past us as we consider this. I say, "I remember once Dick saying that on his fishing trips he'd begun releasing every third catch for Viv. We were all at that Mexican restaurant. Bryan, do you remember what he said?"

"Something like, 'I got the idea from the Buddhists—still trying to figure out that merit concept.'"

Kathy smiles and takes Bryan's hand.

Midway through our journey, we stop in Coeur d'Alene, Idaho, to swim in the endless blue lake. Bryan and Kathy playing in bright sunlight and water, laughing. They seem passionate and broken open, like two people who know it's going to end.

Tuesday, August 10

I spend my last day in Seattle at Green Lake—my ideal, lonely farewell—walking and stopping at intervals to sit beneath the trees with my notebook. I have a deep and enduring fondness for this particular place because, everywhere I have lived, there has always been a path where I go to walk and get my thinking done—a habitual and recursive journey that is like an old friend. After Koun and I returned from Japan that first time and then got married, during those ten brief months we lived in Seattle, I came here nearly every day. Though we didn't know it at the time, we were in transition. We'd just returned from two years in Japan, and we found ourselves slowly realizing that we needed to go back—Koun for his formal Zen training, and me because of a gnawing fascination with that unique Japanese aesthetic.

And now, another time of transition. Or perhaps an arrival.

In the evening, when Bryan comes home, I admit my discomfort about returning to Alaska tomorrow. "I always feel that something bad awaits me there—it's illogical, I know. But the discomfort is real. I'm not sure how to make peace with that feeling."

And so, as a way to calm my mind, he shows me how to do a basic *puja*, which looks and feels very much like one of the ceremonies at the monastery. It begins with both of us sitting on meditation cushions in front of his makeshift coffee table altar. Vishnu, deity of ultimate reality, is invoked through mantra, incense and a candle are lit, and water is sprinkled on a miniature plate of cooked rice. The candle, then, is lifted and circled. The ceremony concludes with a final mantra, and I can't look away from a photograph of a smiling Ammachi, the Hindu "hugging saint," swimming in a white sari in the Ganges River, flower petals floating around her. This is Bryan's chosen guru—a woman who has dedicated her life to hugging strangers as if they are her own children.

When, at last, I begin to enter sleep this night, it is the image of the woman in the flow of a river that stays with me.

Wednesday, August 11

Remarkably, I am on an airplane, once again defying space and time. For much of the five-hour journey, I can't seem to concentrate on anything I've brought with me and so, in neurotic cycles, I flip through a favorite novel, a book of kanji, the materials in the seat pocket in front of me, and my notebook. Nothing offers escape. The oxygen in the cabin seems inadequate, and I feel that there is a slow constricting in my chest as the plane draws closer and closer to the place where I came of age.

But when we hover over countless glaciers and great, jagged, snow-peaked mountains, I experience an extraordinary expansiveness—like a slow taking in of breath. There is a right-ness in that treacherous view below that I can't deny. *Home.*

After the plane lands, I exit into the main lobby and imme-diately spot my mother waving cheerfully from within a group of others (mostly tall, sturdy-looking men with facial hair) waiting to collect and depart. As usual, I'm struck by how alike my mother and I look—it's disconcerting every time. As we move toward each other, I wonder if anyone is observing us as a single subject approaching her future (or past) mirror image.

Together we gather my luggage and then step out of the airport building. A blinding blast of sunlight and remembered smell hits me.

"What time is it?" I ask, squinting into the brightness.

"10 p.m."

Thursday, August 12

The glowing rectangle around the sun-blocking window shade wakes me much too early. My body is already ticking with that manic Alaskan-summer alertness as I lie on one side of a twin bed. It is funny how, even in sleep, I habitually make space for Koun.

I rise and draw open the shade, look out on ocean before turning back into the smallness of a room that houses familiar and unfamiliar objects—a bedspread from my youth; a newer painting of my mother's, of sunflowers; an antique dresser and mirror purchased from a secondhand shop when I was here last; a shelf filled with books on painting techniques and cans and jars of pencils and paintbrushes. My mother has returned to a long-abandoned artistic self since divorcing my stepfather some years ago, in that year before I moved to Japan for the first time, in the year of my own divorce in grad school.

When my mother wakes a few hours later, there is a flurry of welcome distraction having to do with Yoko-san and Satsuki-chan's expected arrival today—mainly, I have no idea how to track them down. The original plan was to meet them at the hotel—and that is where we go—but the hotel desk clerk insists that no such names are on the guest list. A quick over-the-counter peek while we are talking reveals that their names have been horribly misspelled, as are most of the Japanese names on the list. "We are sure that the spellings are correct," the desk person says. "But if this is your friend and granddaughter, they will arrive shortly at the airport, and the tour guides will bring them here."

Finally, we locate them at the airport: Satsuki-chan, a thirteen-year-old with the long slender limbs of a ballerina, looking wide-eyed and in awe of her first moment in an exotic, foreign land; and Yoko-san, as *genki* as always, in awe of nothing. Apparently they will shortly be collected by the guides, and after they drop off their bags at the hotel, they will be immediately off on an all-day tour—a glacier cruise just outside of Whittier. After such a long plane journey, I can't imagine being eager for a long bus ride and then climbing aboard a ferry. "It'll be beautiful, though," my mother says. "It's a great day for the ferry—maybe the glacier will be calving. And the animals will be out."

Our plans of being tour guides thwarted, my mother and I return to her condo to sit on her couch, contemplating from her picture windows a cargo boat's slow movement across the ocean's surface.

"The culture here—I'm trying to put my finger on it. It's like, do whatever the hell you want to do, just make sure you leave me alone."

"And make sure you stay away from what's mine," Mom adds. "People are liable to shoot you if you step onto their property."

"Oh yes! And that kind of collective glee that shows up when someone gets eaten by a bear or dies of exposure. 'Well, that guy wasn't prepared. Had it coming to him.' Not a lot of compassion there. Not a lot of empathy."

"Maybe every culture comes with its own good and bad," says Mom as she rises to brew more coffee.

Show no weakness—the simultaneously great and tragic creed of the Alaskans, I think. I wonder how much of this culture is still mine?

In another time and place and culture, surely Koun is letting himself into unlocked strangers' houses in Takamori today and tomorrow, having been released briefly from the monastery to help his teacher deliver blessings for the Obon season, which honors the spirits of the departed. If someone is home, they will greet him after he enters the *genkan*, and lead him to the *butsu-dan*, the home's Buddhist altar, where he will light a candle and incense, chanting the *Heart Sutra* in the name of each family's ancestors. Afterward, there will be *tsukemono* (pickled vegetables) and green tea, or maybe *amazake* (a fermented rice drink) and *yokan* (sliced sweet bean jelly). If no one is home, he will find the *butsudan* by himself, do the ceremony, then leave. The smell of incense the only clue that he was there at all.

Friday, August 13

I walk toward the center of downtown Anchorage with Yoko-san and Satsuki-chan, my accidental guests in this place where I am now more tourist than local. A prescribed burn in the Interior lends a smoky haze to the sky, obliterating the mountains. And it's much warmer than usual—in the upper seventies.

"It's cold, *ne*," says Yoko-san.

"Yes. Cold," says Satsuki-chan. I think of my mother, who has left windows open and turned on multiple fans to cool the air in her condo.

"Do you want to borrow my sweater?" I offer.

"No thank you," says Satsuki-chan.

"Ohhhh, good English conversation, *ne*," says Yoko-san, as Satsuki-chan smiles and blushes. "You can practice in the store, too."

For Day Two of their journey, the aim is to locate suitable obligatory *omiyage*—for each of Satsuki-chan's classmates and teachers as well as for Yoko-san's various family, friends, and associates. Given Yoko-san's careful attention to proper etiquette, I suspect we'll be at it for a good part of the morning, if not the whole day. Unfortunately, I'm not sure what here will appeal.

"There," says Yoko-san, gesturing wildly. "And there." I see nothing of particular note at first glance—shops, yes, but why the excitement? And then I see it: all of the windows display multiple little signs written with Japanese characters.

"When I walked here yesterday, I didn't notice those signs at all."

"Now you are seeing with your Japanese eyes," says Yoko-san.

Later, when we enter my mother's aging condo building to take in the gorgeous afternoon view of the ocean, I cringe when I see how Yoko-san's gaze moves over the small living room, the cramped kitchen, the dining nook, the many paintings and sketches in mid-process. She pities my mother. I know she sees divorce, a woman who has been "forced" to have a career. But somehow she stops short of commenting directly, and I am relieved. These things will be talked about later, among the pottery ladies perhaps, and they will feel sorry for my mother, and for me, for all the wrong reasons.

Saturday, August 14

I am beginning to realize that the phenomenon of "recognition"—that curious bit of culture shock that prompts the brain to believe that passersby are known—is probably, here anyway, real recognition. This morning as I stroll to Yoko-san and Satsuki-chan's hotel, I see at least two people I went to high school with, only really catching on to this fact some minutes later, when an ephemeral flicker of memory translates the familiar features of face and body across time: a boy who kissed me once, a girl who hated me because she mistook my depression for arrogance.

After I collect my charges, we head to the Performing Arts Center to watch a film on the aurora borealis—the northern lights. It's definitely geared for tourists, but still I am moved by the sweeping displays of green, red, blue, and gold set to over-the-top New Age music. As the sound and images fade and the theater lights come on around us, I turn to Yoko-san and Satsuki-chan. Both appear stunned. "Are you okay?" I ask

"They . . . they are like ghosts. Very scary," says Yoko-san.

"*Honto? Honto?*" asks Satsuki-chan, her eyes wide.

"Yes," I say. "They are real. I have seen them many times."

"Very scary," repeats Yoko-san solemnly. Still, she buys four boxes of photo cards in the gift shop. A necessary proof, perhaps, of this haunted land.

~

In the evening, after I drop off an exhausted Yoko-san and Satsuki-chan at their hotel, my mother and I meet up with Thor—local artist, commercial fisherman, and my mother's long-time sort-of boyfriend. "Bar hopping is all about people-watching," explains Thor who, I believe, looks more or less like his namesake. I wonder if people go to bars to watch *him*. The first place we enter, sparse and clean and nearly empty of patrons, houses a few of Thor's paintings. We collect our drinks, then move to a mural—a lively New Orleans–style jazz scene with people dancing in the streets. Several of Thor's friends— including my mom—appear in the crowd, held fast in an image of raucous nostalgia. On another wall, near the bar, hangs a portrait of Mt. Redoubt looming large. That singular, distinct character. "An Alaskan Fuji," I say. The proprietor agrees with my assessment, reaches across the bar to shake my hand when Thor explains where I live, that my husband is a cloistered monk. "If I were inclined to be a religious man, I guess I'd be a Buddhist," he says.

We continue our rounds downtown in this way—a tour of art and life. A couple cozy hole-in-the-walls with rough-looking locals. And then an over-the-top classy place for wealthy tourists, the walls and fixtures sparkling with brass and mirrors. A final stop to a smoky room filled with people on the edge of youth, save for the old timers sitting at the bar itself, all of them deep in their glasses. As soon as we sit down—me just a little off to the side of Thor and my mom, who have just entered into some kind of quiet quarrel—one of the men on the dance floor releases a woman at the end of a song and asks me to dance. "Don't worry. I'll keep my hands to myself," he says. I refuse— and then accept. What's the harm? He's seen the ring; he's made a fair promise. But he does not keep it, so I walk away before the dance is over. "What's your story?" he shouts after me. Mom and Thor turn from each other as I sit down.

"I should have known better." I can feel my face burning. Thor laughs and orders me yet another glass of wine. I watch from my seat as the man captures a sad-eyed redhead, then, and spins away into the music. I am more than a little drunk, I realize. I've never done too well with alcohol.

When our drinks come, my mother and Thor get up to dance and I drift, trancelike, into memory. Nome. 1979. My mother beautiful in a short gold cocktail dress that she sewed herself for her role in the local theater—an adaptation of Bogart's *Casablanca*. I remember she bought the thing I had been coveting for months from one of the gift shops in town, one of the few places to view and desire objects for purchase: a delicate miniature gramophone music box made of dark wood that played "As Time Goes By" at the lift of a tiny brass lever. She gave it to one of the men in the play as a flirtation. This, too, a pattern with us.

On the way home from this last bar, I stumble, dizzy, and fall over onto concrete. I see my mother leaning over me in a gold dress—but it is just a bit of light behind her in the darkness. A flickering streetlamp, or a ghost.

What's your story?

No story.

That would be the Zen answer—wouldn't it?

Sunday, August 15

Koun calls while out doing *takuhatsu*. He is on his *onsen* break at the end of his day of alms rounds, and we just have these few moments that he has saved by taking his bath more quickly than the others. How lucky that I am home in time for the call. I can hear the exhaustion in his voice, imagine those rope sandals cutting into his feet, those robes bound around his body gathering heat all day long. He tells me about the day's frustrations: "Jisen-san gave us extremely complex instructions about going to Fukuoka and calling some monk and so forth. It was impossible to get right. And Aigo-san is driving the other monks crazy. They've begun mimicking him in Japanese—even when he's in the room. He hasn't quite figured it out yet. 'That is not the way Dogen washes laundry. That is not how Dogen picks his nose.' It's comical, in a way, but there's real tension beneath it." He sighs. "How is it going there?"

"Yoko-san and Satsuki-chan have been a welcome distraction in many ways. Still, it's overwhelming—an assault on the senses. I feel tired all the time."

"Was it like that when I went to Alaska with you?"

"Somewhat, yeah. But we'd only been dating a year. I'm pretty sure that all I could really see was you."

"That was mutual. . . . Maybe people who don't leave have time to grow into a place, or they grow with it. But those who do leave—"

"Yes, yes! There's this sense of a split personality, or of lost time. There is no real connection to that person who was and the person who is. It's terrifying. Like being unable to locate my self, my ego. I'm lost."

"Maybe it's time to shave your head, baby."

~

In the evening, I call Cheryl, my best friend from high school. We have, over the years, kept a slender thread of contact. Her voice, not heard in a very long time, exactly the same as I remembered it.

Monday, August 16

Yoko-san and Satsuki-chan are leaving at 3 a.m. tomorrow, and Yoko-san suggests that we say goodbye now, as the hotel shuttle will deliver them both to the airport at that early hour. So we see them off at the hotel entrance with an armload of souvenirs: a book of Alaskan photography, some coffee and loose-leaf tea, an assortment of chocolates from the gift shop where my mom works part-time. This is followed by lots of bowing, which my mother and I return awkwardly. Then as we get into the car and pull away, we observe as Satsuki-chan and Yoko-san dutifully stand and wave until we are out of sight.

"Wow, that was an elaborate send-off," says my mother.

"If we turn the car around now and catch them before they go back inside, I'm pretty sure that Japanese etiquette will require that they start up again," I offer. Some cruel part of me wants to do just this, as experiment.

"What now?"

"I have no idea. I feel like my purpose has been taken away."

"Is there anything that you know you'd like to do while you're here?"

"Nothing special—just be here," I say. "Take walks, read, write a bit. Oh, and maybe try local Zen—I guess there's a little group that meets in the mornings."

"Okay. How about a drive to Portage Glacier today?"

"Sure!"

And so we shuttle off down the Seward Highway, that great route of stunning vistas—towering mountains and vast sea. When we arrive, it is as shocking as the first time I noticed: a concrete building adjacent to nothing more than a cold lake. Years ago, in my childhood, the lake was mostly glacier. Somewhere, there is a photo of me standing in front of this same building and the massive white-blue river of ice next to it, a small inquisitive hand reaching out to touch the frozen chunks that have settled along the dark riverside sands. Now, we stand before a giant vanished. That great receding, as if a memory erased.

"It's changed a lot, hasn't it," says my mother.

"It shocks me every time. When we last saw the ice—that must have been with Fred." I ask her if she ever thinks of her last ex-husband, the man who served as my stand-in father for most of my childhood.

"Sometimes, but not that often nowadays."

"I worked very hard to put him out of my mind when I first moved to Japan—it was an active forgetting, I think. But sometimes something comes up, and I almost can't believe it's real, that someone could actually treat other people that way."

"Yes, it was like being caught in one long nightmare."

"That's a good word for it, 'nightmare.' Our own personal hell. Nobody could see it but us. Or they chose not to see."

My mother looks at the edge of water, then up toward the mountains. "When you went off to college, I remember having vivid dreams that he was fattening me up to eat me—to devour me—just like in the Hansel and Gretel story. That's when I knew I had to get away."

"I've had dreams like that. Little echoes after I left. Always something about being trapped—terrible." And at the same time I allowed men to build traps around me. I walked into those iron cages knowingly. I shut the door and locked it behind me again and again.

"But you know, there were good times, too. We shouldn't forget that." This odd habit of my mother's, always applying the positive spin.

"He was a bully, Mom. A horrible person. Nothing can change any of that."

I think of a childhood friend, Matt, the son of a minister. His father hunted bear and moose with my stepfather while discussing the mysteries of God. Matt's family moved out of state just after I entered high school—we already lived in different parts of the Valley by then, and we had been attending different schools. Still, over the years, we stayed in touch off and on. I had written him a letter that first year in Japan, and I told him what I had failed to tell so many others. But he hadn't believed me. In his reply, he wrote how Fred, as his fifth-grade teacher, had been a kind of inspiration to both him and his younger brother, and that he would always be indebted to Fred, for showing him how to be strong, how to be a man. I never wrote back, even though he wrote to me again and again. That broken thread of friendship. A boy who had once held my hand as we crossed a treacherous tributary of a river swollen with spring ice-melt and glacial silt. I had thought we would always know each other. Maybe I shouldn't have told, maybe he should have believed. I still don't know which is true. I still don't know.

Tuesday, August 17

My first day of "Alaskan Zen." I rise at 6 a.m., pull on loose, dark clothing, and with my mother's car keys in my hand rush out the door chanting, "Stay on the right, stay on the right, stay on the right." Though directionally challenged, I do succeed in both driving on the correct side of the road and locating the little yoga studio where, according to the Internet, the Anchorage Zen Community meets for zazen every morning.

Still, I feel that I am trespassing as I enter the building. Standing before an empty reception desk that sits next to a large dark and empty room, I weigh my options: call out or leave or just snoop around. Then I register that the hallway extending beyond the desk is lit, and I follow it (thus opting for "snoop around," I suppose). At the end of the corridor is another big room with a single glowing lamp, a few tall bookcases off to the side obscuring one corner, a simple table altar with incense curling around a small Buddha, and a number of square cushions and round *zafu* set out in a long rectangle. No one is in here, as far as I can tell, but at least I now understand what I am looking at. I *gassho* and bow, enter, and seat myself on the nearest *zafu* and let my gaze rest on the wall in front of me.

A few minutes later, from behind the bookshelf comes the sound of cloth—a monk's ample robes, perhaps. I sense an emerging from behind the bookshelf, a settling-in, and then the strike of a bell to begin the session. If I close my eyes, I could be at Tatsuda Center, or at Shogoji with Koun.

After a while, I hear movement again, a kind of pacing around the room, and then the person whom I have now decided is definitely the priest puts his hand gently on my shoulder and presses my lower back to correct my failing posture. I misunderstand and *gassho*, bowing low to accept the firm smack from the *kyosaku* stick, but he whispers, "No, no, no, no, no," laughing a little under his breath. I smile when I recognize the accent—Japanese.

After zazen and then *kinhin* and then zazen again, there is a flurry of prostrations and chanting in English and Japanese from the lone figure at the front of the room. Without other laypeople to guide me, I'm not sure what to do, so I fake it, fumbling through every movement and chant. Finally, we rise and bow to our cushions and to the potential of other practitioners, and then I turn my gaze to the front of the room and really see the priest for the first time: a small, older Japanese man with a wide face, and an easy, broken smile. I like him immediately.

"Good morning," he says. "Are you okay?"

"I'm very sorry. I messed up your beautiful ceremony."

"Don't worry. How about zazen? You are okay? It was not too difficult?"

"I think it's always difficult for me."

"Oh I see."

"Do you need help with this stuff?"

"You can put the cushions away here. And the sutra books go here. There is a special way for the altar things—I will show you."

"Is it always so quiet?" I ask as I gather and stack.

"Alaskan people are always busy enjoying their lives in summer," he explains as he disappears behind the bookshelf. He emerges minutes later, now dressed in plain black *samu-e*. "Please call me Tozen," he says. "Will you come again?"

"Yes. For a couple weeks, anyway. I'm visiting my mother, but I live in Japan. This year my husband is training in a monastery."

"Oh I see. You are lonely like me."

Wednesday, August 18

After a late breakfast, I borrow my mother's car again and drive north through birch and evergreen and across endless mud flats, toward a stunning view of Pioneer Peak in bright sun. In just under an hour, I arrive in Palmer, the small town where I attended junior high and high school. Cheryl, now a high school teacher in the Valley, greets me with a hug at the door of her house—this tall, tan, stunning woman with long brown hair. We stand back briefly and just take each other in. "You look the same!" we both exclaim, and we do, but for that slight angular maturing of the features, that falling away of softness and rounded youth. Her son and daughter, she says, are with her ex-husband this week, so she has the day to herself.

"Let's sit out back—in the sun," she says, and we pass through the living room, out onto a bright deck. "So your husband—how long has it been now?"

"This is the sixth month. Six more to go."

"You know, I was thinking about something you wrote me a while back, something about Buddhism."

"Oh yikes—I hope I didn't say something stupid."

"No, it's just that I was going to counseling for a while, after I got divorced. The more I think about it, it seems spiritual. Not what I expected at all."

"Maybe Zen is like that. A little like that and a little not like that. I'm not sure."

"Hey, do you want to—do something?" Cheryl has often been my guide to perilous outdoor adventure. I know whatever she has in mind will not be boring.

A short while later, we are biking at breakneck speeds along a forest trail that offers views of the glacially silted waters of the Matanuska-Susitna River. Descending a hill, my tire connects with a big rock and I'm neatly thrown into the bushes.

"You okay?" Cheryl asks as she maneuvers her bike to me.

I brush dirt and foliage from my body and pick up the bike. "Nothing broken. But I might need to walk it off for a few minutes."

As we walk, my racing heart and breath begin to slow.

"I love coming here," says Cheryl. "Makes me feel like a kid again."

"Thank God we're not. I don't think I could bear all that teenage angst."

"Yes, angst. . . . I worried about you, you know. Back in high school. I always did. But I had my own problems, too."

I laugh. "I always thought you were the together one. I envied you."

Cheryl stops walking and I stop too. I grow aware of the metal carcasses of vehicles between the trees around us. Ghosts from a distant time, a haunting. Cheryl says, "There was Ms.

P, do you remember her? She once told me that we all have our time—'yours just hasn't come yet.' That meant a lot to me, you know. That meant a lot. And she was right."

We climb back on our bicycles, and I look on as Cheryl rides ahead of me. It is jarring how the memories of others, once revealed, can rewrite our own histories in an instant. Cheryl was tall and awkward and smart and fearless and beautiful in a way that few could see. I was slight and shy and pretty and damaged, and for some reason certain things came easily to me. Self-absorbed in my own misery, I could not fully comprehend the misery of others. I had not been a good friend.

~

As I am driving back to Anchorage, a memory comes to me, bright as the evening light. One winter day into our second year of high school, Cheryl and I walked into the woods near her house. We carried with us the long and painful letters we'd written each other in junior high and that first bit of high school. There were many, and we had meticulously saved every one of them, compiling them in a three-ring binder over the course of those years. We also brought photos—one of Cheryl's first boyfriend, one of a boy I had liked until, in the darkness of a near-empty movie theater, he tried to force me to do something I did not want to do, one of a girl who had called one or both of us "bitch" to all of her friends. We brought matches and a bottle of lighter fluid. We gathered dry branches and bits of yellowed grass revealed by the thaw. After we lit the fire, we dropped the photos in one by one, watching them curl up and burn. The letters, our devastating masterpiece, we could not bring ourselves to burn, so we buried the folder in the snow. Sometime after that day, we drifted apart, each to our own paths.

Thursday, August 19

I feel broken this morning. When I attend zazen, I am vaguely aware of many comings and goings of the participants—but it is all through a sleepy fog. Afterward, Tozen suggests he and I have breakfast at a little mom-and-pop diner nearby. As we walk across the parking lot, he tests my Japanese—a long riff of questions that move from easy to more and more difficult.

When I completely fail to answer, he tells me in English, "I am not only a monk. I am also a Japanese-language teacher."

"Then you know exactly how bad my Japanese is."

"Yes."

"Ha—in Japan I always know I'm doing badly when someone compliments me. *'Nihongo ga jozu desu ne!'* It's a real giveaway."

"Do you get a lot of compliments?"

"So many."

"I see."

Over breakfast, I learn that in Japan he lived in Gunma, "famous for nothing." And that, for a while, someone in his family was desperately trying to develop a *fugu* blowfish with no poison. But this, according to Tozen, was a very bad idea because the mother said he had always been careless. I also learn that Tozen's *deshi's deshi* was at Shogoji recently.

"Tim?" I ask, faintly recalling Koun mentioning something about an American man, someone who stayed there only briefly. It seems everyone knows everyone in the small world of Zen.

As we are about to part ways after breakfast, he asks, "Do you know *Tora-san?*" Tozen has collected and watched the entirety of this long-running Japanese series about an ever-lovesick traveler. He says, "I am like Tora-san—completely hopeless."

Maybe I am like that, too.

Friday, August 20

Sitting this morning is pure pleasure, a rarity: my posture balanced, my respiration measured, a gentle humming in the mechanisms of the body. Tozen is not here today and the atmosphere in the room feels slightly different, though I'm not sure if his absence is the reason. Maybe it's the rain outside and the sound of cars moving through water. Or it's that flash of brightness in my peripheral vision: a pretty blond girl in her twenties wearing all-white, in contrast to the others' dark, demure clothing. A reluctant goddess, she slips away after the first end-of-zazen bow.

That pleasant energy evaporates midway through the morning, and the deep tiredness of yesterday hits me again. Mom and I make plans to go to a movie—a low-key event—but Koun calls just before we step out the door. I tell him about meeting Tozen, and when I mention his *deshi*'s *deshi*, Koun reminds me that Tim was the American monk who decided to leave Shogoji a few weeks ago. Jisen-san was constantly berating him for not being able to "sit like a real monk."

"He has water-on-the-knees. A very painful condition. But she wouldn't hear of it. She called him weak, lazy. I felt bad for him."

He also tells me that he and some of the Shogoji monks had been invited to visit the Kurume temple, a complex nestled next to an unforgettable landmark: a huge statue of Kannon, or Avalokiteshvara, overlooking the city. Some years ago we entered the building and climbed the spiral of stairs inside to peer out from the very eyes of compassion. I remember a scratchy recording of the *Heart Sutra* echoing up and around us and also the *jigoku*, the hell realms at the base of the structure—horrifying yet somehow Disney-like dioramas of demons and figures trapped in eternal torture. Thus we climbed out of hell, and then entered back into it.

"The priest there carves beautiful religious statues," Koun tells me. "He's made a living of it. If we ever have a temple here I'll go to him first for statuary." He also tells me that he served as the babysitter for the priest's newborn son. "Such a happy little guy, his head constantly bonking on my chest. It's the best monk's job I've been assigned so far." I smile at the image of my husband as Kannon with a baby in his arms. I wonder if we will ever be brave enough to have children.

He asks, "How are things there?"

"I don't know. I think maybe I was an asshole in high school."

"I doubt that very much."

"Well, I know for sure I'm tired," I say. "Everything feels heavy."

"I feel the same way."

"Maybe it has something to do with the midway point. Or maybe it's the weather or Alaska—I don't know. Part of me can't believe that we've come this far already. Part of me can't believe we have six more months to go."

Sunday, August 22

Mom and I drive out to Hatcher's Pass today, stopping here and there as we ascend the mountain, snapping photos of each other dipping our fingers into the cold, clear water of the Little Susitna River, or pointing at damp stones laced with fool's gold.

Near the top of the mountain, we've climbed high enough to reveal the blanket of clouds floating above the valley. Here dense foliage has given way to moss, lowbush cranberries, and blueberry bushes. We've brought buckets to gather blueberries, but it's unusually warm this year, and the fruit is sparse and wrinkled. Still, we continue to search, taking pleasure in our rare findings.

On the way back down, we stop at the Motherlode, the lodge our family owned for barely a year before the business lost viability. It is strange to move through this remodeled version of my memories. Very few people are in the building today, and my mother and I comment on each space in hushed voices: "This was here, wasn't it?" and "This is new." I must have been ten years old when we moved in. My second stepfather, an alcoholic, poured away all that we had every night at the bar—rarely charging the patrons for the party. I was forbidden visits from school friends because, as my mother once said, "This is no place for a child." She had been right of course, and so I mostly gave up friendships altogether—the start, perhaps, of a lifelong habit of letting go.

But in brief spurts, I remember feeling great joy here: there were those long, solitary hikes that were my refuge and then lying invisible on soft moss among jagged brambles, looking up at the sky, and thinking, *I am a part of THIS*. Fireweed blossoms, pungent Devil's Club, the sound of the river, and black, black earth offering me up to blue sky. Or, in winter, it was the snow that held me. It was here where I first began to do what I called "The Big/Small"—I'd feel myself expanding to the size of the universe, and then I'd shrink back down to a grain of sand. In this way, I think I discovered some sense of spirituality; my way of seeing was my one true magic power. And it was this sensation, this practice that I would try to articulate to Koun so many years later. He was the first person to ever understand what I was talking about.

As we re-enter the Mat-Su Valley, my mother and I settle into a deep silence. When we are together, I realize, we are two women caught in the same stories—stories that we have rehashed and analyzed so many times before. And I know we're both there now, turning it all over in our minds as we drive through memory and landscape. Perhaps for both of us it is the last character who is most difficult to forgive: my third stepfather, the man who rescued my mother from a bad marriage to a reckless alcoholic, and then pulled her into something more sinister. Fred had been jealous, controlling, cruel—and all of this interspersed with bouts of equally confusing kindness and charm. In this way, through these dualities in his nature, he became the architect of our reality. He put us in our place. And after I went off to college, my mother got the full brunt of it, as I knew she would.

And then there was the last time I saw my stepfather—I was in graduate school in Spokane. It was their first and only visit; I had not returned to Alaska since leaving six years before. In a restaurant, Fred revealed the impending divorce while my mother stared at the ice shifting in her water glass. There had been an eeriness to it all—the constant hand-holding and touching, like a grotesque of newlyweds, juxtaposed with the fear and pain in my mother's eyes. But I was focused inwardly, on my own failing marriage. There were too many echoes there for me to cope. She told me later that everything in the divorce had been on his terms—the unequal division of money and debt, the date of his leaving her life, certain intimacies. And there were also the suicide threats, the veiled death threats. No horror surprised me. This was a familiar territory. Family friends were delivered a story and devoured it; my mother was abandoned by all.

How could they not see?
How much do I not see?

Monday, August 23

In my mother's mailbox, there is a letter from Koun today—a fascinating jumble of events and thought. He says that at last he has "plateaued" to a certain degree at Shogoji because he now understands all of the ceremonies and doesn't have to constantly cram. *But maybe it is better when I am always on my toes, always hyper-aware.*

In addition to this, he has been given the responsibility of translating letters for Jisen-san, so she seems happy with him lately. The other monks have nicknamed him "Solar Man" because Jisen-san decided that no one can touch the solar generator except him. *At the moment, it's funny. But this privilege—this departure from rank—will likely get me in trouble in the end,* he writes.

Also, Jisen-san has warned him about returning to the U.S.: *Women everywhere! You be very, very careful!*

~

I arrive at Cheryl's place in the evening for an informal gathering of teachers. A blond woman greets me at the door in Japanese, and I respond immediately, before registering the improbability of this. We cycle through a textbook dialogue.

"My name is Carla," she says. "It is nice to meet you."

"Where do you live?"

"How long have you lived there?"

"What do you do?"

And then she explains that she teaches Japanese in the same high school as Cheryl.

"Your Japanese is so much better than mine—where did you learn? University?" I ask.

"I was married to a Japanese man for a few years, in Hokkaido."

"They always say, 'Take a local lover . . .' Fortunately or unfortunately, that was never really an option for me."

"Well, it is highly recommended!" She laughs—such friendly, open energy. I have no doubt that she is a very, very popular teacher.

"Hmm. Maybe our students should exchange letters."

"Sure, pen pals—the next best thing to a lover."

Tuesday, August 24

I have breakfast with Tozen at the same little diner as before. When the waitress delivers menus and offers coffee, I ask for tea. Tozen announces, "I am Japanese, so I drink coffee."

I respond in kind: "I am American. So, I drink green tea."

He tells me, "I hate Japan. Everyone is the same. NO individuals." Then, "Do you know Ryokan?"

"Sweet bean jam?"

He lets out a BIG belly laugh. "No, Ryooooookan. He is a very famous founder of Buddhism. A real individual."

After we finish our food, Tozen reaches into his bag. "I have something for you." He produces two books for me to borrow, and two books "as a bribe" for me to come back and bring my husband.

"These authors understand Zen is no striving. Americans always want goals."

Thursday, August 26

I am sitting on Cheryl's couch in her living room. It is near midnight, and both of us are sipping wine and growing drowsy. We have been talking about her dating life, the difficulty of finding love after a certain age, with two children, in a small town, with complication and history. There is this hesitation, a tentativeness. Maybe we both sense that we are now moving into the past.

"It's strange," I say, "as teenagers we were always so raw and yet so guarded at the same time."

"Absolutely, it was painful. Do you remember that summer

we painted Chris with my little sister's watercolors? We were on my front lawn, and his shirt was off, and we painted his body."

"Yes—how could I forget?" I always felt that was a pivotal moment, for all of us.

Cheryl sighs, looks over at me. "I kissed Chris, sometime around then. I don't know if you knew that."

"I didn't know. But it doesn't surprise me."

"He had something, didn't he? A kind of sadness. It was hard not to be moved."

"Yes," I say, "I always felt he and I shared that, that we were the same person in some ways. And there was always a lot of anger there, too. He was my friend and he said he loved me, but I did not love him, not in that way. I felt that he shamed me into dating him for those few months, and then I hated him for it afterward. I hated myself."

"I know. Maybe that's why I kissed him. I think I was mad at you. For many reasons."

"I probably deserved that."

"Sometimes I think about that time, about those first relationships or encounters—or whatever they were."

"Oh yes," I say, "all those devastating sexual games. The boys high on the social food chain preying on the girls below. I did not deal well with any of that."

"No, you didn't."

"I guess I had some issues. Maybe I was easy prey."

"Maybe we all were, in a way. Even those on the top of the food chain. They were caught up in something. That's kind of sad, too, isn't it?"

"Yes, though I wonder how many of them walked away with the scars we walked away with. . . ."

"True. That church boy in Anchorage—do you remember him?" asks Cheryl.

"I remember how happy you were, and how sad when he stopped calling. But I didn't know the whole story, did I? We didn't talk a lot then."

"No, you didn't know the whole story. . . . Tell me, do you really think it is possible for people to fall in love in high school, when we were just kids?"

"Who's to say that kind of love wasn't real? It was immature and chaotic, it was overwhelming, and a good part of it was probably chemical—or the result of some misguided narrative. But we felt what we felt. We were moved in some way that changed us."

"Yeah—almost like waking up, or seeing something that you couldn't see before. Like some kind of recognition." Cheryl swirls the last bit of wine in her glass before drinking it down. "Tracy, did you ever *really* feel that way, back then?"

"No. Maybe once. Though I think I didn't know why until just now. There was an awakening, yes. But I was carrying a terrible burden. And in that moment, it broke me."

"Adolescence. Everything felt so dramatic then—life or death. And we kept so many secrets from each other."

"And from ourselves."

"I wonder where Chris is now?"

"I don't know. I hope he's happy."

"I do, too."

~

Two girls painting the skin of a half-naked boy stretched out in the grass like a lion in sunlight. The girls laughing and teasing inside that last bubble of fading friendship. The boy pretending to tolerate the girls but also finding pleasure in the attention. And a darkness turning in him slowly, like a stone.

How we are marked. How we mark each other.

Friday, August 27

It's been raining hard for much of the day and I can't bear to leave the condo. It seems as if my mood has been translated into weather—an internal and external melancholy.

Koun finally breaks the spell by calling in the evening—he's out on *takuhatsu* again, and he has many adventures to relate: stung by three bees while out working in the fields; poured gasoline down his back when he tried to burn a big pile of weeds and twigs; saw flying squirrels gliding between the trees at dawn, as he rang the temple bell. He says overall he's feeling *genki*—happy because the visiting university students who just left said their three-hour Shogoji stay was hard but inspiring because everyone made it such a good experience. "Lately I've been struck by how easy it is to be grateful."

Also, Jisen-san says that in November Docho-roshi, the abbot of the head monastery in Zuioji, will come to Shogoji to hold a precepts ceremony, in which laypeople take up basic Buddhist vows:

(1) Not killing
(2) Not stealing
(3) Not misusing sex
(4) Not lying
(5) Not indulging in intoxicants
(6) Not speaking of the faults of others
(7) Not taking credit or assigning blame
(8) Not withholding the dharma or materials
(9) Not indulging anger
(10) Not slandering the Three Treasures (Buddha, dharma, sangha)

To participate, I'll need to sew a *rakusu*—that bib-like mini version of Buddha robes—with some of the other laypeople. Our *rakusu* will then be passed on to Docho-roshi before the ceremony, so that he can inscribe a new name—a dharma name—on the back of each. After that, we will formally receive the robe from him during the ceremony.

Which of the vows, I wonder, will give me the most trouble?

Saturday, August 28

My mother and I have dinner at Thor's place—pasta with shrimp, scallops, and a white wine butter sauce. It is all too rich for my now Japanese-y palate. I rub my aching belly while Thor expounds his Theory of Everything: "In our bodies we get to experience a limited perception. Otherwise we are just in the vast flow of everything—we have omniscient perception, but there is no way to experience the individual bits and hone in. I came up with this theory when I was just a kid."

Later, in the middle of the night, there is a horrible, intense pain in my gut. I try to get up, but can't move. Sweat drenching me. Falling into and out of consciousness.

Sunday, August 29

After today's zazen, the Anchorage Zen Community gathers for tea at the aptly named "Middle Way Café." I still feel unwell but am grateful for the distraction of human interaction. There are many new people in attendance—a testament, perhaps, to the rapid change in season. Clutching my tall mug of green tea, I settle in next to Loren, a second-generation Japanese from Hawaii. I have known him for all of an hour and he has taken to teasing me for constantly bowing—I laugh and then bow again, unable to stop. He begins to tell me the details of his family, tracing the history of the one temple on the small island where his father lived, and how his family struggled later during the Internment—losing a fishing boat, all hard-earned property. "But, you know, they got through it and here I am."

With coffee in hand, Tozen and a petite Japanese woman take seats at our table. They begin chatting away in fast, fluent Japanese—something about the woman's recent trip to Hiroshima, about it being her first time home in many years—and Loren joins them in his *nisei* Japanese. I do not know what, exactly, is different in the way each of them speaks, but there is something there, each of them perhaps offering up a language colored by geography and history and time spent away from their places of birth.

Abruptly, the petite woman stops talking, looks me in the eye suspiciously. "Ahhhh—do you understand me?" She asks this in Japanese. Tozen and Loren laugh and introduce me to Rie. She came to Alaska many years ago "for adventure." It is the same reason I so often give for moving to Japan.

After tea, I drive to a walk-in clinic. The pain from the night before stays with me as a dull and sluggish ache and I am worried that something is really not right. Stretched out on white paper, I nervously explain what I've been feeling while the doctor presses her fingers against my abdomen. "Hmm," she says, "let's do an X-ray." A short while later we review the pictures. "Severe constipation—full to the brim," she explains. "Has your diet changed significantly?" Before, I had steady meals of very healthy Japanese food—and now a lot of bread and wheat pasta and dairy. So much for paying attention. How could I miss even the most simple and essential process of the body? How stupid could I be?

I explain the diagnosis to my mother afterward: "I guess I'm just full of shit."

Monday, August 30

In the early evening, Mom, Thor, and I walk around one of the neighborhoods near downtown. Thor names all of the builders of all the houses we pass. He seems to hold knowledge of everyone, of everything about this place. We stop at one of his friend's houses—really just a renovated old log cabin from some distant era. Amazingly, though, it is set in a huge, beautiful, Asian-inspired garden, all of which is surrounded by a high wood fence. "From the outside, you never would guess would ya?" says Pat, the friend, obviously proud of his handiwork. His buddy, Bill, is lanky and tall—unlike Pat, who is bald and tough looking. Both men sit on tree stumps in the garden, drinking beer from cans. They are in their late forties, but in their demeanor and mannerisms they remind me very much of the boys I knew in high school. There is something distinctly Alaskan about them and also something wonderful about this roughness held in such a refined and elegant space. When Thor mentions that my husband is in the monastery, Bill tells us that he is deeply enamored with Ram Dass's *Be Here Now.* "That book changed my life, man. I tell you, that's the only book anyone ever needs to read."

Tuesday, August 31

After zazen this morning, I stand in my mother's spare bedroom gathering various items into a backpack—my ever-present notebook, a few Japanese study materials, and a couple of books and articles that Tozen gave me. My mother has already left for work and I'm feeling aimless and lost. My first thought is to walk down to the park and sit on a bench with a view of the ocean, but there is a chill in the air today—that first strong hint of the season to come—and I opt instead to hang out at a café, someplace where I can be insulated by a crowd while I read and write and study. I aim downtown toward a congregation of what look to be both tourists (identifiable by their well-matched caps and bright windbreakers) and locals (identifiable by their ambivalence to all manner of weather and temperature).

The café I choose is really a full-on restaurant down the street and kitty-corner from my mother's condo, and it soon becomes clear that it isn't the sort of place where people grab a pastry and an espresso and hang out for hours, poring over kanji and old Buddhist poetry and scribbling into a notebook. But I stay anyway, much to the annoyance of the waitress, who keeps asking if I need anything else.

I may need something, I want to tell her. *I just don't know what it is. Please bring me what you think I need.*

Fall

SEPTEMBER
Returning

Wednesday, September 1

It is overcast this morning—drizzly, chilly. For the first time since I have been to this yoga-studio-cum-zendo, tall lamps glow from two far corners of the room, casting deep shadows—a clear signal that the long days of the Alaskan summer are quickly growing shorter.

This new light illuminates those who are present today—Loren, Tozen, Rie—as we kneel before each other after zazen. Funny, I think, just me and the Japanese Americans. Tozen signals Loren to distribute an unfamiliar stack of sutra books, and we begin the *Heart Sutra* together in a language that I cannot call my own:

> *Kan ji zai bo satsu*
> *Gyo jin han-nya ha ra mit-ta ji*
> *Sho ken go on kai ku*
> *Do is-sai ku yaku*
> *Sha ri shi*
> *Shiki fu i ku*
> *Ku fu i shiki . . .*

I trace my finger down the line of *furigana* next to each Chinese character, trying to keep pace, but the rapid rhythm coupled with inadequate lighting is too much for me and my poor second-language reading skills. My voice enters and exits. Glancing up, I almost expect to see Koun half-in, half-out of shadow, chanting along with us.

"Did you enjoy?" asks Tozen afterward as we are putting the cushions away.

"Oh yes. It is difficult but it also feels right in Japanese, not forced into an awkward cadence, as it is in English."

"Hmm, yes," adds Loren. "It's hard to get the same feeling in translation."

"Oh," sighs Rie. "Hearing Japanese sutra—it reminds me of when I was a little girl in Japan. So comfortable."

"I don't think it's comfortable for me," I say. "But I feel like I'm doing what I'm supposed to be doing—being confused. That's my day-to-day experience in Japan. I never completely understand anything."

"Well—that's Buddhism!" says Loren.

Outside, the rain has stopped and the smell of damp concrete rises around us. As we are taking our leave of each other—bowing in that Japanese way—I realize that I've forgotten my keys. Tozen unlocks the door, and I step back inside the studio, move down the long hallway, and enter into the dark solitude of the zendo. My keys are a small lump on the floor where my *zafu* had been. I feel a question forming in my mind as I walk back toward the light at the entrance. When I exit the building, I thank Tozen and tell him, "Sometimes I think I just want to sit zazen because it is like sitting with Koun—this little thread of connection across time and space. Maybe that's all this is for me. Maybe that's it."

"Oh, now I see," says Tozen. He smiles broadly and then turns to amble off across the parking lot, a hand thrown into the air as farewell. I briefly watch his slow gait before turning to the car. Why did I make that confession? And what did his comment mean? As usual, I do not understand anything.

Thursday, September 2

I have decided to make something authentically Japanese for dinner, something that will give my mom a taste of my other home. The aim is to cook what I know only as "Japanese spaghetti"—noodles, tuna, shredded *nori*, grated *daikon*, a bit of onion, soy sauce, and a dash of rice vinegar. Satomi explained the ingredients to me once while I devoured a plate of it at a little café we often frequent. I remember being surprised by the simplicity of it.

But as I peruse the well-stocked local Asian grocer, I struggle with the products; I do not recognize many of them. How often do I rely on familiarity with a certain color and font and shape and nothing more? Take that away and I'm lost. The addition of English is interesting, but it does not give me the guidance I need. What happens, I wonder, to the blind who gain sight?

After I make my choice, I move on to a key ingredient—*daikon*. I spot a sign in romanized Japanese but beneath it is a pitiable little warped gray tuber the size of my fist. "Excuse me," I say to the grocer. "Is THIS a *'daikon'*?"

"Of course," he says.

When I prepare the dish, the root is dry and bitter and adds no depth of flavor.

"It's really unusual," says my mom as she chews the bland food. "Very mild."

"It's not authentic," I explain. "I couldn't find all of the right ingredients. And the Japanese radish should be sweet tinged with spice."

"Well, I guess it's authentic for here. . . ."

She has a point—this is what I'm always doing in Japan: searching for the right taste. I never find it. Maybe I need to own up to the fact that this is reality. Maybe nothing tastes the way I want it to.

Friday, September 3

When the alarm clock jerks me awake, I take in a long slow breath and notice that familiar itchy throat and ballooning pressure behind the brow: the first inklings of a cold

At the zendo, zazen proves challenging. Something— *there*—running out of my nose while I am just trying to sit and be a reasonably dignified being. But sickness always reminds me that there is no special dignity in bodies that are just dirt and water—each of us only holding a certain shape for a short while before breaking down into the essential elements. I hear that Tozen is coughing, too, as a counter to my sniffling. Strange percussion in this spacious room.

Afterward, I say to Tozen, "Nobody is here today. Maybe everybody has a cold?"

"No," he says, "some people came in earlier, and they left because they had to go to work."

How could I not even notice the comings and goings of other people in the room? Instead, I focused inward, my meditation on snot. At least I had a general awareness of Tozen, if only for the sound of his mutual suffering.

"And how are you feeling?" I ask. "It sounds like you are a bit sick, like me."

"I feel fine today. Sometimes I cough, but only because I am old. It is old-man sickness."

"Then I must have middle-aged-woman sickness."

"You are not yet middle-aged. And yes, we are all dying."

Saturday, September 4

My autumn cold has gotten worse, and I'm bedridden today. I try to read the books and articles Tozen has given me—but my mind cannot latch onto anything, the words just flying in and out of my brain in a Buddha-inspired fog. My mother brings me hot tea and sliced fruit, just as she did when I was ill as a child. "Anything else—soup? Hot cereal?" Both of us are easy and comfortable in the roles of caregiver and cared-for. Maybe we are our best selves in these moments.

Koun calls in the evening from the pay phone at the bottom of the mountain; he says a bad typhoon just came through Kyushu. "I was working in the kitchen when the door unhinged itself and it went sliding through. I just picked it up and put it back on. What could I do? Argue with the door? I had to finish with the cooking."

"A practical man—I always liked that about you."

"By the way, did I ever tell you that I tried to break up with you once?—Before we were even dating? You know, I thought I should stop messing around with women, with relationships, and focus on what really mattered, on becoming a monk in Japan. I wrote this five-page letter, threw it away, and then I called you up and invited you to Montana to meet my family the next day."

"I'm glad you called!"

"Yes, it worked out pretty well, didn't it?"

Sunday, September 5

I still feel ill but crave fresh air, so my mom and I venture out to walk the Coastal Trail that stretches for miles along the Cook Inlet. The fireweed has completely gone to seeded white tufts now, and there is that distinct earthy, sweet-and-rotten herbaceous scent of fall. Stepping off the trail, we sort through rocks and driftwood for the best still-life specimens, our pockets filling with relics. "Do you remember beachcombing in Nome when you were little?" Mom asks.

"Of course." Walking that barren strip of landscape had been my favorite thing to do during our five years in the Bush. You'd think it would've lost its allure after a while. But we always found something new—things from the ocean, things from people, sometimes a mix of both. Or a recasting of the two, like the beautiful "sea glass" that was, in a former life, beer bottles thrown into the breakers by drunks.

"Do you remember catching those little fish with your hands? I think the locals called them 'hooligan'—you filled your pockets with them when they came in on the tide one day. We took them home and cleaned them and ate them. There were so many."

"Oh yes, I remember, and that time we found all of those dead walruses with their tusks missing. Mutilated bodies everywhere—like a war zone. Terrible."

"I remember the smell. I remember you cried."

"I wonder if we'll go back someday?" And then, shaking my head as an answer to my own question: "I guess we probably never will. I mean, even if we did, it wouldn't be the same. Or maybe it would be too much the same."

Somewhere in my mother's things are slides and photographs of that distant life. 1978. A creased photo of me at age five bundled in a parka with a fur-rimmed hood, snowpants, boots, mittens. I am perched like a dark bird on a fault of aquamarine ice that juts, dagger-like, from a vast and blinding whiteness, laughing in awe because all around is the violence of the Bering Sea held fast in time—a clenched fist pulled above and behind the shoulder. It is my first winter in Alaska, the idiom of the South still thick on my tongue: *ya'll, UMbrella, YOUston.* My mother, outside the photo, holds the camera. My father, in Texas, begins to build a new life.

Tuesday, September 7

"I've been thinking about retiring," Tozen announces as the two of us sit down for breakfast after zazen. "Maybe I should meet your husband and his teacher sometime. Who knows? Maybe this would be a good job for him and then you could come home."

"Well, I'd like for him to meet you. As for moving here, I don't know about that. But—what will you do?"

"I'm thinking about moving to Costa Rica or maybe Thailand. Someplace not so expensive. I will miss Alaska, though. I like the cold."

"Do you miss Japan?"

"No. Too much formality. But I can enjoy being there sometimes. There are some comfortable things."

"We are both between homes, aren't we? I didn't think that I missed Alaska but now I can feel that some part of me has."

"Even the cold?"

"Yes, maybe even the cold."

"And how is your lonely year in Japan?"

"Honestly, all of this is not quite going how I wanted."

"How did you want it to go?"

"I had an idea—that this would be my monastic year, too,

in a way. That it would somehow be spiritual. I would stay in the present moment. I would pay attention. But honestly I just miss Koun all the time. And my mind is always floating off to the past. I feel like a walking paradox—who I was then and who I am now."

"Two sides of the same paper."

"Well, I just want the one side."

~

As I am walking out to my car, Tozen hands me a photocopy of a Ryokan poem, pointing to the lines:

I wondered and wondered when she would come.
And now we are together. What thoughts need I have?

"I think this is how you must feel now, and also how you will feel when your husband comes home—nothing special."

Wednesday, September 8

With only an hour to spare before we need to head to the airport, I realize that I've misread my travel itinerary. Unfortunately, the packing proves challenging. I thought that I had bought very little, but still nothing fits into my bags without a fight. There always seems to be this phenomenon of coming to the U.S. and thinking I need to buy, buy, buy in order to be comfortable in my home in Japan. But the reality is that I have new favorite products, new daily staples in my diet. Still, I see some old remembered brand and think, "This—I need this; I used to use this every day." The next thing I know, I have a year's worth of hand cream in my shopping cart.

Of course, the trend works both ways—I always bring too much from Japan. My mother looks doubtfully at my new comfort foods spread out on the kitchen counter: the multiple bags of green tea, instant miso soup, and assortments of seaweed. "Thanks for . . . all this. I'm not sure how to use it, but I'm sure I'll figure it out."

As we walk through the airport lobby, I tell my mother about Tozen's remark of yesterday, about the possibility of Koun taking over his work as the AZC resident priest.

"It's ridiculous and I don't think he really meant it anyway, but I do keep wondering, *Where to live? Where will we end up?*"

"Maybe you *should* move here."

"I'm fairly certain that's the one thing we should not do."

Thursday/Friday, September 9/10

Hurtling faster than usual into the future, I experience a delirium of travel. After the first long flight, in which I am held by white noise and buffered murmurings in Chinese, there is the endless layover in Taipei, and I spend most of this time asleep on a bench in a deserted wing of the airport. Then there are two more hours on the plane to Fukuoka, and then another two-hour bus ride to Musashigaoka, the stop nearest my home in Kikuyo.

When I finally arrive, no taxi is available at my insignificant little bus stop, so I set out dragging three bags down an unlit narrow road in the center of night, the sound of cicadas and frogs pulsing through the heavy humid air. Luckily, ten minutes or so later, a taxi pulls up alongside me, and I offer directions in Japanese—the words garbled and strange in my mouth. I am duly delivered to my townhouse. *My own personal monastery*, I think.

I drop my bags inside the door and, after checking for large insects in the bedroom, crash into sleep. Then I'm up again a few minutes later to attend to a nagging suspicion: yes, there is a message on the machine from Koun, welcoming me home. "Come to Shogoji Sunday, if you can—I can't wait to see you. Maybe bring some *kabocha* croquette for the monks."

As I am drifting off to sleep, it occurs to me that international travel is really moving from one vivid dream or memory into another.

Saturday, September 11

My first bout of jet lag wakes me much too early this morning, and the sun has yet to rise. But it is a reasonable hour in the U.S., so I call my mother. "Good—you made it okay." And then, "Oh," she sighs, "we're both 'singles' again." I know exactly what she means. I'd grown accustomed to steady company, too.

Just then the sun's first rays offer a sliver of brightness, and I lean toward the window to catch a glimpse of the neighborhood. It looks eerily wrong somehow, deconstructed. I tell my mother I have to go, that I'll call back later.

I didn't notice anything at all out of the ordinary when I arrived last night. But now, in the light of day, the full effect of the summer's latest typhoon is evident as I step outside and investigate. Trees have been uprooted. Chunks of roofs have been torn from houses. Gardens have been tied into living knots. Most of my neighbors' windows bear big taped X's stretching from corner-to-corner. Half of a heavy white lawn table lies face-down in my backyard. The entire side of my van and the townhome are plastered with green shredded bits of vegetation and dirt. Littered everywhere are broken relics, unidentifiable debris. Men, women, and children are emerging from their homes to clean up the carnage. Huge piles of refuse—no doubt their work from the day before—wait in orderly rows for the garbage trucks to arrive.

And indoors, too, there is evidence of an unusual atmosphere. The mold is pervasive. All of my shoes in the *genkan* are covered in a green fuzz. There is a dusting of black fibers beneath an errant hot pad on the kitchen table, behind pictures hung on the walls, within cabinet interiors. It's a wonder that I didn't die of an asthma attack in the night.

The cleaning—outdoors and in—takes most of the day, the work rooting me back into this place and time. As I am high on a ladder, struggling to free the windows from the organic paper mache that has sealed them shut, one of the women in my complex steps out her back door in plastic slippers. I climb down to greet her. Together we stand and marvel over the broken table in our shared lawn. The other table half is nowhere in sight.

"I don't remember seeing this before," I say. "Is it yours?"

"No."

"Where did it come from?"

She shrugs. "A gift from the sky?" We each grip an edge and carry this unlikely offering out to the huge piles of debris on the side of the road.

Sunday, September 12

I wake too early again, 5:30 a.m.—most likely a combination of ongoing jet lag and deep eagerness to see the love of my life—and so I take my time gathering the things I'll take to him: head oil prepared by Brinda, two boxes of hard *choco* cookies and twelve packages of *kabocha* croquette from the neighborhood grocery store, new men's underwear in regulation white from the U.S.

Koun has warned me in advance that there will be cameras and television crews at Shogoji today, and he's been slated for some sort of interview. "It's possible that we won't see much of each other." My heart sinks at this thought. I suppose I had imagined a more tender reunion.

When I arrive, I am received by a monk who seems to be giggling incessantly at my gift of *kabocha* croquette. "For lunch," I explain. But he continues to giggle as I step out of my shoes and place them neatly against the stones.

Koun emerges from the dining area. "Jisen-san would like you to help in the kitchen today," he says to me in Japanese as he collects the packages of food from the other monk.

In the kitchen he gives me a quick, forbidden hug. I can feel his ribs beneath his *samu-e*. "You've lost more weight! Are you okay?"

"I'm down to 145 pounds, but I feel pretty good. I'm eating healthy food all the time."

"You lost almost 50 pounds?"

"Yeah, Shogoji is Buddhist fat camp."

"Hey, what's so funny about these anyway?"

He looks at one of the packages I brought and smiles. "They're for the microwave."

"What? You guys didn't put in electricity while I was gone?"

It's a little cooler today, but the heavy cloud cover outside makes it twilight in the kitchen. I peel and slice vegetables, using a sense of touch more so than sight, while Koun and I talk quietly. Both of us are particularly unsure of what Tozen's retirement idea means. "Maybe he's just sort of . . . thinking out loud?" I surmise. "Either way, I don't think I want to move back there. Part of me loves it—craves it, even. But there are land-mines of story there for me, too."

"I know, T. And we'll figure all that stuff out when we get to it. You know, I like hearing about all of your adventures. It's one of the few good things about us being apart."

"I think your adventures are more glamorous—after all, I'm not making national television!"

In the afternoon, reporters from NHK, Japan's public broad-casting network, arrive with big cameras to begin filming—this will be a segment on the monastery and its inhabitants, within a longer spot about Kikuchi. As we shuffle into the *sodo* for zazen, I see that one of the reporters will be joining us. He selects a camera-conducive spot two seats down from me, and from the way he gets up on the platform, I can tell he's never sat before. Such a shame that he's being televised on his first attempt. Two minutes into sitting, and I hear his labored breathing and shift-ing legs. I know how he feels—I've been there before.

When the drum sounds, we all rise and move to the Dharma Hall for a ceremony—the monks bowing, chanting, and offering incense—while the camera crew and I bear wit-ness. Through it all, I am observing Koun in this new role, his seamless movement through what now must be becoming com-monplace to him. I don't know if he has changed in any dramatic way. But there is possibly a grace that I've never seen before. A new way of holding the body. As he moves among the other ten or twelve monks, I'm not sure that I would immediately distin-guish him from the others, except that he is a full head or more taller.

Later, during the break, I rest on the steps outside the kitchen watching from a distance as Koun is interviewed at length by the NHK reporter. They look, I think, so very far away.

Tuesday, September 14

It's pottery Tuesday, and it feels like ages since I've touched clay. As I slide open the glass door of my teacher's house, I am greeted by Sensei, Megumi-san, Yoko-san, and Baba-san, all unusually on time this evening. *"Ohisashiburi!"* they shout collectively. Sensei pours me a cup of tea and asks how my mother is, and when I say she is well, the other ladies proceed to ask about Alaska, the questions coming in rapid succession. When I take too much time to answer, Yoko-san translates.

I sigh. "It's not the questions that are difficult. I just can't seem to catch the right words for what I want to say tonight. . . ."

"Oh," says Sensei in Japanese, "so you forgot all of your Japanese while you were away! Tsk!"

We settle into making pots, and working at a steady and semi-confident rate, I manage four passable cups of nearly equal size. *"Jozu,"* says Sensei, as she leans into the table, inspecting my work.

"Yes," I say in fast English. "It was easier tonight for some reason. I mean, I just sat down and *made tea cups*. But shouldn't I feel more artistic? More inspired or something?"

"Wow, you really did forget Japanese!" replies Sensei.

The other ladies laugh while Yoko-san translates her version of my lament.

"They're just cups," says Sensei, looking at me quizzically.

Friday, September 17

A postcard in the mail today from Koun—I've been given permission by Jisen-san to stay at Shogoji over the long holiday weekend. This way, I'll get a chance to better experience what the monks experience; plus I'll be able to start making my *rakusu* for the upcoming lay ceremony.

During the lunch hour, I peruse one of the tiny cloth shops that I've spotted a thousand times in passing but never once visited. I'm searching for Koun's suggested first-time *rakusu* cloth: mid-weight dark blue or green cotton. An old woman, the proprietor of the shop, greets me and begins pulling out every kind of blue and green, some of it tucked beneath bolts of other fabrics. "What's it for?" she asks.

When I say "*rakusu*," I see that I need to explain: "*Bukkyo no mono desu.*" (It's a Buddhist thing.)

"*Aaaa . . .*" she says knowingly, as if my explanation was adequate.

Finally, with cloth in hand, I'm driving back to school when Koun calls from the Shogoji phone. He tells me that Jisen-san is now concerned about my visit because

(1) I will distract the monks,
(2) It will hurt Koun, and
(3) It will be too challenging for me.

So, I may only stay one night . . . or maybe not at all. She will decide after I arrive Saturday. "I guess this is a test-run," says Koun.

"What? Surely she recognizes that we're adults? We know what we've gotten ourselves into. We're not going to behave badly!"

"I know, I know. I'm not sure what's going on. Probably we don't get to know."

Saturday, September 18

I'm driving up the mountain to Shogoji after my morning Japanese class in the city, my mind grappling with the many challenges of a foreign grammar, when I must suddenly negotiate the one-car road and sheer cliff by backing down when a gray van approaches from above. I'm flustered by the time I actually reach the parking lot, but Koun's smiling face is the first I see as I lift my eyes to the top of the stairway and it brings a sigh of relief. "You're just in time for some weeding," he says, taking my bag and handing me a pair of gardening gloves. "Check in with Aigo-san over there—he'll tell you what to do." And then a little quieter: "Probably shouldn't work near each other because of—whatever it is."

Aigo-san instructs me to pull delicate green shoots from around big stones. "But NOT the moss—moss is very precious."

"Why is it precious?"

"It takes a very long time to grow."

How unfortunate to be fast-growing, I think. On the other end of the courtyard, across a sea of pebbles, a pair of monks kneel over their work. They wear their requisite uniforms—black work *samu-e* and thin white towels tied around their heads to halt sweat and sunburn.

A little while later, Jisen-san emerges from the main building and instructs me to attend to the wilting flowers throughout the temple. Feeling like a wilting flower myself, I am grateful to get out of the sun. However, Jisen-san's manner is especially stern and brusque today, and the seemingly very simple responsibility assigned makes me nervous: I am to collect the many vases in the monastery, discard the old flowers, arrange fresh flowers and greenery, and then return all of the newly filled vases to their *exact* original positions throughout the buildings. "You must take vases from one area at a time—so you remember," says Jisen-san.

"If the placement is important, why not take them one-by-one?"

"No—too slow."

After my first attempt, Jisen-san is not pleased. On one altar, I've placed two pairs of vases in opposite positions. She reverses the vases, then beckons me to stand a few paces in front of the altar. "Tracy-san, look. Do you see? He is a face. You can't move the parts. He will not be the same face. He will be a completely different man."

On the next attempt, I pause to really look at each altar and imagine the distinct features on its surface. The eyes, the nose, the mouth. When I put the vessels back, I am confident of the placement. Jisen-san finds me again while I am gathering more greenery outside. "Tracy-san, come." I trail after her, this tiny and fierce bald woman in cheerful purple-pink *samu-e*, as we retrace my work. "Not like this—like this," she says, moving each vase just slightly to the left or right. "You must remember the face exactly. It is important."

I sigh as she walks away. Is it possible that, in my careless-ness, I have altered the character of a monastery?

After informal dinner in the evening, I sit in my room, waiting. I haven't seen much of Koun all day—not that that is too surprising, given Jisen-san's expressed concern. I scribble in my notebook. Consider the kanji I'm supposed to be learning. Watch as a black spider the size of my hand slips through a crack in the fusuma. The wife of Koun's teacher once told me not to worry about spiders in the house—"They look scary but really they are lucky; they kill bad things." But still . . . I jump at a knock at the door. It is Koun, standing outside with a towel over his arm. "I heated the bath," he says. "Ladies go first tonight."

As we walk along the open corridor in the twilight, mist moves over the mountains. "I can't believe how beautiful it is here—like being in a painting or a dream or a scene from the past. It's another world."

"It *is* another world. I'm happy you're able to visit, even if it's brief."

"How long can I stay? Did she tell you?"

"One night. No more."

"Okay."

"I'm sorry."

"I know."

"Lock the door to the bath. There'll be trouble if one of the monks walks in on you."

"Okay."

After the bath, I return to my room to wait for the final zazen bell of the evening. It's raining outside now, a soft patter against the roof. Some of the monks are engaged in *shodo* prac-tice, and as I step out of my room into the open-air walkway, I see them far across the courtyard, beyond the wide-open doors of the generator-lit informal eating area, leaning over ink and paper. All else is pure, disorienting blackness. Frogs and insects sing from the darkness.

"T." I startle at Koun's whisper behind me. I turn and see nothing. There is just the gentle tug and the brief, wordless kiss. "Okay," he says, stepping back so that I wonder if this small transgression was only in my mind. The bell rings. I flick on my flashlight, and we make our cautious way to the *sodo* to join the others for evening zazen.

Sunday, September 19

2:55 a.m. I rise just before the patter of a monk's feet running the length of the hallway outside, a high-pitched bell rattling in his hands. And the low, heartbeat-like *taiko* drum felt before it is heard. Last night, I was in and out of sleep as heavy rain fell. There was also the sound—and sting—of mosquitoes taking cover in my room. Where was that lucky spider when I needed him?

I dress quickly in the thin beam of a flashlight, step outside to wash my face, and then proceed to my cushion to sit. There is a lot of rustling-cloth movement behind me—I keep raising my hands in *gassho* because I think maybe it is Jisen-san doing morning greeting, but of course I can't turn around to check. At the completion of the session, we move together to the Dharma Hall. Koun is the *doan* for the ceremony. I know by the sound of his voice—loud, full, clear. He sits somewhere in the shadows, hitting the wooden block in time with the chanting. The *Heart Sutra*. The lineage. Layers of sound filling a room. The black-robed monks all in semi-darkness, the few lamps failing to illuminate much of anything, and then morning light begins to trickle in. At last, the ceremony ends in a flourish of *taiko* drumming. I feel that we all have just now woken up.

During breakfast, I recall Koun's reminder that I'm expected to finish everything that I take, and to eat very quickly. Unfortunately, I put too many *ume* in my bowl because I can't identify much in the poor lighting of this room. I swiftly swallow my salty-sour meal of rice and pickled plums and am then led to my first chore for *samu*, the work periods that fill out a monk's day. My task is to clean the wood floor of a long hallway. Koun provides me with a white towel and shows me how it is done. "You get the cloth a little damp like this. Fold it, place it on the floor, put both hands on it, stick your butt in the air, and run." He scoots a few feet down the wood floor to demonstrate. "The trick

is to balance your weight between your hands and your feet—
too much pressure either way and you'll lose your balance." And
then he's off to attend to his own chores, leaving me to contemplate the hallway that seems to be getting longer and longer as I
stutter-slide along it.

When the bell rings the cleaning period ends, and I see the
first few arrivals for the sewing group—the *fukudenkai*—walking up toward the main building. Among them is Otani-sensei,
a priest and our soon-to-be sewing teacher. I remember her well
from the international ango last year. She was not ordained
under the Soto sect, and her teacher has forbidden her from
attending Soto events. Still, she comes to Shogoji on the sly to
teach people how to sew the traditional Buddha robes—*rakusu*
and *okesa*.

Under Otani-sensei's guidance, we slide open closet doors
and produce long, low tables, *zabuton*, *zafu*, and well-stocked
plastic sewing boxes. Together, we quickly turn one of the monastery's back rooms into a suitable space for the work ahead of
us.

Suddenly Sakamoto-san, the sometimes-attendee of the
Tatsuda zazenkai and one of the lay regulars of Shogoji, arrives,
sweaty and defeated-looking. Otani-sensei chides him for his
lateness. "I biked here," he explained. "I didn't realize how far
away it is."

"You biked—from Kumamoto City?" she asks. "Famiri-boi,
are you crazy?"

"Did she call him . . . Family-boy?" I whisper at Koun across
a table we are adjusting.

"He works at Family Bank," he explains with a smile.

After a brief pre-sewing ceremony, Otani-sensei and Koun
move around the room, helping everyone measure out the pieces
of cloth to cut and sew for the mini Buddha robes.

Koun shows me the length of cloth he's been sewing as an
example. Each stitch is perfectly spaced. "You have to angle the
needle just so. The stitches are said to resemble bits of rice."

"Wow—that seems very . . . precise."

"As Jisen-san says, this practice will make you straighten
pictures on walls."

"It makes you have OCD?"

He laughs. "Well I don't know, but it does make you pay attention."

Before I leave for the day, Sakamoto-san brings his pack to my room. I give him my bug spray, spare flashlight, Kayumi Baibai (Itch-Be-Gone), and extra purified water. I also warn him about the fierce mosquitoes.

"What do you do?"

Smack! I kill one on my arm in reply.

"We're in a temple!—You can't do that!"

"Oh—right. Sorry about that."

Sakamoto-san laughs, but I notice too that he just gently waves the annoying insects away instead of harming them. I am, as always, a terrible Buddhist.

Monday, September 20

It's a holiday today, and the neighbors have been arguing all morning—the volume of their voices, if not clarity in meaning, is carried through the paper-thin walls of the townhouse and through open windows. I, meanwhile, am standing at my kitchen table, working a knot of stubborn clay. Outside, a bright line of laundry flutters beneath a darkening sky. When the rain comes, the shouting pauses, and I expect a frantic Jennifer or her husband to come tumbling out in plastic house slippers to gather the bright flags of cloth. But there is only a rising drumroll as water falls and falls and falls to earth.

This evening, we all forgo zazen at Tatsuda Center. Only Stephen and I can meet—Richard is too busy—and it is beginning to seem excessive to make a trip out for only two people. Instead, I sit in the evening by myself at home and then watch the moon light up the trees. Around 11 p.m. Satomi calls: "I'm so sorry, but . . . can you pick me up at the bus stop? I got off work late and my mother can't collect me."

"I'll be right there!" My voice is just a little too loud. I wonder if she noticed the eagerness? Such a lonely day. And the neighbors' wet laundry still shifting along a line in the darkness.

Tuesday, September 21

Sensei canceled pottery this week for a family trip. I feel restless after work. I want my routines.

There's a call from Tatsuda Center—the woman very angry and incoherent, and I'm having a terrible time understanding why. All I understand is "you didn't come" and "money."

"Okay, okay, I can come now and pay you the 500 yen." This, apparently is the wrong answer, as she gets angrier and more incoherent.

I call Richard and he sorts it out for me: "It seems that the watchman stayed at the Center the other night just for us—when none of us went."

"But there are always other groups in the building when we're sitting. And don't they have open hours during that time?"

"Yes, well maybe nobody was there this one time, or there is some other reason. . . . We don't get to know."

"I'm never going to win, am I?"

"No. There is no winning here."

Wednesday, September 22

During after-school seminar, one of the girls in the Art program, my homeroom student, gives me a beautiful *shodo* gift—my name written out in elegant *katakana* on rice paper. "Don't tell my teacher or I'll be in trouble."

"It's beautiful—why will you be in trouble?"

"I'm still a student. I'm only allowed to practice."

Perfect for me, I think as I tack this unsigned art to my office wall—a gift from one student to another.

Thursday, September 23

Today is another holiday, and Satomi and I are driving into the city on a mission to locate *okesa*-worthy dark blue cloth for Koun. My previous sewing lesson has given me a better idea of what is needed for the project. The difficulty is that the cloth must be of a natural fiber, not too heavy or thin, nothing too flashy. Ideally, it should have a broken weave. I explain the desired aesthetic to Satomi: "Back in the day, monks made *okesa* using only found cloth—rags from the garbage, or the cloth from corpses. They'd dye it all one color and then sew it together."

"So we're trying to find something that looks like it's been roughed up a bit? Or . . . died in?"

"Yes, that's the idea."

Satomi proceeds to explain in detail my peculiar request to a clerk at one of the better cloth stores downtown. A few moments later, the clerk produces a possibility: a super-soft broken-weave linen in indigo.

"Hmm. Satomi, what do you think?"

"I don't know if a corpse would wear it, but maybe it will work for Koun's purposes."

Satomi and I part ways, and I drive solo out to Kikuchi. Brilliant red spider lilies, the *higanbana*—known to old Japanese women as the "flowers of death," according to Satomi—trace along the edges of green rice fields.

The monks are attending to their daily chores when I arrive, so I only get to see Koun for a moment (he loves the cloth!) before I am led to the back "sewing room" where Kenpu-san, Jisen-san's son, is working diligently on an *okesa*.

"Does this mean you are planning to be ordained?" I ask him.

He shrugs. "I'm not planning on it, but I'm here. Maybe it is simply the thing that will happen."

Saturday, September 25

"You're always rushing off to somewhere after class. I think you must have a secret life." This from Chris, one of my American classmates from the YMCA. "You sure you don't want to come to lunch with us?"

I decline but promise to explain "my secret life" some other time. And then I am out the door, hurrying along the sidewalks to the parking garage, and then in my car speeding down the highway to Kikuchi. I have been given permission to stay a night at Shogoji again.

Arriving just in time for *samu*, I sweep leaves and debris from the stone stairs and take boxes of it all down to feed the bonfire, which sends clouds of smoke tumbling down the mountain.

Koun is the *doan* in the rotation today, and so I help Aigo-san in the kitchen when it is time. Like me, he also became a vegetarian at age sixteen, so he has no problem with vegetarian cooking. "But," he explains, "it is a little difficult here because there is such a strong link between food and emotion, and this can create a problem when Japanese and foreign monks must dine together. Strong tastes, too much spice, mixing foods and colors incorrectly for the Japanese palate. . . . Sometimes there are very big problems when we get it wrong. Sometimes there are fights."

"But I thought the goal was to transcend such mundane worries."

"People get upset—it's human nature. If it's not something trivial in the outside world, then it's something trivial here."

After lunch, most everyone has gathered in the sewing room and Koun and I go to work on his *okesa*—he'll need it for a ceremony at Zuioji soon. As we cut, iron, and sew, Koun tells me about a man from Oita who visited him yesterday morning. "He'd recently lost his mother, whom he had never liked very much, and then he saw me on TV. He said he immediately got into his car and drove here from Oita, just to see me. We talked for thirty minutes or so, he gave the temple some boxes of *yuzu* from his grove as an offering, and then he left."

"What did you tell him?"

"What could I say? His mother is already gone. But we did talk about practice and compassion, what he can do in this moment to relieve the suffering of others."

"Does everyone have a complicated relationship with their mother?"

"Probably."

As the day shifts to evening, I think of the famous writer Junichiro Tanizaki and his assertion that all the splendor of a Japanese temple is best revealed in shadow. How right he was. As I step through the *gaido* doorway for zazen, I stop and watch as Koun chooses and then plumps up one of the larger *zafu* for me. A mosquito coil has already been lit next to my spot—the smoke rising in a thin, protective cloud. *So this is true love*, I think. I shuffle in oversized slippers to my cushion. Koun and I bow to each other before settling in. Three deep breaths. The rustle of robes behind me as others enter and take their places. The flicker of oil lamps. Outside, the living music of the night.

At nine, the *taiko* signals, and I'm off to bed. Slipping into my futon in the guest room, I switch off the flashlight. Brilliant light from the nearly full moon streams through the window as I drift off to sleep. My secret life.

Sunday, September 26

Zazen is weirdly intense in the monastery this morning— perhaps due to such a short sleep cycle. Bright flashes of my mother and I in Nome, standing beneath the northern lights on some distant winter night. Of wandering alone through the brush in Hatcher Pass in summer and finding that unexpected purple flower—monkshood—against endless green. All the colors of my youth.

Just as I settle in again for the second half of zazen, a fat cockroach bumps against my bare foot. Do I stay still and let the thing crawl up my leg? Or break the rules and brush it away? I opt for the latter, but it returns again and again. When the *taiko* starts up near the end of the session, I breathe a sigh of relief.

As I return to my room, I touch the switch on my flashlight, feel a wet smushy thing against my thumb and drop everything. The lamplight reveals a small, stunned frog on the floor. I pick up the flashlight and discover more frogs clinging to my bedroom door and all along the walkway.

"In the mountain, you live with the creatures of the mountain." I startle at the voice behind me. Aigo-san. He bows, moves beyond me, the light of his headlamp quickly swallowed by darkness.

~

Koun and I sit together in the open back of our van. The door is popped up and our legs swing against tall grass. I'll need to head out soon.

"I've been thinking about when we'll actually leave Japan," says Koun. "We have these special skills now. We're very good at being foreigners in Japan. But these skills don't necessarily translate well in America. And my time here in the monastery is like that, too. I can't expect that my skill set will transfer, even if I do become an expert at all of this. I can't hold on to that one expectation."

"Yes, I feel that, and also how other habits and ways of being are always slipping away. For both of us."

It becomes dark as we talk, and Koun realizes that he hasn't switched on the generator. I turn the car around, aim the headlights at the stone steps to the monastery, and off he goes into the night. That last image of him turning and waving at the top of the steps. This, among the string of moments that makes up a life. I can't let go of what I don't want; I want to hold on to what I can't keep.

Tuesday, September 28

In pottery class there is much speculation about the nature of the "Alaskan tea"—a commercial brand from the supermarket—that I brought for Sensei as *omiyage.* "Perhaps it has cinnamon because of the weather or because of recurring sore throats or . . ." The cups of tea are sniffed, then tasted, between each comment. I am enjoying listening to the speculation so much that I don't bother to explain that it's a common tea blend, and it is not Alaskan in origin.

When we get down to work, the cone I form from new clay is not at all well-centered, so the walls of my first cup are uneven. I decide to keep it anyway because it still looks fairly pleasing. Sensei gives me the evil eye. *"Renshu!"* (Practice!)

"*Hai, Sensei.*" The verdict is clear, so I cut the form off the hump, discard it in the scrap bucket, and keep going. When the exact same thing happens again, she allows me to fold the rim over and back into the cone so that I'll still have plenty of clay with which to practice. I precisely repeat my mistake again and again. Clearly, my sense of balance is off today. Giving up early, I go outside to clean my things, and Sensei follows.

"The radio says a typhoon is coming again."

I look doubtfully at the sky. "Really? It looks calm."

"Help me protect things so they won't blow away."

"*Hai, Sensei.*"

Thursday, September 30

After yesterday's typhoon, cold last night and this morning too. I move through yoga poses in that delicious air before settling into zazen with a blanket wrapped around my shoulders. Flipping through the goldenrod pages of the sutra book that Koun has lent me, I find the *Heart Sutra*. The sound of my voice and the thin stream of incense smoke is pulled in a slow curl out the window and to the neighborhood beyond.

Kan ji zai bo satsu
Gyo jin han-nya ha ra mit-ta ji
Sho ken go on kai ku
Do is-sai ku yaku
Sha ri shi
Shiki fu i ku
Ku fu i shiki . . .

When I finish, I sit in the center of my doubt. I am no monk. I know that I am trying this on. I know that I am pretending. What happens when we dedicate our lives to pretending to do or be something? When does the unreal become real—the dream a reality? And does any of it matter?

OCTOBER
Monastics

Friday, October 1

On my way to work, an overwhelming cloud of scent thickens around me as I draw close to campus. It is, like memory, unrelenting. Pausing along the path, I do a slow turn in search of the cause of that powerful perfume and, when I find nothing out of the ordinary, look up into blue sky. *There*. Koun and I in Hawaii on the day of our wedding, the fragrance of exotic flowers ebbing and flowing through the open-air temple. We stand in formal posture, our hands held in endless *gassho*. His teacher chanting in long, soothing riffs. The few attendees growing drowsy in their uncomfortable metal chairs. Me thinking, *Is this America or Japan? America or Japan?* And also:

What is real?
What is real?
What is real?
What is real?
What is real?
What is real?

"*Kinmokusei*," says a voice behind me. I startle and turn to find one of my students investigating a neatly manicured shrub covered with clumps of tiny yellow flowers. "Gold olive flower—it has autumn smell. My mother says is stinky. But I like. Do you like?"

"I like it, but I think I might be just a little bit allergic."

"*Arerugi?* But still like?"

"Yes, I seem to love many things that I'm allergic to—cats, dogs, flowers, certain trees. It's a big problem for me."

"Oh, very big problem! Paradox?" This, a word we recently encountered in English class.

"Ironic. Mother Nature played a joke on me."

Her head tilts in that Japanese expression of surprised contemplation. "You LIKE things that are bad for you?"

That, I think, is the most common paradox of all.

Sunday, October 3

While driving to Shogoji early this morning to assist with what I have only been told is "an emergency sewing project," I am greeted by rice fields turning to yellow. Last week's brilliant red spider lilies have almost all withered away—the "flowers of death" are dying. The sky is half-cloudy, the air cool and breezy. Fall, it would seem, has arrived.

Rolling down the car windows, I savor the slight chill before taking on the final treacherous climb up the mountainside. When I reach the top, I park and sit with the view of a valley. *What an unexpected life*, I think.

As I step out of the car and gather my things, I see Koun descending the stone stairs in his blue *samu-e*. "What took you so long?" he asks when I meet up with him on the last step. "Meditating?"

"Something like that."

"You've come to the right place."

"So I hear." We stop at the top of the stairs and smile openly at each other. The face of a loved one—one of many transmissions beyond words. And then we continue onto the stone path, slipping out of our shoes at the temple's entrance before it strikes me that we have yet to see or hear another soul. "It's quiet today. Where is everybody?"

"Most of them have gone to visit with the Catholic monks. Those of us who need to sew were left behind. Jisen-san is here, too, but that's about it, until the *fukudenkai* and Otani-sensei arrive."

"So for the moment we have the place to ourselves."

"Yes—well, almost."

"What's the emergency anyway?"

"A transmission ceremony. The date has been moved up. We have to finish sewing the new *okesa*."

"Right. Monk problems."

"Yes. It's interesting what becomes important when all else falls away. Getting the rice cooked just right or the bath heated on time can feel like a life-or-death situation. It feels that weighty."

"Maybe being able to see you, here, on weekends has become that for me. Such a small thing, but also a really big deal."

"I know, T. It's the same for me—a huge comfort. We're very lucky that it worked out this way."

Together we shuffle along in our slippers to what I now think of as "the sewing room." One monk, Aigo-san, is present. He is pulling a needle and thread through muddy-gold *mokuran*, the color only a priest who has been given transmission may wear. He greets me warmly—"Ah, Tracy-san. Welcome!"—and then turns back to his work. I imagine he is taking refuge in his mind, in the proper way of sacred sewing, as he forms each stitch:

Namu kie butsu (I take refuge in Buddha)
Namu kie ho (I take refuge in dharma)
Namu kie so (I take refuge in sangha)

Koun and I settle into assembly-line work on the *okesa*—him ironing, measuring, and cutting, while I push thread through cloth. Both of us share a permanent smile, a silent communication between us. At some point I become aware that the members of the *fukudenkai* have filled the room, talking in hushed tones with occasional spurts of muted laughter.

"It seems there is a bubble around us today, or around whatever it is that we're doing."

"Yes. This is a new kind of intimacy, isn't it?"

Tuesday, October 5

It is early evening, and I am in the back yard, lost in thought as I labor over a big plastic bucket of clay scrap and slurry, pounding at it all rhythmically with a found chunk of wood. There are splinters in my hands; both arms and shoulders ache. I know I'll pay for this violence to the body later, when the rush of determination (or whatever it is) wears off.

I am thinking about Koun, about hypothetical conversations. *Something I have never told you—maybe because it points to some wickedness in me or some belief in magic—is that I touched the groove of your back once in passing, the palm of hand against cloth and the smooth muscle beneath, and there was an electricity there, a little shock that startled me. An awakening or some spark of desire. The touch was not intentional—something to do with moving chairs and desks around in a closet of a classroom and I lost my balance. That was early in our program at the university. I was married to another man then. I didn't look you in the eye for a week. I'm sure you had no idea why.*

KA-CHUNK. A screen door yanked open on a rough track. Jennifer emerges from her home, gathering one of her cats to her as she approaches. The smell of cooking wafts after her, something tomato-y and Italian. "Still working on that clay?" She asks, looking doubtfully at my bucket.

"Yes. I'm pretty sure it's hopeless but I have to try."

"How many months now until Koun comes home?"

"Five."

"That many."

"That's right—not until March. Possibly later."

"Do you have any plans for travel at least? Something to fill up the time during the winter holiday?"

"No, I think I just want to be right here for a while and just see what I can learn or experience or—I don't know exactly."

"What have you learned so far?"

"Well, clearly I'm a terrible potter."

"I don't know about that," she says. "But you might want to rethink that bucket."

Bending down, I see for the first time that the blue plastic has begun to crack—a wild set of hairline tributaries from top to bottom.

"That might be sexual frustration," I explain, laughing.

"A vacation, Tracy. Think about it."

~

In pottery class, all of my energy is focused on trimming the only two surviving cups from the last session. Sensei barks orders the whole while, urging me to do every step in proper form. While she is helping another student, I stop the wheel, try to etch away at a stubborn bump that just won't give.

"Don't cheat!" Sensei appears at my side, slapping at my hand. "You must trim it as the wheel turns."

"Wow. Sensei has eyes on the back of her head," I mutter in English. To my dismay, Yoko-san interprets my words into Japanese, and the ladies all begin to giggle.

"Hai!" replies Sensei. "Eyes all over!"

Wednesday, October 6

Between classes, I encounter a small group of my first-year students moving en masse along the hallway. When they spot me, there is a collective scream of delight, which is followed by joyous shouting: "Tracy-sensei! On TV! Husband too! Famous, famous!"

It seems the local NHK program about Kikuchi and the Shogoji monks is being rebroadcast over and over throughout the country. This, in and of itself, is a bit surprising. What is more surprising is that somehow my students were able to spot me at all—from what I recall, there is just a brief periphery clip of my profile in the introductory credits. I am sitting zazen beyond the pained posture of the show's host as he tries to lean and shift out of his agony.

Koun is the primary focal point throughout the video— much of the program features him working on the temple grounds or talking about his experience of monastic life in Japan, a thin line of text below him "translating" his already good Japanese. So that, in the end, it is clear that the real star of the show is his and others' foreignness set in such a traditional place. It is a much-enjoyed juxtaposition in a nation that takes great pride in its impenetrability.

What was it that Koun said in one of his letters? *No matter that most Japanese do not know the slightest thing about the workings of a traditional Zen monastery, let alone having ever stepped inside of one— they will claim an inherent knowledge of it as birthright. On some level they are correct. But not entirely.*

In pottery this evening, after much discussion about Koun's rise to TV fame, there is disgusted talk of yet another typhoon— Japan is now on number 22. It may become a record year for the violent windstorms. "Such a nuisance," says one of the ladies. "I'm always repairing my roof."

"Tracy-san, do you have *taifu* in Alaska?" asks Makiko-san in her cautious English.

"No, I have only experienced them in Japan. I remember there was a typhoon the first night that I moved to Kumamoto City. I thought it must be a very windy place! My apartment was on the third floor. There were terrible sounds all night long, and I was scared because I lived alone and also I did not yet have a phone, so I couldn't call anyone. In the morning I found a thick plastic door on my balcony—something from a greenhouse, maybe."

"Oh yes. That year—was it 1999? I remember. An outhouse appeared in my grandparents' garden. Nobody in our neighborhood knew where it had come from."

"Typhoon. Such a nuisance!" Sensei repeats as she scoots her stool in close and examines the cup I've just formed. "Looks okay," she says. "Let's try making a vase now."

"What?" Surely I did not hear correctly. Or I've misunderstood her Japanese.

"Let's make a vase."

"So—not . . . not cups?" I ask, pointing to the creation still attached to the wheel in front of me. This cup had formed beneath my hands as if of its own accord, my fingers the conduit for its simple, pure expression. I had already imagined sipping perfectly brewed tea out of this perfectly formed cup, a perfect thread of steam curling up from within.

Sensei doesn't answer. Instead, she puts a palm-sized flat

wooden *kote,* a shaping tool, in my hands, leans down, and pushes my foot down hard on the wheel pedal. The clay form whips around crazily. "Let's make a vase," she says again. And when I don't do whatever it is she expects me to do, she nudges me aside in her usual way and takes my seat. The *kote* (now in her hands) disappears into my beautiful cup, stretching it wide. Then she sets the tool down and begins to pull the clay up and in—a hollow ball. Finally, she lifts the slender opening into a short neck, flaring out the top lip with her fingertips. "Okay, your turn," she says, rising from my seat. "Begin with a cup." And so I do—one perfect cup after another is destroyed by my belabored attempts to turn them into vases.

In the last minutes of class, I lean back from my work to behold one particularly lopsided Dr. Seussian creation as it spins sadly on the wheel.

"What are you doing?" scolds Sensei.

"Waiting for Typhoon 22 to come and blow it away."

Thursday, October 7

After the day's classes, I am slow to leave work and so when I arrive home the shift to twilight has already begun. Still, I know I need to get out and walk tonight—a necessary purifying of the mind. Fifteen or twenty minutes into my journey, an ordinary and known landscape becomes alien as light drains away. I walk slower and slower, unsure of my path through a barely lit old neighborhood. Time, like my gait, lags and I grow accustomed to pixelated gray vision. I begin to see that the dark is populated. A slender figure drifts cautiously by on a creaky old bike, full plastic bags swinging slowly from each handlebar. A cat or some other creature races past my feet. Tiny bats—what else could they be at this hour?—tumble through the air.

After a while, I realize that I am completely lost in a place I have been exploring every evening for two years. At the moment I recognize exactly where I am, a swirl of black cloth emerges from an iron gate to my right and then I sense-see a priest with his back to me as he shuts the door behind him.

Having just emerged from light, he must be seeing even less than I do. I know I'll startle him when he turns. And when he does—both of us jump. I bow and *gassho*, and he—a second or two after—mirrors the gesture before moving beyond my range of vision, black robes disappearing into black night.

Which one of us, I wonder, was bowing to a ghost?

Saturday, October 9

I am staring out the window on the bus this morning, watching passively as both time and place slip by, when the bus slows for the light and I spot the inexplicable: maybe eighty high school kids in uniform poised over bicycles in the empty parking lot of a closed *manga* shop. They are all near-motionless and neatly spaced and pointed in the same direction—the effect is a kind of living sculpture of youth in repetition. As the bus starts to pull away, I scan the passengers around me, but none appears to have noticed the unusual scene. They are looking down politely, or they are sleeping. Sometimes I feel that no one sees anything here. Or, in contrast, they see everything that I do not see.

When I return home in the afternoon, there is a message from Koun on my answering machine: Jisen-san would like me to drive him and Aigo-san to the ferry terminal, as both are being transferred to Shikoku after the ordination ceremony tomorrow. My heart rises and then sinks.

Sunday, October 10

As I prepare for going to Shogoji, I have a nagging sense that I've forgotten something important. *Ah well*, I think as I toss my things into the car, *I'm sure it will come to me.* And it does—just as I'm pulling out of my parking spot, I see that the gas gauge is hovering near empty and, unfortunately, nothing beyond the ubiquitous convenience stores are open at this hour on a Sunday.

I repark the car, consider my options—take the risk, or wait a couple of hours for the gas stations to open. For Koun and I, today is our last chance to see each other in who knows how long. I think of him, up at dawn, certain that I'll be there soon to greet him. I think of myself, sitting alone in my kitchen, sipping tea and waiting for time to pass. *It's mostly downhill into the valley*, I tell myself as a kind of pep talk. *It's coasting, really.*

As I drive, my eyes flick from road to gauge and back again. I begin to imagine scenarios of being stranded in some lonely spot, a naive American girl with lousy local language skills. I start to work out stories—some of extreme inconvenience, others terrifying. I wonder if everyone has such a violent mind?

Finally, I enter the temple grounds on what, I can only imagine, are fumes. My heart thumps like I've just run the race of a lifetime. I'm breathless as I step out of the car.

"What's the matter?" asks Koun as I bow into the temple doorway.

"Is it that obvious?"

"You've got wild eyes."

"This is stupid, but I've spent the whole drive being terrified that I'd run out of gas. I started cycling through all these possibilities in my mind. Now everything's okay, and I can't shake the feeling. I'm a wreck."

"I'm sorry—I know that's a bad feeling, but I do think that tank is endless." He leads me to the dim, shadow-filled kitchen, and points to a ceramic bowl filled with just-cooked sesame. "Here—grind this. That should take your mind off it." The bowl is warm in my hands, the pestle awkward.

"It's a slow circular motion. Crush the shells against the ridges in the bowl to release the flavor."

Working the pestle over the sesame, I clutch at a lost metaphor. "Isn't there some kind of Japanese proverb about this? Something about relationships?"

"Yes—there's a process involved. It takes hard work and attention."

"That's lovely. Probably a lot of truth there, too." I contemplate the grains of crushed sesame, now fine and delicate as sand, and the smell rising earthy and delicious from the bowl.

Aigo-san slips in the door behind us, collecting things for

tea. "Ah, you are 'grinding *goma*'? I believe this phrase means 'brown-noser' or 'ass-kisser' in English, yes?" He exits as Koun and I stifle our laughter.

"So much for beautiful Japanese proverbs," says Koun.

"Oh no, it's great—two versions of the same thing. I think I must now dedicate my life to grinding *goma*."

"You would make a good monk."

After our collective meal, I join the *fukudenkai* while the monks leave us to prepare for today's ordination ceremony. Everyone seems giddier than usual. Sakamoto-san is in particularly good form, offering a running deadpan commentary on our various failings as vestment makers. "Ah, Otani-sensei. Tracy's holding the needle different from me . . . am I doing it wrong?" And this is always followed by a firm and detailed correction by Otani-sensei. Sakamoto-san circles around the room, getting everyone in trouble in this way. I sense that Otani-sensei is completely charmed by whatever it is Sakamoto-san is doing, even though her demeanor is serious, unsmiling.

Shortly after sewing in the afternoon, the members of the *fukudenkai* gather in neat rows on either side of the big altar while monks flow like sunlit specters in their long dark robes, preparing for the ceremony. Jisen-san sits in a raised seat near the base of the altar, a tiny and severe feminine Buddha. When she begins to chant, the sound is as lovely as it is eerie. Kenpu-san enters in his white under-kimono and kneels over a bowl of clear water while two monks run razors over his scalp, saving one small clump of hair up top for Jisen-san to scrape away in one final symbolic motion. The monks then dress him in the black robes of a priest and he bows to formally receive the *okesa* he's been so dutifully sewing in the back room. With this knotted over his robes, the transition is complete: Kenpu-san becomes "Senpo-san," and he is now officially a Soto Zen monk.

In the hallway afterward I catch him examining his new haircut in the glass reflection of some framed photos, his hands moving over bare scalp as the photographed participants of years past look on. Without the hair, he is all cheekbones and eyes. *Deerlike*, I think.

"How does it feel?"

"The same—but different."

"It must be a little awkward to have your mother as your teacher."

"Yes. My therapist is going to kill me."

~

Koun, Aigo-san, and I begin our drive to Kokura in Kita-kyushu to make the 10 p.m. ferry. It is the same ferry I delivered Koun to last March, when he left. From there, the two of them will journey on together to Zuioji, the main temple in Shikoku. Now is my big chance to be "alone" with Koun, "but with a chaperone," as Aigo-san cheerfully points out.

As I drive, Aigo-san and Koun talk animatedly about the day-to-day politics of temple life. I understand very little, but am happy to be immersed in their company. I am transported, for these brief hours, to the many road trips taken with Koun and Bryan—usually between Seattle and Montana, to visit their parents. Two brothers revisiting a family landscape that only they can understand.

In Kokura, in the remaining time before the ferry will leave port, we search for a restaurant. As we walk the streets, I am flanked on either side by the two foreign monks. "I'm beginning to feel very important," I say. "It must look as though you two are my bodyguards!" Indeed, passersby are staring more at me than at the monks.

At last we spot a trusty favorite Indian food chain restaurant, Nanaak. We order several spicy curries, garlic naan the size of elephant ears, thick mango lassi. "These flavors must be outside of temple regulations," I chide.

"In Japan, a thing that is not seen is a thing that did not happen," says Aigo-san.

When the food arrives, they devour it at the speed to which they've grown accustomed. Two monks who've become thin as bamboo poles. I lean back into the booth and sip my lassi as the food disappears.

"The Hindu traditionally said mantra when preparing meals," says Aigo-san, now sated. "It is made with God's love." Before we rise to leave, the turbaned chef comes out and bows to us and thanks us in Indian-accented Japanese, a kind of punctuation to Aigo-san's comment.

At last, I must say farewell to Koun at the ferry parking lot in the dark and the rain. Aigo-san stands some paces away, allowing us this space. "I feel that I'm always saying good-bye to you."

"I know, T. I'm sorry."

As I am driving home, I wonder if what Jisen-san said a little while ago was right. Seeing each other is too hard. Maybe today was a lesson for us.

Tuesday, October 12

It is a drowsy busy and not-busy day—finals are scheduled for the entire school, and I am slated to co-proctor additional exams for professors with particularly large classes. Overall, there seems to be a collective sense of discomfort. Between sessions, both teachers and students complain of testing fatigue and many are sick with minor respiratory ailments, perhaps due to the recent dramatic change in weather. After a couple periods, my eyes grow lazy and inevitably settle on one student, who then feels my gaze, looks up, and we both startle and look away. It is after one of these moments, while assisting with the final class of the day, that I look up above students' heads to a faint line of English printed on the wall clock there: *The stream of silent silky time makes you feel graceful.* The text is set beneath the image of a fluffy bunny in a field of pink-and-green flowers. A surreal and unexpected cuteness. And then, as if in response to this observation, the grandmotherly professor for whom I am proctoring begins pacing around the room, patting each young woman on the head affectionately—each pat a slow tick on the clock.

In the evening, there is a lot of sympathy from the pottery ladies about Koun having to go up to Shikoku. "It's harder when he's farther away, isn't it."

Wednesday, October 13

In pottery class, I sit down before my lump of fresh clay, take three deep breaths, and decide to get it right. An hour and a half later, Sensei scolds me as the walls of my lovely and delicate vase fold inward, collapsing. *"Abunai!* Too much water! Too slow! You need to work carefully AND quickly!"

I cut away the failed form, and Sensei stands over me as I begin the second, barking out orders for each stage: "Not so tall to start! Push down! Pull to the side to form the bottom! Pull the sides up! Thinner! No—thinner! Use the *kote* to make a round shape! Now, make a waist! Make a lip!" After ten minutes of this, I complete a passable little vase. I also feel as if I've finished a race.

"Good," she says. "Do it like that every time."

Thursday, October 14

It's actually cold this morning—I can feel it in my bones, and it's more difficult than usual to leave the warmth that has gathered in my nest of bedding during sleep. I ascend cold stairs, enter a cold kitchen, flick on the portable heater. There is the whoosh of the pilot light and the smell of kerosene. Already, I can feel the grumble in my belly, the approach of what the Japanese call "the winter appetite." I know my breakfast of miso soup and rice will taste unusually rich and delicious.

Before leaving for work, I rummage through closets to find thick winter blankets and then hang them on the laundry pole outside to freshen in the air and sun. The day will grow considerably warmer, but I'll appreciate the extra weight of this bedding in the cooling nights ahead. There will be no extra body in this room this winter, no human furnace flaming beside me. I think of the bare feet and hands and heads of the monks at the monastery—that required exposure. I think of how they sleep at night, nothing more than a single futon folded over them.

I must remember to send Koun more underlayers soon.

Saturday, October 16

When I meet Mimaki-san and Tsuda-san at the Budokan for karate practice, we spend the entire session trying to re-create a complex *kata* that we all had begun to learn just before Koun left for the monastery.

"We watched the DVD of Chinen-sensei, Koun's teacher, over and over. But it's just too fast," Mimaki says. "I can't catch the last bit—even when I watch it in slow-motion. Maybe like this?" He begins the *kata*, hesitating before moving his body into each new stance.

"It's close—but something's not right," I note. "I remember seeing the full version so many times, but I didn't learn it myself. Hmmm. Maybe it's more like this?" I demonstrate my version, failing miserably.

We simply do not have the right feel, that body-memory. We haven't earned it yet. If we were better students, we would practice what we already know instead of moving ahead of ourselves, thirsting for exciting newness.

Sunday, October 17

I am late this morning to the sewing group at Shogoji, somehow getting it in my head that I need to arrive at 9 a.m. and not 8:30. Unfortunately, this seemingly insignificant error means that I must do the sewing sutra by myself, and not follow (mumble) along with the *fukudenkai* members as I usually do. While others begin their work around me, I kneel before the small altar with sutra book in hand and begin stumbling over syllables.

Sakamoto-san walks up to me and considers my reverent posture. "Tracy-san, what are you doing?"

"Um, the sewing sutra."

"You sound terrible."

"Thanks."

"You're welcome."

"You Japanese really need to learn about American sarcasm."

"What?"

"Never mind. I was being culturally insensitive."

I expect a joke from him in return (surely he is always joking?), but instead he sits down next to me and begins to chant in a loud, clear voice. I follow along, mumbling in my usual way, and am grateful for his help. We return to the main room together, my face red with shame, no doubt. I feel as if I've just copied someone's homework.

I settle into my sewing, then, but immediately see that something is not quite right. Otani-sensei confirms that I've mismeasured many sections of my *rakusu*, sewing each piece neatly together a precise quarter inch out of alignment. "You'll have to start over. There's no other way," she says. And so I spend my afternoon pulling out the threads before re-measuring and beginning again. When it's time to pack up for lunch, I'm more behind than when I started some days ago.

"Don't worry," she says. "Come to my house next weekend, with Famiri-boi. I will help you both."

During the noon meal, there are many unknown faces at the table—new monks from Zuioji. They fill the seats left behind by Koun and Aigo-san as if it has always been this way.

As we walk to the sewing room afterward, the big temple bell begins to ring outside. The monks, usually so careful in their movements, startle around us, looking to each other in confusion. A peek through the window reveals a couple and two young boys playing with the big bell in the courtyard.

Sakamoto-san steps next to me and explains, "In a temple, all of the bells have a special meaning."

"What do these bells mean?"

"Tourists are here."

Tuesday, October 19

The rain is a low rumble on the roof of the pottery studio as I struggle again and again to right the little upended vase that refuses to stay fixed in the mouth of the slice of PVC spinning on the wheel before me. How am I supposed to trim this awkward thing? For a second or two, I think I've got it all under control, and then it rolls around like a ball bearing in that socket of plastic, despite the thumbprints of scaffolding I've applied where plastic meets pot. Each time this happens, I stop the wheel, right the vase, and recheck it with the level. I can feel Sensei's constant disapproving eye on me as I do this, which probably—absolutely—contributes to my incompetence. She lets out a little sigh. "Spin the wheel and carve a dent for your finger in the center of the base—like this." Her rough, powerful hand over mine as she pushes the sharp tool into clay. *Puppet and master*, I think. "Now," she says, "put your finger there and push very hard but not too hard." I do as I'm told, and it's better—there is, finally, something like a centered stability.

A few minutes later, though, my hand cramps, and I have to stop. Shaking out the pain, I watch Sensei at work on her own project—a huge serving platter. I'm beginning to appreciate the truly uncanny sense of balance she has, her understanding of what will hold and what will not. Perfection is a given; she makes everything look effortless. Sometimes I think true genius rests in the body and not the mind, or perhaps somewhere in-between—when there is no longer a translation from one to the other.

Returning home after class, I find that Tozen has written me a brief email, from Alaska. *It has been a long time. Do you remember our conversation? I think I will retire soon. I am ready. Maybe you will come home and your husband will be the new resident priest. It is time for a change.*

Friday, October 22

Alone in my quiet townhouse, I spend the evening drinking tea and sewing in the tatami room upstairs, a warm sense of gratitude or accomplishment rising in my belly. Just after midnight, I've almost finished the *rakusu*'s main quilted section, the part that takes the most time and skill and concentration. When I spread the last few pieces on the floor in front of me, I have to rub my eyes. How can it be? The last bit of cloth is cut too short. Way too short. And this piece comes from the last of a bolt of fabric from the shop down the street. There is no spare from the same dye lot. The only person who has the exact same shade of indigo is a single monk, my husband, now sequestered on a different island.

The postal system here is good, but not that good.

Saturday, October 23

After Japanese class, I attempt to locate Otani-sensei's house near downtown Kumamoto City, a hand-sketched map held open in front of my nose. Despite the artistry of the priest's drawing—or because of it—I am deeply and desperately lost in a labyrinth of narrow, tributary-like roadways and jigsaw residences. Bicycles, K-cars, vending machines, sheltered Jizo statues, and bits of cultivated foliage seem to cling to every spare nook and cranny. I round a bend and nearly run into Sakamoto-san, who is standing in the middle of the street staring at a small two-story complex.

"Oh, Tracy-san," he says nonchalantly in English, as if expecting me to be there. "I think this is Otani-sensei's house. On the second floor."

"You think? Didn't you say that you visited her before?"

"Yes. Many times."

"So is this her place or not?"

"I think it is her house."

We climb the stairs and Sakamoto-san opens the door, steps inside, and announces himself, a Kumamoto custom that always feels like an invasion and leaves me a little disconcerted. I tentatively follow him in as soon as I hear and then see Otani-sensei emerge from another room. We put on slippers, and she beckons us to settle around the low table in the small main room. In one corner stands a full clothing rack and a dressmaker's dummy on which a partially completed suit hangs, absent an arm and a lapel.

"I am a seamstress in my spare time," she explains.

"It's lovely," I say, inspecting her careful work—the invisible stitches and precise creases—before settling into my cushion at the table.

I begin to take out my things from my backpack and try to explain the problem with the cloth.

"Let me see," she says, then makes that familiar air-through-teeth sucking noise that can only mean one thing: I'm screwed.

"It'll be okay," Otani-sensei assures me in slow, measured Japanese. "I'll be back shortly. Help Famiri-boi with his sewing. Famiri-boi, you make coffee."

"Yes! I am coffee *tenzo*."

Otani-sensei tucks a bit of my cloth into her purse and then, in a swirl of gathered items and self-chatter, she is out the door.

"Okay," I say, "so I guess we'll start on your *rakusu*."

"We have not yet chanted."

"What?"

"We must chant before we begin."

"We're not in a temple—surely we don't need to? And besides, we don't have the sutra."

"In my mind," he says, tapping his head.

"Oh good."

"I am happy you are happy."

"I am not happy."

"I do not understand you."

"Remind me to teach you the finer points of American sarcasm."

"In here," he says, ignoring me. I follow him down the short hallway and enter a room in which Otani-sensei's priest's vestments hang from another clothing rack. Against the main wall of the room, an altar has been carefully assembled. A framed photo of a cat sits prominently next to the Buddha statue.

"These are the bones," says Sakamoto-san, pointing to a small ceramic urn.

"She must have been very close to her cat."

"Yes." A solitary, then. Like Sakamoto-san. Like me.

We burn incense, chant, and bow to the bones of a much-loved pet.

A short while later, Otani-sensei returns, a bag of new indigo cloth in her hands.

"You must begin again—there is no other option."

"Argh." I throw my hands over my face. Sakamoto-san, finding this amusing, begins to laugh and cannot stop.

"Don't worry. It gets much faster and easier each time you do it," says Otani-sensei.

"Maybe she should do mine, too," offers Sakamoto-san. "For practice."

"Make coffee," replies Otani-sensei.

"Yeah, Famiri-boi," I say. "Make coffee."

My lungs have begun to burn by early afternoon—I suspect the ghost of a black-and-white cat. I explain and Otani-sensei opens the glass doors in the big room, and I sit on the balcony in the warm afternoon sun, listening to bits and pieces of the conversation drifting in. Lots of scolding from Otani-sensei. Lots of (jokey? not jokey?) questions from Sakamoto-san. *Mother and son*, I think. Otani-sensei, softening into this other role, has perhaps taken on Famiri-boi as another of her projects.

As I stand and stretch, from the nonstop conversation in Japanese emerges a single, clear sentence in English from Otani-sensei: "This is a chrysanthemum." A burst of laughter from both of them when I lean in through the open door.

Sunday, October 24

At 7:30 a.m. I meet Sakamoto-san in front of Fujisaki Hachimangu, Kumamoto's most famous Shinto shrine. After locking his bike in my van, we walk over to the nearby Rinzai temple to sit. It had been Sakamoto-san who got the idea to visit this temple; neither of us is sure what to expect. He is, as usual, cavalier and unafraid. I am, as usual in such situations, a ball of nervous energy. As we enter, the temple wife greets Sakamoto-san and then looks doubtfully at me. "The foreigner will need to remove her socks," she says. And then for emphasis: "It is very rude to wear socks in a temple." I look down. How could I have forgotten this detail?

"I'm so, so sorry," I say in Japanese as I remove the offending items and tuck them into my shoes.

"Does the foreigner speak any Japanese?" she asks Sakamoto-san.

"I speak a little, though I'm not good," I answer in Japanese.

"The service will be in Japanese only. We do not offer English for foreigners."

Sakamoto-san, stepping toward a wall to consider a calligraphy, says nothing.

"Follow me," she says firmly and leads us into the main hall to join twenty or so others. I wonder which of us puts her off more—the awkward foreigner or the unapologetic (and somewhat un-Japanese) manner of Sakamoto-san.

After we are duly seated on cushions, the woman hands us booklets for the ceremony. "Can the foreigner read this?"

"Her? Read Japanese? *Saaa*... how should I know?"

"It's fine," I say, giving my odd friend a sideways look. I don't know if I should hug him or bop him in the arm.

The room grows quiet as the priest enters, a kind-faced middle-aged man wearing rough indigo robes. (Koun, no doubt, would love the cloth.) The service starts with a flourish of ceremony and then an explanation of zazen basics, which is followed by a short bit of sitting, and then a lecture on the energetic merits of Tai-chi. "We will now do Tai-chi," concludes the priest. Wait—have I heard correctly? I look over at Sakamoto-san who, phased by nothing, simply stands and awaits instruction. We begin following the ancient Chinese postures—Sakamoto-san with an unexpected grace and agility, and me, clumsily, as is befitting my bumbling "outsider" role.

We settle into zazen again and this time the priest makes slow laps with the *kyosaku*. As he approaches, nearly everyone holds their hands in *gassho* and leans forward to request the stick; our blissful meditation is punctuated by bursts of rhythmic violence—bamboo striking flesh again and again. *Thwack ... thwack ... thwack ... thwack.* I can't help but smile as I think of women beating futon in the morning sun. If I let him hit me, would a lifetime of dust fly out of my body? Would I be purified?

Afterward, there is *matcha* and delicate sweets, a lecture on "the three vehicles" which I cannot follow at all, as well as a much longer discussion that I do not wish to—something about how Christian foreigners are interested in visiting temples nowadays and how nice it is that they have an interest in Japanese culture (a kind of apology or explanation—or both—for my presence to the others).

After we put on our shoes and walk back to my van, I ask Sakamoto-san what he thought of our Rinzai Zen experience.

He shrugs. "It was the same—but different."

"Indeed it was. I wondered if he would give us a koan or something, but I guess that's another venue. By the way—thank you for . . . standing up for me, or whatever that was you were doing earlier."

"What? I do not know what you are talking about."

"My friend, you are a true enigma."

"What is 'enigma'?"

"A person of a contradictory nature."

"Then I am not the enigma."

"Touché."

"What is touché?"

"Never mind."

Monday, October 25

"I think we should postpone our sitting group at Tatsuda," says Richard over the phone this afternoon. "Clearly the schedule is no longer working for people."

"Okay," I say with a sinking heart. "*Shoganai.*" (It can't be helped.)

Always the encouraging optimist, he offers, "We'll get it started again. Maybe when Koun returns. But now is just not the time."

After I hang up, I climb the stairs and enter the little spare room that has served as my sitting area for the past several months. Sunlight glints off the small Thai Buddha in the window seat.

Closing the curtains against fading light, an idea comes to me. I begin to move around the house—opening and closing closets and drawers to find whatever is necessary. There are a couple wooden boxes, some lengths of cloth, a few workable pieces from my pottery efforts, the items from our zazenkai. With these, I fashion a new and improved altar. I add a sprig of greenery collected from the backyard to one of my tea cups and fill another with fresh dried rice and insert a stick of incense. Thanks to my various monastic cleaning assignments and Jisen-san's fierce insistence on precise placement of every item in the monastery, I have a pretty good idea of what goes where.

When all is assembled, I light incense and a candle, pull out my *zafu*, settle in, and ring the bell as a gentle rain begins to fall against the roof. *This is exactly what I need,* I think. And my mind, for once, is still as lake water. . . .

Suddenly, a yowl and then a crash against the window causes me to leap up from my seat in terror. What could this be? I edge toward the window to pull back the curtain and reveal Jennifer's cat clinging to the second-story window screen, meowing pitifully to be let in. I blow out the candle and oblige.

Tuesday, October 26

It's another rainy day today—there's that patter against my umbrella as I am walking home from school, but the usual percussion has been altered by absence: no frogs, no insects. The season has shifted again, slowing into the coming winter. I see this settling in my students and in myself as well.

In pottery, there is lots of talk about going to Aso to view the cosmos, that final, elegant flower of autumn. My experience of this backdrop of conversation, as a non-native speaker of Japanese deep in concentration in my own work, is that the women are talking about "cosmos" in the larger sense—and this transforms the meaning of each utterance: "Go to Aso. You will find the cosmos." Ah, who knew? The mystery of the universe revealed in that great volcanic caldera, my first home in Japan and Koun's second.

During the last bit of class, Yuko-san shows up, youthful and glowing and very, very pregnant. Her sunny nature defies the season, and the women gather around to stroke her belly and ask questions. It strikes me that her new form is not unlike the roundness of the pots that have been shaped by those same hands this evening.

Somehow it grows later than usual and as we are packing up, Yoko-san asks, "Tracy-san, when will you have children?" It's not the first time this has come up. It's a common topic, especially with my advanced age, thirty-going-on-thirty-one.

"I'm not sure. . . ." I offer vaguely. What can I say? I never know how to answer this question.

"That is difficult without her husband," laughs Baba-san.

"When he returns," Sensei says. "Then there will be a baby."

When I get home, it is well after 10 p.m. Light is in the windows when I arrive and, as suspected, I find Satomi sitting at my table drinking tea and grading papers.

"I had to stay late again at work," she explains. At this hour, the bus only goes as far as my neighborhood.

"I'm glad you're here." I put the water on for more tea and sit at the table.

"A bad day for you, too?"

"Not exactly. Satomi, do people ask you about having children?"

"Yes—often. Sometimes it is about getting married. Either way, it is very annoying."

"I find it painful. I don't know if I want children, or if I should have them, even. My own childhood was so complicated. I guess the possibility of failing in some way is terrifying to me."

"I think everybody's childhood was complicated. But the possibility of being trapped is my worry—a wife and a mother with no possibility of anything else ever again. That is a Japanese problem."

Thursday, October 28

It is cold again this morning—not only outside but also in my office, where I sit with one of Koun's big, thick sweaters pulled over my suit jacket, my fingers slow and stiff as they move over the keys at the computer. At intervals, I stand and pace the length of the room in order to pull feeling back into numb limbs. An Alaskan in Japan. Sometimes I wonder how many varieties of cold have I experienced in my life.

The official day for turning on the university's heating system has not yet arrived, and no matter how often I argue the poor logic of this common local practice (which extends even to preschools!), the Powers That Be refuse to alter that official date. In Japan, comfort is never the point. The ritual of schedule is everything.

It is the same in the monastery, or so Koun has told me. *What do we do today? I don't know. Let's look in the ledger.* A hundred years ago, on a warm sunny day, the temple gutters were precariously cleaned by a half-dozen monks in black *samu-e*. A hundred years later and to the day, a half-dozen monks in black *samu-e* clean gutters as the rain falls hard around them, so that their skeletal bodies are revealed by the irrelevance of wet cloth—wood ladder and ceramic shingle slick under foot and hand. This is *gaman*—follow the rules and do what must be done, no matter what.

Is Alaskan "show no weakness" the same as Japanese *gaman?* Sometimes I think there is a connection—and also no connection. In Alaska, you are not allowed to show your misery. In Japan, it is essential.

Friday, October 29

Today, as per my students' request, we hold a Halloween Party during class. Ironically, the same students who will sport all manner of bizarre dress-up paraphernalia for festivals and even everyday wear seem shy about the concept of costumes in a Western context. In fact, despite our lengthy discussions about the fun possibilities, not one student brought a costume, whereas I, misreading that previous enthusiasm, am wearing a full-on Japanese Tare Panda suit, complete with thick padding. Many, many photos of me are taken. It is a well-documented humiliation. After class, I pass by one of my coworkers, who gives me an odd sideways look. "American culture," I explain. He simply nods in response. *Crazy gaijin.* By this time, though, I've decided the suit is brilliant—it delights my students and it keeps me toasty warm. What more can I ask for?

After work, I trade my bulky panda suit for more traditional wear, and I'm off to Otani-sensei's house to continue *rakusu* sewing—there is much to finish before the precepts ceremony this coming weekend.

When I arrive, she welcomes me in, and then disappears into the kitchen, from which a delicious smell wafts. I see that she's neatly set out our things and the windows are opened to release the ghost of her cat. "We can turn on the *kotatsu,* if you like," she calls from the kitchen. "I know it's too early in the season, but . . ." Otani-sensei, it would seem, truly *is* a rule-breaker!

As I sew, we both sip tea and chat about the various coming pleasures of winter: *mikan* oranges and *kotatsu,* the *onsen.*

"How about in Alaska?"

"There are other pleasures," I say. "The snow is very peaceful. I miss skiing the trails alone. I miss the feeling of a winter day."

"Sounds cold. And lonely."

"Yes. But still, I miss it."

~

Sakamoto-san arrives an hour or so later, bursting through the front door in his usual abrupt manner. He is dressed in his Family Bank uniform and brightly striped toe socks, his hair a shock of black fuzz—presumably styled by the swift removal of the bike helmet tucked under his arm.

"So what did you talk about before I got here?" he asks in Japanese as he takes his place at the table.

"Lots of things."

"Really? You could understand each other?"

"We can communicate just fine," says Otani-sensei.

"Um—I do understand some Japanese, Famiri-boi," I say in English.

"Oh yeah? Good. Let's only speak Japanese. I'm tired."

"*Hai,*" I reply.

"Oh! I will bring beer. Just a moment," says Otani-sensei.

"Yes, that would improve my Japanese considerably. But I am driving today so I can't drink."

"That's okay," says Sakamoto-san. "Your Japanese will sound better to us, even if it is not better."

"Great."

For dinner we eat homemade *oden*—a simmered selection of vegetables, egg, tofu, and processed fish flavored with dabs of spicy yellow mustard. Otani-sensei lifts a bit of food with her chopsticks and asks what *gobo* is in English.

"Burdock," I reply.

"What??" says Sakamoto-san, "Bulldog?? *Honto??*"

When I explain the pronunciation, he doesn't believe that native English speakers can really tell the difference between the two words. I assure him that both my translation and pronunciation are accurate.

"How about this? Can you understand it?" He switches on the small TV, to a news report, and tells me to interpret, and so I do. I don't know exactly what I'm getting wrong, but whatever it is, it is very, very funny. More beer and food appear, disappear.

"Tracy-san, your Japanese is now VERY good!" Laughs Sakamoto-san, as Otani-sensei, lint roller in hand, begins to "roll up" the hairs along his arm.

After our extended meal, I offer to walk Sakamoto-san to a taxi.

"*Daijobu,*" Otani-sensei says, and then in English, "He is Japanese woman—*samurai!*"

"Ehhhh?!!" responds Sakamoto-san, "I am *woman??*"

"*Ah—gomen!*" giggles Otani-sensei. "Always mixing up those words . . ."

Both pause to take in their breath—one, two, three—and then another volley of laughter.

Saturday, October 30

There's Japanese class in the morning, but a terrible pain in my lungs prevents me from getting up in time to meet the bus. Most likely I've had one too many visits with the ghost of Otani-sensei's cat.

When I at last rise and open the windows, I find a beautiful clear day with a warm breeze—the final taste of a fading season. There is that initial urgency to do something different—something exciting and out of the ordinary, something to make use of this precious time—but there is just sewing and reading and walking and studying and working clay in solitude. And when I'm in it, really in it—nothing is lacking.

I write Tozen and tell him about this new understanding. *I am such a solitary. Sometimes I think I should become a monk, or that I am a monk already. Maybe I should shave my head.*

Sunday, October 31

It is late morning at Shogoji. Sakamoto-san and I stretch our legs after three hours of intense sewing among the other members of the group. We slip out of the room, pace along the hallway, and then peek in the open doorway of the *sodo*, now empty of meditators. "What is this?" asks Sakamoto-san, gesturing toward the side of the room.

"What is what?"

"This. Where we sit." He sweeps his hand out again. "I do not know the word for this thing."

"Are you joking?"

"I am not joking."

"*Tan.*"

"Oh. *Tan.*" He says this with reverence, a holiness against the tongue, and then moves off down the hallway.

How my competencies in this country are uneven—those bright spots of unexpected knowledge surfacing like vivid memories from a vast darkness, the unknown, the constant murky pool in which I live my life as a foreigner in Japan.

Later, when I return home, there is a new email from Tozen. His comment is short, cryptic. *I will visit you in Japan sometime,* he writes. He also says my head would not look so bad shaved.

NOVEMBER
Practice

Monday, November 1

All day, I seem to be wading through a tide of nonspecific memory, almost a nostalgia—I don't know what brought this on. It's a heavy, painful feeling, a burden that I can't quite let go. One minute I am chatting with one of my eager, sweet students in the hallway—something having to do with the many moods of English verbs—and the next I'm looking out the window in my office, seeing a landscape that has nothing to do with the expanse of manicured lawn and trees and sky before me. I am in Alaska. There are flashes of my mother, and of my father, and of my stepfathers, and of all those boys and men who entered and left my life. There are quips of poisonous dialogue. Fred saying, *I married your mother, not you. I don't have to love YOU.* And then a boyfriend who took too much, who took everything, and later told me, *You are beautiful when you don't smile.* And then a man— once a boy I knew in high school—who said I probably deserved what I got. And then a jealous first husband who had a thing for other women and who lied to me so often that I did not know what was true and what was not. I see now the great connectedness of all of these things. How they repeat and repeat and repeat in a spiral that deepens with each turn. At the center could have been the absence of a father. Or something in my fragile nature. Or it could have been a handful of lessons with a piano teacher in Nome, when I was five or six—that first devastating loss of innocence turning what should have been natural in later years—a touch, the intimacy of a kiss—into a kind of grotesque. Sometimes I think it is not people who haunt us, but only moments of encounter.

After work, I pass through the gates of my university, still riding that terrible flood. I remember Koun slipping a strand of *juzu* prayer beads over my wrist outside the little Balinese import shop on Shimotori. The faint corkscrew grain on each bead and the scent of sandalwood. He told me the story of koi who do not know that they are really wise and powerful dragons, how the bright fish become their true selves as they pass through the river gate. That was my second year in Japan. And now . . . how long have I worn that famous Zen story? A protective talisman knotted at the wrist and heart.

Tuesday, November 2

In pottery class, I quickly produce two vases that are undeniably pleasing to the eye. Sensei, rising from the stool across from me, leans over the table and squints at my work, considering it from various angles. *"Kihon,"* she says finally. "You are still not doing the basics properly. You should go back to tea cups for a while."

"Hai, Sensei." I sigh. So this is the feeling of pure failure.

I clean my things early and then sit and watch as Baba-san manipulates a tall and impressive form gone wrong. She playfully—but with great concentration and seriousness—works the clay for a good thirty minutes. Various lovely objects reveal themselves before being folded back into nonbeing. At last, she settles on a shape—a tall, tapered vessel. I imagine it holding a few well-trimmed lengths of the season's much-celebrated pampas grass. She slices her creation from the hump in one quick motion and maneuvers it to the table.

Sensei would never let me work with just one object for so long, the walls inevitably giving way beneath my fingers, an excess of water, and all those poorly reintegrated faults. When I look over at her, this question forming in my eyes, she says simply, "Baba-san can do that because she knows what she's doing."

Friday, November 5

When I return home from work, there is a letter from my ex-student Yamada-san. *It has been a long time since I wrote to you last. I am so tired, so busy.* Much of his letter recalls the day-to-day happenings of his business. The usual complaints. As always, there is a pragmatic sense to his writing—I can see that he is practicing his English, and I think I've already read a lot of what he's written here in previous letters. How we always return again and again to our same familiar motifs.

But the second half of the letter, written some days later perhaps, is a little brighter . . . and different. He's been feeding stray cats twice a day out behind his workplace. *I've been doing this for a while. What would they do without me? More all the time. Such a nuisance. Feeding them will make me broke.* I can imagine his exasperated sighs, but I know that he's happy to be depended upon. A big sunburned man with rough hands stooping to pour chow into a bowl. The bodhisattva of skittish, shred-eared alley cats.

Saturday, November 6

A gift for Docho-roshi. A gift . . . a gift . . . I search all—ALL— of the stores in downtown Kumamoto after Japanese class this morning, looking for something to offer to the head priest of Zuioji who will be at Shogoji tomorrow for the lay ceremony. He is no doubt spending his day writing dharma names in elegant black strokes on the white silk backings of the *rakusu* we lay-people have spent so many weeks preparing. As for a gift, nothing seems quite right. *Bring something nice, but not too nice,* Koun had told me in a letter. *It should just be a token of your gratitude. All of the standard local gift-giving rules apply.* So knives and clocks are out, I guess, as both allude to death. Green tea may or may not be okay—but it's definitely boring. Handmade items are not really acceptable, unless I am a master at my craft (I am not). The value should be appropriate to the occasion and to the status of both parties (I am in no way culturally suited to evaluate this). And then I remember something Koun mentioned during my last visit, a little anecdote about Docho-roshi's assistant once sneaking off from the Shogoji kitchen with a *second* plate full of homemade chocolate chip cookies that I'd sent the monks. Docho-roshi has a sweet tooth and a certain appreciation for my Western-style baking.

As I'm folding chocolate chips into buttery batter, Sakamoto-san calls. There is some confusion about when all of us are supposed to arrive at the monastery for the ceremony tomorrow, and—in typical fashion—no one can get through to the Shogoji phone. "I assumed 9 a.m.," I say. "Isn't that what we were told? Did I miss something? Was that code for some earlier or later time?"

"I don't know. You're the monk's wife. Don't you know exactly?"

"Be there at 9. Then we can be too late or too early together."

"I will go at 8:30."

"Fine. 8:30 it is. Oh—what did you get Docho-roshi?"

"What are you talking about?"

"The gift?"

"There is no need for a gift. *Jaa . . . shitsureishimasu.*"

I hang up the phone with a sigh and return to my necessary or unnecessary project.

Sunday, November 7

I arrive at Shogoji just before 8:30 a.m. A great number of cars have completely filled the main parking lot, and I have to squeeze into a non-space near the entrance to the grounds. It is a good thing I have a small vehicle. Ahead of me, an older couple dressed in crisp black business-style suits slowly work their way up the long stairway, and I regret my choice of simple zazen clothing—dark blue cotton *samu-e.* It hadn't occurred to me that I would be expected to wear something other than what I usually wear at the temple. This, of course, is "common sense" in Japan. Formal events require Western business suits. I should have known.

A monk greets me as soon as I reach the upper grounds,

bowing deeply and gracefully in his long black robes and *okesa*.
It is certainly a different atmosphere at the monastery today. I
trail after the monk to the entrance to sign in, where he takes
my gift of cookies—then leads me past a seated group of temple
supporters to an altar in the back room where the others, the
fukudenkai members, have gathered. Clearly they have all been
waiting for me to join them in the initial chanting and bowing.

Sakamoto-san, wearing a neatly-pressed black suit, is among
those present. "You wore the wrong clothes," he says.

"Um, yeah. Thanks for noticing. I thought we had decided
on 8:30."

"Yes," he replies, with no further explanation.

Collectively, we are led into the Dharma Hall to practice
the ceremony. It would be poor form, I suppose, to get it wrong
in front of Docho-roshi. Sakamoto-san sits on his knees next to
me, and then each of us takes turns practicing walking up to the
altar seat to bow and then receive the *rakusu*. "I'm nervous," he
says as we return to our spots. "Maybe I will trip. Or—maybe
you will trip."

"Or maybe I will trip you," I offer.

At last, the guests are ushered in, and the actual ceremony
begins. We chant, promise to abide by the layperson's rules, bow
repeatedly, and nobody trips as each of us moves forward to officially accept our *rakusu*. Docho-roshi, looking ancient and regal
in his maroon robes, swirls each quilted cloth over a bowl of
smoking incense, blessing it, before delivering it into our hands.
The ceremony is over in a matter of minutes. Such formality and
fanfare to frame this brief moment.

Afterward, we gather to have lunch, picnic style, beneath
the color-changing leaves on the Shogoji grounds. The weather
is unusually warm and sunny—a lucky last good-bye, perhaps,
to a season. As we eat and drink, each of us passes around our
rakusu, and the Buddhist names we've been given are discussed
at great length. My new lay name, in particular, gives everyone
pause. "What does it mean?" I ask, again and again.

The answers are vague: "Well, it's very profound. . . ." and
"It's a little difficult to explain, but it's a very good name. . . ."
and the common and wise-sounding, "Ahhh . . ."

I find Sakamoto-san and ask him to explain. "I don't know what it means," he says. "You should ask someone."

Monday, November 8

While walking the university hallway during one of my breaks, I discover a huge praying mantis tucked into a corner, legs bound in a mess of dust and fibers. I put down my stack of paper and books, and squat on hands and knees for a better look. Its heart-shaped head moves side to side as I peer at it—like a quizzical dog. It's among the largest insects I have ever seen.

"Tracy-sensei, what are you doing?" Yukari appears next to me, and then drops to her knees when she sees the insect. "So BIG!"

"Yes . . . and I think it has a problem."

"Oh!" she says, and then, "Just a moment please!" She leaps up, runs down the hallway to the ESS room, and then returns a few minutes later with two sets of convenience-store chopsticks.

"For take away the dirt," she explains, handing me a set. Careful as surgeons, we pluck bits of fluff from the insect with the chopsticks.

"Tracy-sensei, what is the name in English?"

"It's a 'praying mantis.' It is similar to *obosan* with hands held together in *gassho*."

"It is '*kamakiri*' in Japanese—cutting the grass with big knife, like a farmer."

"Sensei—"

"Yes?"

"Can I take a paper?" She points to the notebook paper stacked on the floor next to me.

"Of course. Why?"

"For little *obosan*."

Yukari, my kind and fearless student, scoops up our farmer/ monk friend with a sheet of paper and releases him into the grass outside. True compassion is no hesitation.

Wednesday, November 10

After pottery this evening, I cannot sleep. Instead of preparing for bed, I brew a pot of tea and sit curled up on tatami in front of the television, watching a videotape made by Senpo-san—Jisen-san's son and now disciple. He shot the film using the little video camera I lent him some months ago. A box—with the camera and video inside—arrived from him this afternoon, with a simple note: *Thank you, Tracy-san. I hope you enjoy. If it's not too much trouble, can you make a copy for me?*

So far, the tape is a collection of moments at Shogoji, all gathered during Senpo-san's many months at the monastery. The observing eye rests a long time on each scene, just taking it in:

> a breeze working its way through tall rice fields
> monks laughing at tea time
> *takuhatsu* through some unknown town
> chanting rising out of the darkness—an invisible night
>   ceremony
> a sunlit pond
> an impossibly miniature frog balanced on the tip of a
>   large leaf
> monks meditating in flickering lamplight
> Koun sewing alone in a room

I watch almost the entire tape—nearly three hours of footage—when the scene cuts to what must be one of the Latin dance studios in downtown Kumamoto. Loud salsa music echoes from the speakers as Japanese and Latino men and women writhe to the beat. A conga line forms, and the camera shakes as it is passed to another cameraman. Senpo-san appears then—for the first time in the video. He grins and waves from the tail of the conga line. Thick hair still on his head, civilian clothes—a snapshot of a previous life.

Saturday, November 13

This morning I meet the karate boys, Mimaki-san and Tsuda-san, at the Budokan. The room is cold, and, like my body, my *karate-gi* feels stiff and inflexible. Only movement and sweat soften it.

As usual, we begin our practice without much small talk. Tsuda-san leads us in warm-up stretches, and then we work through the *kata* together, pausing after each set to critique each other's form. Several times we find ourselves puzzling over the "correct" way to do something, our flawed memories leading us astray.

"That does not look right," says Mimaki-san.

"But the other way does not *feel* right," I reply.

"Practicing without a teacher is too difficult. Maybe we are learning many mistakes."

"Bah, it's okay," says Tsuda-san, swiping away our conversation with his hand. "Our bad form will give Koun-sensei something to do when he returns!"

Tuesday, November 16

No work today—it's a national holiday. Still, I take no pleasure in this thought as I dig through the closet in my bedroom with a chill in my bones that won't go away. On go the long underwear, the layers of shirts and sweaters, the thick socks. The ancient air-con heater in my bedroom wheezing out barely enough warm air to dress by. Downstairs is an icebox, and I've run out of propane for the portable heaters there. Breakfast, then, is taken upstairs, directly beneath that frail but endless outbreath.

A short while later, I collect Satomi in my K-van.

"So cold today!" she says.

"How do those school girls manage in their short skirts all winter long?"

"*Haramaki*," explains Satomi. "It is a secret warm cloth that wraps around your middle. And also heating adhesive patches.

These can be hidden beneath clothes as well." This, she tells me, is a throwback to the days when monks carried hot stones beneath their robes as personal heaters.

"I imagine the new ways are considerably safer."

"Yes," says Satomi, tapping her middle. "My tummy is safe AND warm."

"So you are not cold at all now?"

"No, I'm still cold. But I am less cold. If you want to be completely warm, you must go to an *onsen.*"

Thirty minutes later, we are soaking in a massive outdoor tub filled with languid women, great clouds of steam rising around us. There is a deliciousness in that boundary between cold air and warm water, the pleasure almost spiritual.

"Satomi, what is the meaning of this holiday anyway? I've never really understood my students' explanations."

"Japanese Labor Thanksgiving Day. I think it used to be a way to celebrate the rice crop, to be thankful for the effort that went into growing it. Now, maybe it is for labor in general."

"So, no big turkey feasts."

"No."

"Well, I am thankful for national holidays."

"I'm thankful for *onsen.*"

"I'm thankful for hot noodle soup."

"I'm thankful for long underwear."

"I'm thankful for the existence of central heating, but I wish it would hurry up and come to Kyushu."

"Yes," says Satomi. "Oh yes. That would be good, wouldn't it?"

Wednesday, November 17

Sensei spends the latter half of pottery class sorting through recently fired items from the kiln, locating our much-awaited wares. Each time she opens the studio's sliding glass doors, there are initial squeals of delight over the goods that are delivered. Again and again, we pause in our work, wipe off our hands, and lift each piece—turning it to inspect the weight, shape, and design, before passing it to our neighbor. There is a certain reverence or ritual in this slow consideration, in the comments that are passed around the room with the ceramics:

"Beautiful."

"Amazing."

"How did you make that? Please teach me."

Most of the exterior design work has been done by Sensei, each piece reflecting a subtle and traditional aesthetic, that *wabi-sabi* elegance I've been unable to capture the few times I played with slips and glazes.

When I ask Sensei if she will teach me more about decoration, she replies, "Yes, I will teach you. First, *kihon*. This is most important. The other stuff is extra; it is just the surface." She sets one of my cups in my hands. "Do you feel it? Better balance now, but still too heavy. Air bubbles in the walls can destroy it while it's baking in the kiln. You must be more careful."

As we wrap the ceramics in newspaper, Sensei ducks out again and emerges with a tea tray filled with New Year's rooster figurines for all of us, and these garner a round of *"Kawaii!"* (Cute!).

The ladies begin talking animatedly among themselves, something having to do with the characteristics of their Chinese New Year animals. As usual, the discussion is too fast for me to track well, but I understand when there is much laughter about the animal characteristics of the ladies' husbands.

"Tracy-san, what is your animal?" asks Sensei as I'm rinsing off my things outside.

"The ox."

"Ah. That is good for a potter."

"Why?"

"Stubborn. The ox keeps trying even when it is hopeless to do so."

"That is a good thing?"

"Yes. A good thing."

Sunday, November 21

The annual Shokei School Festival is just beginning to get underway when I arrive on campus. I locate a couple of the office ladies, Katsue and Michie, standing off to the side of the main lawn, chatting and taking in the "girls' fashion contest" currently in progress on stage. "Look at that," I say, nudging Katsue. "The girls aren't the only ones putting on a show." Here and there, lone "visual boys" with carefully mussed-up locks and baggy-butted pants look sullenly over the crowd or stare into their cell phones. It is an unusual sight to see so many young men wandering about in this normally all-girls context. "Let me guess, are they looking for hot chicks?"

"Oh yes, hot chicks . . . LIKE US!" says Katsue.

"*Nani? Nani?* Hot-to chicken? *Nani?*" replies Michie, looking alarmed.

Katsue explains, and Michie nods with an air of exaggerated understanding. "*Hai.* We are hot-to baby chicken!"

As I make my rounds, one of the ESS girls, Naoko, spots me and hands me a huge bowl of curry rice from their club stand. "Tracy-sensei, don't worry, we took out meat." It is very thoughtful that they remembered this detail about my diet. I don't have the heart to explain that the sauce is made of beef and that, yes, this counts as meat. "Try! Try!" I take a huge bite and proclaim it "delicious."

"Thank you, Sensei. I will tell ESS!"

She slips back into the crowd, and I enter my building with the aim of discreetly disposing of the remaining curry when I see that the festival is not confined to the outdoors only. One of the classrooms has become a tea ceremony room, complete with portable tatami flooring and beautiful kimono-clad ladies. Another room displays student-created pop-culture manga juxtaposing fantastical images of cuteness, sex, violence. The cafeteria has become an elegant *shodo* calligraphy studio, and it is here that I spend a long time gazing over the black-and-white displays of ancient wisdom/art that only a few can readily read.

"Can you understand?" asks one of the *shodo* sensei in Japanese. "It is a very famous koan written by a monk," he explains.

"But I think you can tell the true meaning just by looking at the way it is written." He moves away, then, not explaining the words.

As I exit the hall, another teacher approaches me. "Did you like the exhibition?" he asks in careful English. "It is both teachers and students. But maybe you cannot yet tell the difference between their work."

"That's true," I say. "What is the difference?"

"The teacher is a master."

"And the student?"

"The student is practicing to become a master."

"Does the teacher still practice?"

"Of course."

"So the teacher and the student both practice. . . . What is the difference between them, between their work?"

"The teacher is a master."

"Oh, I don't understand." I laugh.

"My English is so bad. I am very sorry."

"Your English is perfectly clear, my friend." I bid him goodday with a smile and an awkward bow.

And with this, I leave with the intention to rest in the much-needed solitude of my office. But my hope is short-lived. As soon as I enter, I look through my wall of windows and see (and hear) that a karaoke contest is about to get underway on the stage outside. The overamplified sound begins to rattle the glass at heartbeat-like intervals. A group of girls begin to sing, "We will we will ROCK YOU, ROCK YOU!" I turn, sit at my desk, rub my forehead, and try very, very hard not to see the bleachers of my high school.

When I look up again, a young woman in full kimono glides past my open doorway. The past and the present exist in the same moment.

Tuesday, November 23

It is teacups again in pottery class. "To remember the *kihon*," as Sensei puts it. Working through each step very deliberately,

I produce a near-identical set of four cups. As I rise to begin cleaning up, I see it for the first time: I have somehow managed to NOT smear wet clay all over everything in my vicinity. The mess stays in a neat little circle on the surface of the spinning wheel. "Huh, that's good," says Sensei when I point it out to her.

There is a postcard from Koun when I get home. He writes, *I'm being sent back to Shogoji. I'm not sure for how long.*

And: *Your dharma name is "Myoren"—"exquisite lotus."*

And: *If you ever spill a large quantity of black ink on tatami, be sure to cover it in salt immediately.*

Wednesday, November 24

This evening, after I trim my first cup in class, Sensei uses it as a sample for Mikiko-san, who's trying to make a nice tea set. This is the first time that anything I've made has been used as a model.

"I feel that I'm moving very quickly, today. It is automatic."

"That is a sign of improvement," says Sensei.

"My cutting is fast and deep. I don't feel worried."

"That is a sign of improvement," she repeats.

Thursday, November 25

There is an opaque mist dragging across campus and big pink flowers blooming on some of the trees—a kind of camellia, that autumn beauty. I keep returning to a vague e-mail I received from Tozen this morning. The text was short, perfunctory: *I'm going to a confidential location, so I may not be able to write for a while.* Another cloistered monk. Another solitary. And then later, when I return home after work, there is a package—also from Tozen. Inside, a German film, *Enlightenment Guaranteed.* No note accompanies the package—there is just the film itself arriving in a little nondescript box from Anchorage, Alaska.

In the evening, Koun calls. He needs my measurements for something having to do with a sewing project. Also, Shindo-san, a tall and elegant monk, seems to be randomly chanting sutras while pacing the halls of Shogoji. The other monks think he's losing his mind.

Saturday, November 27

This morning I meet the students from my Japanese Culture class at the bus stop in front of the university. Our plan is to visit Kikuchi—specifically Kikuchi Shrine and Shogoji. This will round out our unit on local religion. The students have prepared brief explanations on aspects of Shintoism and Japanese Buddhism, to be delivered at predetermined spots on our itinerary. Previous years' field trips have been to the "typical" famous sights of downtown Kumamoto, but my class voted unanimously for this unique option. "We always go to those places. We want to go to a new place. We want to meet real monks!"

Koun, it turns out, will be our personal guide at the monastery today. He has often been required to serve as the host for events like this, for schools and groups of businessmen, many of them coming to try zazen for perhaps the first and last time in their lives. His foreignness, I imagine, adding that extra bit of exotic flair.

Given the distance and rural location of our destination, our group travel plans are somewhat complex, requiring multiple bus changes, taxis, walking, and a little bit of luck to make it all gel with the monastery's strict schedule. I have to admit that I'm nervous, maybe about a number of things beyond getting the timing wrong. There's seeing Koun after more than a month. And the possibility of annoying Jisen-san so much that my husband is sent away to Shikoku again, reigniting that nagging question and worry: Am I the reason he was transferred last time? Will my bringing a group of beautiful young women to the monastery precipitate a worse punishment yet?

My students, meanwhile, just seem happy to be on an adventure together.

"Is everybody ready? You didn't forget anything? Do you remember the rules?"

They reply collectively; we've gone over it all before: "Stay together! Have good manners! No sexy clothes!"

Naoko, standing next to me, points at her outfit—dark jeans, a T-shirt, a jacket. "Look, Tracy-sensei. No sexy!" And this brings on a playful scrutinizing of each other. "Maybe Arisa is too sexy!" Arisa, dressed in tight black jeans, tall cowboy boots and a slightly off-the shoulder shirt, waves away the accusation. Her normal wear is undeniably skimpy. This is her version of conservative. If that bare shoulder and bit of leg is all it takes to break a monk . . . ah well. To be sure, it might be enough to annoy Jisen-san, but I hope not.

After the bus collects and then delivers us to Kikuchi Shrine, we pose for photos in front of the great stone *torii* gate. Brightly colored autumn leaves fall around us in the breeze, and it's sunny but chilly. I'm glad for my wool sweater. As I step through the *torii*—moving from the ordinary world to the sacred—Sanae takes my arm, tells me in a hushed tone that I should not walk through the middle of "the gods' road." We must walk on the side of the path to the shrine, to show our humble nature.

Together we climb stone stairs to the top of the hill. Yukari and Sanae protectively flank Fumiko, who, with her slight limp, has some trouble navigating the uneven surface. That unflinching kindness.

After rinsing our hands beneath cold water at the purification fountain, we enter the shrine grounds. A few parents and children in formal kimono move around us, the parents taking photo after photo. These must be the stragglers who didn't make last weekend's 7-5-3 event, that yearly Shinto celebration of children's birthday milestones. My students take turns delivering their mini-presentations on various aspects of the shrine, and then preemptively on Buddhism, for the temple visit. I ask questions, playing the role of uninformed American tourist. I do not, however, ask the hard question that Westerners would be most compelled to ask: How is it that you can belong to two religions at once—one that worships many gods, and the other that has no gods at all?

We return to Kikuchi proper to have lunch at a family

restaurant, and then we hail a couple taxis to take us the last few miles up the mountain to the monastery. Koun is waiting for us in the Shogoji parking lot as we arrive. He looks, I think, even thinner than before. "You made it!" he says, and then more quietly, "Jisen-san is not here today."

"Oh, good. I was a little worried that this would somehow be a bad idea."

"No, no, everything should be fine."

After a tour and a brief demonstration of zazen, we gather in one of the tatami rooms with the others for formal tea. With the women on one side, and the men on the other, we sit in a circle. One of the newest monks serves everyone—his hands shaking as he offers cups to each guest and host.

"Do you have any questions for us?" asks Koun.

"Yes," says Naoko. "This seems like such a difficult life. Why did you all decide to become monks?"

No one speaks, so Koun volunteers his own answer, in English: "This kind of practice strips away everything and reveals the mind very clearly." The other monks look down intently, perhaps struggling with the English, perhaps desperately avoiding having to answer. The Japanese monks look so young yet, I think. Like teenagers. Koun repeats the question in Japanese, and then stares at the monk across from him until he speaks.

"A-ahum. I don't know. It just seemed like a good idea, and now I'm here."

He stops speaking and we sit, looking at each other or down at the tatami for a few moments, before the monk next to him begins, "My father, he owns a temple. . . ." But then he loses his train of thought, trailing off, breathless and flustered. So that there is nothing but silence and a strand of dark hair resting against the revelation of a bare shoulder.

Tuesday, November 30

I only have a few cups ready to trim in pottery class and I finish my work quickly. Instead of throwing a new set, I begin clean-up early, stepping outside to wash and then returning to the studio again and again to gather items that others have finished using. In this way I catch snippets of discussion about the upcoming *bonenkai*, our end-of-year party and farewell until February. Outside, the water is icy cold as I rinse and scrub the tools beneath the spigot, and my hands turn pink and numb. I think of the common ritual in Japan—standing in *gassho* beneath a winter waterfall to show *gaman*, that spirit of enduring through the misery.

"Hey," snaps Sensei as I return again for another load of dirty items. "It's too cold outside—stay inside and stop washing others' things. You'll make yourself sick."

"I'm young and strong and from cold Alaska. It is no problem for me." I realize that I'm sulking a little. I do not want to take a months-long break from pottery class.

When it is time to go, Sensei hands me bits of ceramic wrapped in newspaper. "I forgot to give you these last time—rooster chopstick rests to celebrate the New Year. Oh, one more thing . . ." She disappears into her house and minutes later returns with yet another bag brimming with sweet *mikan*.

"Please wait a moment. My husband is putting one of my old electric pottery wheels in his truck. It is too heavy for you to carry."

"What?"

"So you can continue to practice. He will drop off the wheel at your house."

"Thank you, Sensei. But how will I fire the pots?"

"That is not important. Improve your technique."

"*Hai, Sensei.*" It seems my long holiday will be spent in the spare company of my constant failure. A winter solitude.

Winter

DECEMBER
Impermanence

Wednesday, December 1

Fog, that harbinger of winter, drifts across the broad field
that I walk every morning on my way to work. I hesitate at
the gap in the fence that marks the entrance to the university
grounds, contemplating clouds that touch earth. Next to me, the
neighbor's cat appears and leans into my ankle, her tail curling
up to my calf, and then she leaps away, disappearing into fog to
chase real or imagined prey. I step in after the beast and find
profound pleasure in walking through air that obscures but is
not obscured. Maybe every place becomes transformed when
viewed in a different light. Maybe every person becomes transformed when in a different place. A lion in the skin of a house
cat, or vice versa.

Moving through these unlikely clouds, I follow a memory.
The final weeks of graduate school. Garrett and I standing, as
close as lovers, in the arboretum near my then-home. On the
ground around us, fallen blood-red blossoms of *tsubaki*, "Camellia japonica"—I knew the name because I stopped to read the
descriptions every time I walked among the trees. Picking
up one of the flowers, I felt that fleshy waxiness of the petals
between my fingers.

"I can't follow you to Japan and watch you date other women.
I can't be that kind of friend for you. I'm not going to be that
kind of friend for you."

He reached out and lifted the flower from my palm. "I'm not
going to date other women."

"Okay, then. I'm going to Japan."

In this way it had been me who first pointed out what was happening between us; it had been me who first leapt across that line in the sand. He could have said something else, and then I would not be in Japan. What takes us to one place and not another? Who would I have become if I had simply left Spokane and gone home to Alaska? If I had matured in the center of that echo of youth and devastating memory? Or—if I had gone to some other place entirely? Who would I have become? A petal can fall and be carried anywhere by wind or water.

Sunday, December 5

This evening, the pottery ladies pick me up and we carpool to the Canadian restaurant for our yearly *bonenkai*. Among the many wonderful—but surely not actual—Canadian dishes, the proprietor has prepared a traditional Japanese celebratory food: a fish cooked in a thick crust of salt. The name of the fish, *tai*, sounds like the Japanese word *omedetai*, or "congratulations."

"What is *tai* in English?" asks Mikiko-san, in her near-flawless accent.

"I don't recognize it. I grew up mainly eating Alaskan salmon and halibut. This is a new fish for me."

Mikiko-san produces an electronic dictionary from her purse and rapidly keys the word. "Sea bream," she announces, and the others at the table mouth the foreign word—a slow, fishy mantra around the table: *"Shi-bu-ri-mu . . . Shi-bu-ri-mu . . . Shi-bu-ri-mu."*

"Sea bream," Mikiko-san says again, brandishing a utensil as she prepares to break open the salt crust. "And what do you call this in English?"

"Spatula."

"And this?" She points to a fleck beneath the salt, lifts it, and brings it closer to me for inspection.

"Ah—that's a 'scale.'"

Together we compose a sentence for remembering these new words: "I removed the *scales* from the *sea bream* with a *spatula.*"

Makiko-san coaches the other ladies on how to say it, and the difficulty of this becomes a theme for the evening.

"Maybe I can say it," says Sensei gruffly, "after I have more beer."

While we are gathering our things together after the meal, Yoko-san leans in close to me. "My husband has been sick lately. I think I will quit pottery class. It's secret. Maybe this is my going-away party."

"I'm so sorry, Yoko-san." Terrible news. I feel defeated. Yoko-san, who so often annoys me, has also been one of my kindest allies.

She smiles, pats my hand. "I removed the scales from the sea bream with a spatula. I will never forget."

Wednesday, December 8

Today is Bodhi Day, the day of the Buddha's enlightenment and the culmination of the intense week-long Rohatsu *sesshin* practice period for the monks. It is also my birthday. A large box comes for me in the late afternoon, from a store in Fukuoka—I recognize the characters for the place that sews some of Koun's monk's clothing. Inside are what must be birthday gifts for me: matte black *hakama* and a heavy indigo kimono. Two shades of night. I unknot my hair and remove my work suit, that stripping away of the professional self, and then slip into this other self, this costume of the devoted. With hands in *gassho*, I bow at the regal image in the mirror. Somewhere, an American Zen monk is sitting on his meditation cushion, thinking and not thinking of me.

Thursday, December 9

"So where do you want to go?" asks Satomi after I pick her up from her house in my K-van. We are taking the latter half of the day off from work. Both of us have huge stacks of student papers with us, and the plan is to find a quiet spot to hang out and grade.

"I do have an idea," I tell her. "But it's probably too difficult. Koun and I happened upon this adorable restaurant in Oguni Town, in Aso, a few years ago. It must have been just after we got engaged. It was next to an apple orchard. The building was very elegant, very *wabi-sabi*. I remember the menu was all about apples, and there were journals at each table, for the customers. We wrote something in one of them."

"What did you write?"

"Something totally profound and meaningful. I can't remember."

"Let's find out!" With Satomi as chief navigator and question-asker, we quickly identify the name of the restaurant—Ringo no Ki (Apple Tree). However finding it requires not one but four additional stops at convenience stores in and around Oguni Town. The directions are all haphazard, never pointing us directly to our destination. "It's over there a little ways. [vague wave] Just keep going. You can't miss it." In a last effort, we pull over next to an old woman walking her tiny dog along the street. "Over there," she says, gesturing to a brown structure nestled among a stand of cultivated trees. It is almost immediately in front of us; we'd been passing by and around it the whole while. "It seems we were lost in the place we've been searching for," says Satomi.

Entering the restaurant is entering a history. Koun and I, giddy on our new plans to get married, saw this place as an auspicious find. We'd been hungry, and on an unlikely whim, turned down a road and discovered the building of our mutual aesthetic dreams—a building made elegant by the passage of time.

Now, I take in the cabin-like wood of the interior, the repetitive and enduring geometrics of Japanese design. "Satomi, isn't it funny how a place can look different from your memory of it? Do you know what I mean? This restaurant looks so much smaller and more humble than my extravagant mental image."

"Oh yes, I have memories like that. But I think I visit some places from my past so often now in the present. The memories changed as I changed."

The server—a woman in dark *samu-e*—greets us and Satomi tells her our aim. "We're looking for something that was written in one of the journals. It was a few years ago."

"Hmm . . . that will be difficult, but you are welcome to look. The old journals are on the shelves. Sit wherever you like."

It's early afternoon and no other customers are around, so we choose a big hand-hewn wooden table set apart from the main eating area and next to the tall, open shelving displaying hundreds of journals. We order tea and snacks, set aside our work, and begin pulling down colorful stacks of notebooks, scanning through each. I understand very little of what I'm reading or attempting to read, which probably keeps me focused on the task of finding the odd bits of English, but Satomi bursts out laughing ever so often, engrossed in every narrative. After a few hours, we have graded no papers, nor have we found the mystery message from my and Koun's former selves. We have learned only that many people have come to this place. Many have left their mark.

"Should we write something?" I ask, when it is nearly time to leave.

"Yes, and then we can come back in a few years to look for it."

"How will we ever find this restaurant again, let alone our message?"

"Maybe we should write that."

"We could write 'ichi-go ichi-e.'"

"Oh yes. You can never go back."

Sunday, December 12

At Shogoji's monthly *nichiyo sanzenkai*, the kerosene heaters blast behind all of us sitting in zazen, the warmth and slightly toxic air coaxing many out of consciousness. On either side of me, there is the unmistakable sound of sleeping men followed by the occasional break in breath as the sleepers nod and snort themselves back to reality. The comedy of this keeps me bright-eyed for some time, but eventually I am claimed too. At the end of the session, the booming vibration of the *taiko* drum pulls us all up from the abyss.

During informal tea afterward, the women in the group

examine my new zazen outfit. Some of them leap up and tug, straighten, tuck, and retie until I am "properly" bound up in the kimono and *hakama*. Koun, entering the room and grinning, takes this process in for a moment from a few feet away, me at the mercy of these wonderful and opinionated women—before returning to his daily duties. Breathing will surely be more difficult in the next zazen session—but I have no doubt that my posture will be as rigid as a stone Buddha.

After lunch and clean-up, I have a few brief minutes to take tea and strawberries with Koun in the now-empty informal dining area, and to give him his early birthday presents—layers of warm "legal" items (all that can be hidden beneath a monk's daily wear) and a bag of American snack foods. "I'm sorry I didn't get you something more interesting—but I realized you wouldn't be able to use any of it. So I went with the basics."

"No, this is great. You come to appreciate the simple things here. A bit of fleece, wool socks at night, the taste of winter strawberries . . . It's as if all the excess from before, all that abundance, covers up the basic pleasures."

"And the absence of a lover or a friend or family? There's something to that too, isn't there? A rawness. It brings clarity."

"Maybe there's a kind of paying attention that is not so easily possible in the presence of comfort and attachments. But there is the danger of escapism, too."

I consider the single strawberry left on my plate, that fleeting sweetness. "I wish I could talk to you more often about not getting to talk to you very often."

Just before I leave the temple grounds, Jisen-san waves me back. "Tracy-san, you are working over the winter holiday?"

"No—I have some weeks off."

"Good, good. You stay here, yes? Think of something festive for celebration. This time of year is very difficult for monks—maybe especially foreign monks."

An extended stay at the monastery, near Koun. This thought keeps me smiling all the way home.

Tuesday, December 14

I am sitting in my office after a phone call with my mother—rather, I am sitting in the pause between breaths, after one phone call and before I will begin to make many more. My mother had just heard from her doctor. There had been a biopsy that confirmed breast cancer. "I'll know more in a few days," she said.

Now, there is much to do. I need to talk to my travel agent. I need to sort things out with work. I need to let Koun know what is going on. I need this to not be happening.

Beyond the windows in my office, it is just starting to rain again—a cold winter's drizzle. Earlier, during a lull, I had stepped outside with one of my students and collected a handful of fallen ginkgo leaves—delicate yellow fans clinging to wet pavement. I brought some of the leaves back to my office and put them in a tea cup.

It's raining hard now. I don't know why I can't stop thinking about the leaves.

Thursday, December 16

For two days I have been trying to get hold of Koun, but the Shogoji phone goes direct to voice mail each time. Between classes, finally my phone rings.

"T, I got your messages just now. I'm so sorry I didn't get back to you sooner. There's been—some drama here, and Jisen-san's sick. Are you okay?"

"Just trying to get the flight sorted out."

"Yeah, but are you okay?"

"I'm okay. I'll get to see you this weekend, that's something. And—I wish I could talk now, but I better get back to class."

"All right. I may not be able to talk to you again, not until you get here."

"We have terrible timing, don't we?"

"Always have."

Friday, December 17

I sit with my colleagues in a huge faux-European dining room with a view of a centuries-old Japanese castle. Tonight is Shokei's annual *bonenkai*, though I'm in no mood for it. Today is also Koun's thirty-second birthday, and this fact, on top of my mother's recent diagnosis, feels especially heavy. Last night and the nights before, I couldn't sleep—the insomnia of a too-active mind. I can't bring myself to eat much, either. And there is also the constant game of impotent phone tag with my travel agent—I'm on several waiting lists, but nothing confirmed so far. I have no idea when I'll arrive in Alaska.

As soon as we finish the speeches and the alcohol begins to flow, some of the older men, faces flushed, begin singing and dancing. "*Enka*. Ballads of suffering," Hiroe-sensei, seated next to me, explains. "Some songs are about missing home or a lost love or some other misery. Maybe this is the Japanese blues."

One of the singing men takes my hand and pulls me to my feet. He holds me too tight and does an awkward parody of ballroom dancing with me as kind of reluctant life-sized rag doll. When I sit down again, I can feel the burn in my cheeks.

"You made him look good," says Hiroe-sensei, leaning in too close. What is going on with the men tonight?

After the *bonenkai* (which, as always, is really only the first of several follow-up parties to come this evening), I make my excuses and veer away from the crowd of others. Kumamoto night life is just getting started on the main arcades. The youngsters strumming their guitars and crooning for spare change, or love, or the illusion of fame. The fortunetellers. The hostesses in their gaudy prom-like Western dresses—and the boy versions in shiny suits and pointy-toed shoes and yellow, matted hair. I move away from all of this, toward the shadowed streets surrounding the castle and the looming tangle of tree branches overhead. The koi swim just below the surface of the moat like small, glowing ghosts. I pluck a yellow ginkgo leaf from the pavement, offer it to the fish, watch it drift away into the pure darkness beneath the bridge.

Some time later, after I settle into the smoke-scented interior of a taxi, I notice a message on my cell phone. My flight has been confirmed. I'm going to Alaska in six days.

Sunday, December 19

I drive out to Shogoji one last time to see Koun before I leave for Alaska. All is silent when I arrive. As I climb the stone stairs, no monks can be seen moving around the grounds, or through the open-air corridors. When I turn to look back the way I came, there is only that stunning view of the valley, and then the parking lot, and then a single charred bottle glistening from the center of the burn pile. I move on to the entrance of the main building and as I'm slipping off my shoes, Koun steps out of the kitchen.

"What's going on? It feels wrong here."

"Jisen-san is still sick, so she's been away a lot. The other monks are sleeping or hiding out in the guest rooms. There's some cultural tension, I'll put it that way. The Japanese monks are mad at Jisen-san and Aigo-san for being pushy—and me for being in proximity, I think."

"That does not sound good."

"It's not."

"Is it safe for you to be here?"

"For now, yes." He hesitates. "I think so."

"Okay, I'll have to trust you on that one."

"I'll be fine. You have your own stuff to worry about."

"So what are you and Aigo-san doing?"

"We're trying to keep up the schedule as best we can. But there are only two of us. We focus on the essential tasks, mostly."

"And the other monks? Are they eating?"

"They are eating. Not at mealtimes. Sometimes they steal the keys and take the car into town."

"I don't like this."

"I know. That's just how it is right now."

"I think you'll have a lot to tell me when you leave this place."

"Yes, that's probably true. Come on—let's go to the *hatto*."

Aigo-san, seated on the floor of the Dharma Hall and sur-rounded by odd metal tools and a tray filled with ceramic incense burners, rises and greets me as I enter. "Ah, Tracy-san. I'm very sorry to hear about your mother."

"Thank you. . . . What's all this?"

"I am preparing the incense. Come, you can help me." I sit next to him, and he hands me chopsticks and an incense holder filled with ash. The small bowl is a gorgeous Japanese ceramic with a blue flame of glaze swallowing dark earth. And that smell of incense—always present in the monastery—is sud-denly so much stronger.

"Here, pick out the bones," says Aigo-san.

"The bones?"

"The, ah, leftover incense sticks. The parts that did not burn."

"What is it with you Zen monks and death?"

"Death is our business, Tracy-san. It is the truth of life."

"That kind of makes it everyone's business, doesn't it?"

"Yes." He places another bowl before me, lifts a metal object that resembles the top of a can, but with a little handle attached. "Watch, this is how we make it new again." He presses the metal gently against the ash, smoothing it out across the surface.

"Death and then rebirth?"

"You've got the wrong Buddhists," says Koun with a smile as he rises to slide open the shoji walls, so that we are now both outside the building and within it. A slight breeze begins to move around us like a slow river. In this way we begin the work of six monks.

~

At the edge of nightfall, Koun walks with me to the van.

"How are you feeling, about your mom?"

"I'm okay. Parents—those relationships—are so compli-cated, aren't they? There is this overwhelming sense of love and blame and guilt and sadness. Lots of helplessness. It's all so mixed up. It's also nothing new really, it's just more with me right now. More present."

"I'm sorry I can't go with you, T."

"You were with me today. Take care of yourself. Be careful."

It had been a beautiful day. A perfect day. But as I'm driving home all I can think about is the glint of a charred bottle that should not have been there. And the conversation with Aigo-san while Koun was boiling tea:

"Tracy-san, do not go walking alone here."

"What?"

"On the grounds, where others cannot see you. Do not walk alone."

"Why?"

"I overheard something."

"What did you hear?"

"Not a good thing."

"Okay, Aigo-san. I understand."

~

When I get home, I order a feast of snacks for the monks from the American Costco in Fukuoka, all to be delivered on Christmas eve: giant apple pie, spiced cider, cookies, tins of salted nuts, instant chai, hot cocoa. A little bit of positive currency for Koun, I hope. I don't know what else to do.

Monday, December 20

There are many calls today while I am in my office. First, Jisen-san, who, now back at the monastery, is pleased with the warm clothing and rose-infused head oil I left for her. And then Sensei, who dropped off some sort of mystery gift from Koun on my front step (I'll see it when I get home). And finally Koun, who tells me that somebody delivered a truckload of *daikon* to Shogoji. "An entire truckload! We aren't allowed to waste food so we've been putting it in everything. We've been making a game of it, to see what we can cook." Also, on behalf of Aigo-san, he asks which of my mother's breasts is afflicted. "It's something to do with a prayer or special ceremony, I don't know. Aigo-san is mysterious about his religion. It might be a Hindu thing." And when I call my mother to ask, she tells me that, thanks to her siblings in Texas, the southern Baptists and Catholics are praying for her, too. And also, "the right one."

"Don't you mean the wrong one?"

"That, too." My mother's staccato, static-y laugh through the phone.

After work, on the front stoop to my home, as promised, a stout box is waiting for me. Despite its somewhat small size, it contains a very, very heavy object. I carry it inside to the kitchen, set it on the seat of a chair, and open the flaps. A forest green *te-rokuro*—an iron wheel for hand-turning pots—is tucked inside. How had Koun known that I had been longing for one? I used a *te-rokuro* in Yamanashi a couple of years ago, with my first pottery teacher. He always got me mixed up with another of his foreign students, carving the *katakana* character *ri* (for "Linda") into the bottom of each of my pots. I didn't mind this misrecognition, actually—there was something freeing about not having to own any of those first attempts. Perfect or imperfect—they were all my egoless practice.

Lifting the iron wheel from the box, I place it on the table alongside a big bag of clay. Next to the table rests the electric wheel that Sensei's husband so carefully arranged for me. I've been navigating around these objects for nearly a month, seeing but not seeing.

Wednesday, December 22

The day before I leave for Alaska, Koun calls in the evening while I'm working clay in the kitchen. "Jisen-san is still not well—I've been driving her to the hospital and back." His voice is exhausted, strained. How strange to know that he's been traveling back and forth through town these past few days, along the road a few hundred feet from my door. "I can't stop thinking about my mother—and yours. There is this teaching in the Catholic Church about how we get what we deserve. It's ruthless. And the other version is just as terrible—we are brave and special if we have some terrible burden in our lives. I could never reconcile either of those views. My mother loves the Church, but I watched her endure all of those sermons and comments, on either spectrum, for so many years. We are not special. God does not give us gifts for good deeds or take them away for bad behavior. Everyone suffers. That is reality. Every single person suffers or will suffer deeply at some point in their lives. Recognizing this is cultivating compassion."

"You've been thinking about this a lot."

"Sorry, T. I'm writing speeches in my head. I have no one else to tell it to."

Cultivating compassion. That Buddhist turn of phrase. As if it were a seedling to be coaxed from earth and water.

After we hang up, I survey the delicate clay bodies arranged on the kitchen table. Five tea cups formed on the electric wheel this evening—mostly of the same size. And now I'm trying to achieve the same effect with the *te-rokoro*, by first building coil pots and then hand-turning them to smooth away the imperfections. It is a slower process, a different process, and there is considerably less precision—I'd forgotten that. After my second coil pot, I give up. *I don't know what I'm doing,* I think. And, *Why does everything have to be so difficult?*

Thursday, December 23

A day of travel delirium, and then somehow I am pulling my luggage off the conveyor in the Anchorage airport, stepping out of one reality into another. I move through a sea of holiday travelers toward the tall windows that frame the darkness of the Alaskan winter. The glass, at the touch of my fingertips, is cold as ice. My mother's mastectomy—that cutting away of the rogue element—was some hours ago, in the morning. A woman's breast. A mother's breast. It is hard not to fixate on the metaphorical weight of this affliction. I hate that I cannot stop thinking about it.

I turn and spot Thor's big frame moving toward me, his hand held up in greeting. When we meet, he gives me a quick hug and takes my bag. "How's Mom?" I ask.

"I guess the surgery went all right."

"So she's doing okay?"

"They let her go home, but she's moving pretty slow." Driving through darkness, we don't talk about my mother and what she's going through—just about my travel, about Japan. Thor, still the on-again-off-again boyfriend, seems out of his element in this situation, whatever "this situation" is. It's probably not quite what he signed up for. Then again, what do I know? I do not understand anyone's relationship.

When we arrive, my mother greets us at the door of her condo. Despite her sickly green aura and the agony in each movement, there is a genuine smile. "I have some good news," she says. "There seem to be no lymph problems, so maybe no extended course of chemo. Maybe just radiation."

"That *is* good news," I say. My mother has already explained to me the gifts and plunder of various cancer treatments.

"Oh yes. I'm very lucky. Today is my Christmas."

Friday, December 24

How light comes and goes so quickly here. A day, already fleeting, is even more so in an Alaskan winter. My mother moves cautiously around her condo to lift, carry, and place. A book, a mug of tea, a sketchpad. She takes her painkillers at the prescribed intervals, wincing as they begin to wear off at the bottom of each cycle. "Let me get that for you," I offer again and again.

"No, that's okay." Somehow—through it all—she maintains her sunny mood.

In the early evening, we cook a simple meal of pasta and salad, which we share with Thor. Afterward, there is an exchange of gifts—an antique Blazo box and flowers hand-painted on recycled cardboard from Thor, packages of *washi* handmade paper and *ukiyoe* art cards and used-shop *obi* from me, home-sewn clothing items from my mother.

After we consider each gift and then set it aside—forming a kind of still life in the center of my mother's living room—Thor leaps up suddenly from the couch to examine an old wooden crate leaning against a book shelf, a relic taken from the cannery where he delivers his fisherman's catch each summer. "What is this? It's Japanese writing, right?"

I lean in and examine the kanji. "Yes."

"What does it say?"

"I'm no expert on kanji. But I'm pretty sure it's 'roe.' Well, 'child of fish' and 'goods,' to be exact."

"I like that. Something about those characters. I could put that in the painting I'm working on now."

"Those kanji? Are you sure that's what you want your painting to say?"

"Why not? It's the shape that I like. The aesthetic. That's all that matters to an artist."

I wonder about the rawness of a wound when he says this, the depth of meaning there. I think about the eventual scar knotting against my mother's *wabi-sabi* chest. I think about how I got it wrong earlier. It's not a *still life* we've assembled here in the living room—it's just *life*.

Saturday, December 25

Christmas morning. My mother and I rise late and then sip from steaming mugs of coffee while we consider our plans. Some days ago, my mother's young neighbor invited her to attend Mass at her church on Christmas day. "She's a singer," my mother explains. "We've talked about it a few times, how she's hoping to go professional eventually. I'd like to be supportive."

"Are you sure you're ready to go out?" I look doubtfully at her. She's still moving slowly.

"I'm sure. I just want to get back on my feet, back to living my life as usual. I think that's the best thing."

"Okay. But—can we really just go to the church? We're not Catholic."

"It must be okay. Maybe." Just to be sure, mom calls her Catholic sister in Texas, who assures us that we'll be welcome.

A few hours later, we enter the church in a flood of people. Filing into the very last pew at the back of the room, we sit just as things get started. Excited children squirm and chatter adorably next to me. I can't hear or see much of anything. And then the singing begins. A pure voice fills the space—completely fills it with expansive sound, and yet the distinct instances of commotion are there as well. Aural zazen?

Afterward, I tell my mom about Lisa, from Seattle. "My friend—she recently converted to Catholicism. She told me it was 'for the music.' Now maybe I can understand why."

I email Tozen a brief message in the evening. "Merry Christmas! I'm in Alaska. I'll see you at zazen tomorrow." He emails me back almost immediately: *"Bikkuri shimashita"* (I was surprised) and "Have you shaved your head yet?"

Sunday, December 26

Early this morning, I step outside into darkness and the singular clarity of true Alaskan cold. In Japan, I find the comparably milder winter chill annoying and ever-present, not unlike the vague discomfort that is the constant second-guessing of self and language and cultural habit. However in Alaska, the cold offers up a different teaching: every winter trek outside of a well-heated space is a stark reminder of the possibility of death by the elements. No slow death of the ego and self-identity, this. It's just . . . death.

There is that familiar crunch of footsteps on ice and snow as I trek across the parking lot to my mother's car. When I open the door, I find a small yellow sticky note on the steering wheel: "Unplug!" Right—of course I forgot. I move to the front of the car and oblige my mother's command. Struggling with the stiff plastic of the electrical cable that provides warmth to the car's engine block, I am reminded that even the nonliving can be killed by a night in this cold. I turn on the engine, begin to scrape the ice from the windshield—a full-bodied affair. Two cars down, another early riser is working on his own windshield, a gloved hand raised briefly in greeting.

Arriving at the yoga studio, I enter into an outpost of safety from the elements. The zendo is already populated with people

I met briefly on my previous visit—Jon, Annie, Susan, others whose names won't come to mind until later, when I step back outside and fully wake up again. Tozen is here, too, sitting at his usual spot.

After zazen and our final bow of greeting to each other, Annie, standing next to me, leans in for a hug. "Tracy, it is good to see you. What brings you to Alaska?"

"My mother—she has a health issue. There was a surgery. I wanted to be here."

"Is she okay?"

"I'm not sure. I think so."

"Good, good. You know, today in zazen, I just couldn't stop thinking about it all. How life is so fleeting."

"Oh, I know," says Susan, joining our conversation. "That tsunami. It's quite a thing. It's all they're talking about on the radio this morning."

"What tsunami?" I ask, confused by this sudden shift.

"A big one—in Indonesia. You didn't know?"

As I drive back to my mother's condo, I gather bits of information from the radio. A huge earthquake early this morning in the Indian Ocean triggering tsunami throughout the region. Many unconfirmed deaths, and the confirmed deaths rising by the hour. I think of my neighbor Jennifer and her family, who are spending the winter holiday in Phuket, Thailand. I think of getting engaged to Koun on the same beach that was inundated by water some hours before now. I pull into Mom's parking space. Sit in the heat of the car for a few brief minutes before stepping out into dangerous nature.

Monday, December 27

It snowed all night and continues this morning, the steady fall of white making for treacherous roads. It is really nothing more than a terrifying slide from one destination to the next. After zazen, the few others quickly disperse and Tozen suggests that he and I go for coffee near his apartment. I offer to drive. "The roads are very bad, and I'm not used to driving in snow anymore. Are you sure you trust me?"

"Eventually we all die—one way or another."

"That doesn't sound like a vote of confidence."

At the coffee shop, we mostly talk about my mother, about Koun. "Sometimes," I say, "I think my truest desire is to simply know the outcome of things, some kind of guarantee that it will turn out one way or another. If I could just have that. Then, I could relax."

"There is no such guarantee."

"I know."

"Well, do you know the famous saying about death and taxes?"

"Yes, I believe I do."

"There is your guarantee."

"I'm scared. I want my mom to be okay."

"That is normal."

As we are gathering our coats to leave, Tozen pulls something from his bag. "Oh, this is for you. It is a small thing. Happy Birthday." Tozen hands me a card with cherry blossoms painted on the front. "I remember the day of your birthday because of Rohatsu and also because it is the day of my ex-wife's birthday."

We step outside together, the snow continuing to fall from a blanket of gray sky. *"Mo, yuki ga furimasu ne,"* says Tozen.

"Sakura ga furimasu ne," I reply, holding up the gift card. Snowflakes—like cherry blossom petals—fall. Both are a transient beauty.

In the evening, there is an email message from Jennifer. Their hotel was on high ground and they were not on the beach when the tsunami struck. "Others were not so lucky." The death toll keeps rising dramatically—doubling, in fact—on the news. I can't turn away from the images. So many lives erased by the weight of water.

Tuesday, December 28

My mother and I arrive too early to the doctor's office. Both of us make small talk and pretend to read fashion magazines until her name is called. As she gets up and follows the nurse,

I put down my magazine and stare at my hands. I don't know what to do.

At the bookstore afterward, we spend the afternoon looking through books on health, cancer, alternative medicines. "I want to consider everything," says my mother. "I need to know my options." The doctor cannot yet confirm what additional treatment will be recommended—this diagnosis will come later. "I'll make the decision when it's time."

After the bookstore, we park the car back at her condo, drop off the books, but continue our shopping in the downtown streets nearby. Perhaps for both of us there is a certain need for distraction today. We move from shop to shop, taking in the wares like tourists. We enter a tiny store that carries nothing but Baltic amber jewelry. A woman with a Russian accent explains it to us: "This has a very strong healing power—no amber is stronger than Baltic."

"A stone that heals? That seems unlikely." I bend down to look at the bits of dark and light amber in her display case. They look, I think, like captured sunbeams.

"Not a stone—resin from ancient trees."

"Of course. It's very pretty. What is it supposed to heal?"

"It reduces pain and increases the healing speed of wounds."

My mother smiles, shrugs, and selects a bracelet and a pair of simple earrings from the sale rack. I choose ruby-colored drop earrings with silver beads.

As we leave the shop with our tiny bags of overpriced jewelry, my mother says, "I think I like these because she told me *why* to like them."

Wednesday, December 29

I am driving alone in my mother's car on the way to pick up groceries. I am worried about her and feeling sorry for myself too—the two feelings a single weight. I am also inexplicably lost on streets that should be familiar to me. I've been driving fifteen or so disoriented minutes when I spot a building that I had imagined long since gone. I turn the car around and pull into the parking lot. The structure before me is small, nondescript. Years of wear have stripped the paint. Still, the business appears to be in operation. Why have I not noticed this place before? Sometimes I think everything here is memory for me, stories waiting to be revealed and written and rewritten. I had just turned eighteen when I entered this box of a building to get my first and only tattoo. It took me just a few minutes to choose what I wanted. I knew it had to be that rose—thorny stem, blood-red blossom. I recognized the obvious cliché but didn't care. I just wanted to mark what had already marked me. The artist—a woman with a shaved head, like a nun—asked, "Are you sure you want this one? That you want to do this?" There was something like worry in her eyes. The look of an older sister, or of a mother.

"Will it hurt?"

"Yes, it will hurt. But we can take small breaks, if you like. I have time."

"Okay. I'm ready."

The woman bent low over my ankle as she worked, as if forming the most delicate of clay vessels. That distilled concentration against my distilled pain. I saw tiny, bright blue forget-me-nots tracing along her collarbone, encircling her neck like a beautiful noose. Alaska's official state flower. *Wasurenagusa*, in Japanese—"the grass of not forgetting."

Everything is memory. Everything.

Friday, December 31

New Year's Eve, and it is another bitterly cold night. My mother and I struggle over a cork stuck fast in a bottle of red wine. Thor, big and strong and handsome, laughs at our womanly weakness, and then disappears into the bedroom briefly, returning with his most recent painting-in-progress: a beautiful classic blonde, head thrown back and hands spraying her slender neck sensually with a bottle of perfume. The kanji from a canning crate are painted neatly in a corner of the picture. *Child of fish. Goods.* Characters without a context—or with so much context that I can't understand. My mother sucks in her breath and doesn't say anything—and then, "Who was the model?"

We leave a short while later, my mother's silence against the sound of fireworks. Like sudden realization, they again and again illuminate the darkness.

JANUARY
Ikasu

Saturday, January 1, 2005

This morning I am skiing fast through trees and over ice and snow on the deserted trails of Kincaid Park, a place I often visited in high school, a place I visit even now in my dreams. It is overcast and cold and quiet. There is only the rhythm of movement and breath.

I found these old skate skis a few days ago while searching for a box of winter clothing in my mother's storage shed. Pushing aside all those carefully tucked-away memories, I gathered up my old red ski bag and made a plan. Now, moving like this through landscape, I see that it was a good choice. The *right* choice. The body, in motion, is fully engaged. There is both a singular focus and a diffusiveness. There is balance. In Japan, certain monks will begin the New Year seated on a black cushion; I begin mine gliding over white snow.

As I reach the top of yet another hill, I pause. Light breaks through cloud cover overhead. I feel, suddenly, like crying. It is surprising how so much can be bound up in the body-memory of movement. It is not unlike the awakenings brought about by a smell or a fragment of music. Had I been at the top of this hill or some other when that obvious solution to my adolescent misery hit me? Take the family car in winter, at the deadliest of temperatures, in the dead of night. Drive and drive and drive and then park in some inconspicuous area, well out of sight. Hike as far as possible into wilderness and then drink from a bottle of hard liquor to take away the survival instinct (how I hated the taste and sting!). Remove the life-preserving warmth and fall back into snow. Pull the whiteness like a blanket over me.

I can see now how all of this appealed to some part of my teenage vanity, that such an act might preserve the image of the body while expelling whatever pain it carried within it. I can marvel at the stupidity of all of this now. I know the preciousness of this life. But then, but then . . .

The truth is that I remember standing in the kitchen. I remember the weight of the backpack on my shoulder. I remember putting on my boots. I remember the sound and feel of the car keys in my hand. I remember that I never got past the front door. I remember, also, being terrified of getting into trouble and so in this one way it could be said that my stepfather, or my own fear of being caught by him, saved me.

I have not thought about any of this in a very long time.

Monday, January 3

"Mom, why didn't we tell people what Fred was really like? Why did we keep secrets for him?" My mother and I are driving home from yet another of her doctor's appointments. All night and also today, rain pours out of the sky, melting snow and ice. I don't recall ever seeing an Alaskan January quite as fickle as this one before.

My mom leans into the steering wheel and sighs, seems to contemplate the unlikely weather surrounding us. "I was afraid. All those stories from Vietnam, from the police force before he became a teacher . . ."

"I guess those veiled threats were pretty clear, weren't they. He was always letting us know what he was capable of."

"Yes, and not all of the threats were veiled." My mother, the ex-wife of this man, knows things that I do not know.

"Sometimes I think we were just trying to be good girls. We were well behaved."

"It was like that, wasn't it."

"And if you think about it, our good behavior was rewarded. Until a mood or a misstep made it all go to hell again. There was no real winning, only a staving off of something. Some beast."

"Yes, there were definitely cycles. Good times for a while and then . . . not so good."

How we learned to define ourselves within the treachery of those moods—stupid or smart, good or bad, ugly or beautiful. I want to ask, *Do we still keep those secrets? Do we have to carry this burden forever? What are we supposed to do?* Even now, I always want to know what I'm supposed to do. A good daughter. A good partner. A good person. What am I supposed to do?

My mother turns to me, smiling as if in answer. "But why focus on all that negative stuff? I want to think positively from now on. It's healthier. It makes me feel better. I want to enjoy all the life I have left."

So lighthearted, I think. We look so much the same, but inside we carry vastly different emotional landscapes. I envy her.

Thursday, January 6

I drive through a winter sunset, out to the Valley to visit with Cheryl and her kids. Tomorrow I'll go in with her to Wasilla High, to talk with the students in her coworker Carla's Japanese-language classes. "It's been a long time since we've had a sleepover," I say as I step into her house.

"That's true! But it might be a little different with the kids."

"Right. I guess that makes us the adults now." We quickly settle into chatting and playing a board game with her four-year-old daughter. Cheryl's son, who is somehow already in grade school, sits cross-legged on the couch, arranging thick stacks of Pokémon cards.

"I need to travel more," says Cheryl. She seems, I think, lighter than the last time we spoke. "I keep remembering how I had such a great time hiking with my dad in the Grand Canyon. Something about that trip—it just cleared my mind. And it really got my dad talking, too. I felt that I saw a new side of him. He was lit up."

"What did you talk about?" I ask as her daughter gleefully moves a game piece several squares along the path.

"Oh, lots of things. Nothing important, really. He kept going off on 'liberals this, liberals that . . .' He had a lot of opinions about what you and your husband are doing."

"Ha! Opinions about hippies like me?"

"Yes. . . ." She gives me a cautious, sideways look—unsure, perhaps, if we've ventured into unsafe territory.

"Okay. You can tell me—is it the Japan thing in general, or the Buddhist thing specifically?"

"Well, both."

"I know it all sounds weird, everything we're doing. It is weird. Unless you're in it. Then it's just what's happening now. It's a new perspective, a new definition of normal."

"I guess that makes sense."

"But your dad wouldn't buy that, would he?"

"Not for a second."

"It's just wrong, what we're doing."

"Yes."

"Well, he's certainly not the only person who feels that way." I smile, swallow this small hurt, and roll the dice. Some part of me—that lonely inner child, perhaps—is always desperate for approval from one parent or another.

Cheryl's daughter—her twin in miniature—looks up from the gameboard. "Mom, what's a 'hippie'?"

"Um, someone who has crazy-long hair and weird clothes," says Cheryl.

"Oh boy. What's the PG version of 'free love'?" I say.

"A hippie is someone who takes a lot of very, very bad drugs. . . . Don't you ever take very bad drugs!"

"Definitely *not* a Zen monk, then!" I laugh. "Or, at least, not one in Japan, who follows the rules. Though, come to think of it, the hair and clothes can be pretty weird."

"Ha! You'll have to show me pictures. . . . All right, guys, it's about time for bed. School day tomorrow." Her daughter squirms, protesting the ending of our game but also happy in her mother's arms.

"I still can't believe you have kids. I'll need to get your advice if we ever get around to having them."

"I wouldn't know what advice to give. You just deal with things as they come up. I don't know any other way to do it."

"Like everything else, then."

"Sure."

~

Kneeling on carpet, I gather game pieces, fold the board neatly into the box—this journey in miniature of luck and choice to play again some other day. From the back of the house, a mother recites bedtime prayers with her two children. A moment, a universe.

Friday, January 7

At Wasilla High, I stand in a room that looks and smells very much like one of the classrooms in the high school I attended a few miles away, in Palmer. I've just finished presenting to one of Carla's Japanese-language classes, sharing tips on communicating with their pen pals at Shokei, and a number of Carla's students surround me, some with questions, others simply eager to share their knowledge of Japanese culture. One tall and awkward boy says, "Tell me about Remi. Is she . . . is she beautiful?"

"She is very good at *kyudo*, Japanese archery. You should ask her about that," I say.

A girl with bright eyes smiles and hands me several pieces of lined notebook paper on which anime characters have been drawn in careful detail—mostly big-eyed girls in high school uniforms. "Can you give these to my pen pal?"

"Nao is an artist, too. She will be happy to receive these. But don't you want to send them with your letter?"

"I'll make more. I draw one every day."

"That's good practice. I'll look for your work someday."

Another boy with sandy blond hair approaches and tells me his name is Trinity. He holds a fake Japanese sword in one hand. "I wonder if you can help me with something. I need to know how to do *hara-kiri*. It's for a play."

"A play?"

"*Rashomon*. You know the movie? We had to change some of it, obviously."

"Well, I don't think I'll be much help to you—I'm no expert in disembowelment, or Japanese film, for that matter. What is the movie about? It sounds familiar."

"It's about many versions of reality."

"Many versions?

"Yes, there's this monk who stands by a gate in Kyoto. He listens to different people explaining an event—a rape followed by a death. Each person tells it in a completely different way."

"Oh, I almost remember this story. Remind me—which person is telling the truth?"

"All of them."

"Right, right." I nod and close my eyes. I am sixteen. I am thirty-one.

Saturday, January 8

My mother and I bundle up and trek down the street from her condo to the museum to see the latest: an exhibit of Tibetan Buddhist artwork. There are paintings of the Dalai Lama at various ages, and also a number of mandalas. It's the latter that really pull me in—those intricate and prismatic depictions of the cosmos—while my mother, drawn more to the portraits, notes that the Dalai Lama, at age five, "looks exactly like himself." I see that she's right, and also that the mandala and the portraits are perhaps not such different things. I think back to my experience as a child living briefly in Hatcher Pass, when I first began to really see the "Big/Small." The infinite universe. The tiniest molecule. And here in this room, a mandala of people (each a mandala him/herself) move around and through and out into the cold of an Alaskan winter. Alaska, too, a mandala.

On the way back to the condo, Mom and I stop at a café and order a berry cobbler to share. It arrives shortly after—a big steaming bowl with two spoons, and a generous scoop of vanilla ice cream melting on top. We each take big bites, and then I set down my spoon, drink most of a glass of water, and slump back into the booth.

"Are you okay?" asks my mother.

"I don't know. This is the kind of thing I crave all the time in Japan. But here, now that I can have it, it's much too sweet. I can't bear to eat it. I don't remember once feeling that way before moving to Japan. There was no such thing as 'too sweet.'"

"Your tastes changed. Maybe all those new flavors had an effect on you."

"Yes. Honestly, I feel that I've been altered in my DNA. Everything has been changed. Everything. This cobbler might be the best evidence I have for that. Before I liked sweet things, and now I don't. I'm a person who *doesn't like sweet things*. How can that be?"

"You know, over time, I think my tastes have changed, too. Maybe it's something to do with aging. But it's there. It's a subtle shift."

"Is this cobbler too sweet for you, too?"

"Not really. But I am also a changed person."

"Changed but the same?"

"That's right."

Sunday, January 9

It seems that true winter has returned, and with a certain violence. After morning zazen, Tozen and I shuffle in our thick coats across the frozen parking lot and tuck ourselves into my mother's car. The engine has been running for at least ten minutes, but it still feels like the inside of a freezer. Tozen removes his gloves and rubs his hands over the lukewarm blast of air from the vent. "I will visit you in Kumamoto soon," he says. "I will arrange to meet Koun's teacher. You can move back to Alaska and take care of your mother."

"But what would you do? Where would you go?"

"It is time for me to retire. This is work for a younger person, someone with energy. I have no more energy."

"I think you have lots of energy."

"No, not so much. Not so much now."

"Honestly, I'm just—I'm not sure if that is the right path for Koun and me."

"That is for you to decide. I will go to Japan and open a door. Then you will make a choice."

In the late afternoon, my mother and I work together in her small art room. I pack my suitcase for my return home, while she cleans and puts her supplies in order for her next project. "I need to get back to painting. It's time," she says.

"That sounds healthy," I say.

"Oh—I almost forgot." From her closet she produces a *zafu*, a pattern of dragonflies flitting across the bright purple Chinese silk. "I picked it up at the bookstore. Maybe you can show me how to use it before you go? My doctor said meditation might be good for reducing stress. At least, she said it couldn't hurt."

I take the *zafu* in my arms and squeeze it tightly against me. "It's a nice one," I say. "Sturdy but not too hard—a good foundation for sitting."

"Oh good. I wasn't sure if it was a real one."

"This doesn't mean you're becoming full-on Buddhist, does it, Mom?"

"Well, I don't know."

"You'd be a better one than I, I'm sure."

"Why do you say that?"

"Just a guess." My mother's heart—light as a dragonfly. I set the *zafu* next to the wall.

"How do I start?" she asks.

"It begins with the breath," I say. "In." We breathe in. "Out." We breathe out.

"Well, that doesn't seem so hard."

Thursday, January 13

The horned cow is your mind. The horned cow is your mind. The horned cow is your mind. . . .

Last night and also the few nights before I dreamed of walking down an abandoned hallway of an airport—the words of a stranger on a loop as I catalogue the ink paintings hanging along the walls:

A man searching along a path in the woods
The hoofprints—a hint—in the mud
From behind a tree, a bit of leg and tail revealed
The man looping a rope around an ox's thick neck, fighting against the strength of the animal
The ox following the man, who carries a whip and the rope lead
Now playing a flute, the man sits astride the ox, riding it along the path
The ox gone, the man rests peacefully in his home
A single *enso*—the Zen circle a kind of mandala that points to transformation, interconnectedness, wholeness, emptiness
A river flowing through the forest
A man walking along a village street, immersed in the normalcy of daily life—the trees around him in full bloom

~

It has been a few days since I arrived home from Alaska. The luggage from my trip sits mostly unpacked in my bedroom, and I feel out of sorts. Maybe I haven't quite arrived yet; maybe I am still traveling. The feeling is not quite a depression but more an idea that won't form—or a riddle not yet solved.

Koun, meanwhile, has been calling constantly from pay phones while out on some long journey with the monks. I barely miss him every time he calls and so there is this other nagging discomfort, this near-miss longing. Finally, in the afternoon, I am standing near the phone when it rings and I jump at the sound.

"Oh, it's you," I say. "I'm so glad to hear your voice."

"Same here, T. How was the trip? How's your mom?"

"She seems well, herself. I'm not sure what else to say. We had a nice visit."

"That's pretty much all you can hope for, isn't it?"

"You're probably right."

He tells me he's been talking a lot with various people at Zuioji, translating difficult conversations for Aigo-san, in order to arrange Aigo-san's finishing ceremonies, transmission, and so forth. "I'm pushing the limits of my language and cultural abilities. It seems to be going okay so far, so that's good at least. I'm gaining a kind of competency."

He also tells me that they've all being doing a lot of *takuhatsu*, a twenty-day run of it to be exact. Usually, they get to take turns resting, but he is the driver, so there is no rest for him. "I don't know if I'm coming or going. It's exhausting. Everything starts to run together. Sometimes I realize I've forgotten the name of the town as we're marching through it, chanting and holding up our bowls."

And then I tell him about my discomfort, the non-arrival, of being on the edge of an idea. "I want to say it's like your experience—my brain is moving so quickly through different places that I can't put my finger on what it's all pointing to, or where I'm at."

"Maybe," he suggests, "you should make something."

In the evening, I sit in my kitchen and form pot after pot after pot. But nothing comes to me. No grand idea. Just *now*, nothing but *now*. I finish well past midnight. After cleaning up, I slide open the back door, slip on shoes, turn off the kitchen light, and step out into cool darkness. I know there is a stand of cherry trees a few paces away. Beyond that, the field I walk through on my way to work each morning. Beyond that, vast plots of cultivated earth. But who's to say that any of that exists in this moment? I could be anywhere. I could be nowhere—or everywhere. As my eyes adjust, I begin to regain my vision. Maybe it is time to unpack my bags.

Saturday, January 15

In my email this morning I find a single thumbnail photo of bamboo heavy with snow, hanging low over an ice-covered pond—a tiny window into cold beauty. No text accompanies the photo. I recognize neither the sender nor the scene.

And then around noon, Koun calls. "Did you get the picture? It's the frog pond behind the main building. It's probably bad to use up the monastery's data, but I had to show you."

"It looks so different, so cold."

"It IS cold. But it's beautiful, too. I wish I could show it all to you. Everything is snow and ice right now. We're freezing and in awe at the same time."

He also tells me that the monks are slated to go to Nagasaki, but the new snow has rendered the mountain impossible to drive.

"So you're trapped up there?"

"Well, we thought so, but when we called to cancel we were told that others are expecting us."

"What does that mean?"

"We're trapped, but we're not allowed to be trapped."

"But how will you get there? You can't drive that mountain—it's bad enough in summer."

"We'll hike down the mountain and make our way to public transportation. It'll take up most of our *takuhatsu* earnings to do it."

"That's crazy."

"Well, it's not ideal."

"Tell me if you run out of food."

"It will be okay. It always works out somehow."

"Do you still have *daikon?*"

"We will have *daikon* forever."

~

I bundle up against the cold and walk to the little movie rental store several blocks from my home. My student, Mizuho, shouts out a greeting as soon as I walk in the door. She seems very amused by my many layers. "Find a movie for me, Mizuho. I will watch anything you want me to watch."

"First I must find you, Tracy-sensei."

"What?"

"So many coats! Why? You are from Alaska."

"Yes, but in Alaska at least it is warm inside our houses. Here, I can never get warm in this season."

"I don't understand you, Tracy-sensei. But, don't worry. I will find you funny movie."

"Why funny?"

"Laughing to make you warm!"

On the way home, a copy of *Shaolin Soccer* tucked tightly under my arm, my attention is drawn again and again to the absence of leaves in the trees. Bare, bone-like branches moving and creaking in the breeze.

Sunday, January 16

"I keep trying to see everyone as their child selves lately. A compassion practice that Koun told me about," I tell Satomi as I spread *okonomiyaki* batter over the hot grill between us, forming a large savory pancake. We are tucked into a booth in a cozy mom-and-pop restaurant that caters primarily to high school kids and university students.

"What do you see when you see me?" asks Satomi.

I watch the door across from us. Any minute, young people will begin pouring in for the after-school rush. What if the child Satomi were one of them? A girl on the verge of adolescence. "I see pigtails."

"Pigtails?"

"Definitely pigtails. And a blue-and-white uniform, the sailor design. Also, one of those mandatory bright red backpacks."

"I hated pigtails. Too much trouble."

"Maybe I'm not very good at this."

Satomi reaches into her bag, produces a few scraps of lined notebook paper. "Let's see. . . . When I was a child I often used to make origami."

"Cranes?"

"Many things. I liked boxes—they are good for keeping small objects, very practical. But I don't know if I remember how." She creases an edge of the paper, tears it away to reveal a square, and then considers it briefly before beginning to fold. A few seconds later, a small paper box rests next to her cup of tea.

"Wow! How did you make that? It happened so quickly."

"I'm not sure. I guess my hands remember, even though my mind does not." I turn off the burner, and begin to dress our *okonomiyaki* with sweet, thick soy sauce, *nori* sprinkles, mayonnaise, hot mustard, and *bonito* flakes, while Satomi folds paper again. She produces two cranes, setting them gently in the box as I serve our meal.

"I get it," I say. "Birds in a cage."

"Well, an open cage. They can fly away. See?" She picks up the cranes, mimics them flitting off to distant lands, before setting them back in the box and pouring more tea for the both of us. "Oh, after this let's get ice cream. Children like us *love* ice cream."

"My inner child likes this idea very much."

"My inner child also likes *onsen*."

"Excellent plan—I know a place that has both."

~

As we drive back from the *onsen*, we pass one of many well-tended Jizo near my townhouse. An elderly woman, a neighbor, bows low to the stone deity, that patron saint of women and lost children. In my rearview mirror I see that she stays in *gassho* for a long time. An old woman, a girl.

Wednesday, January 19

For my students, I am the bearer of good news after lunch—I carry a big box from Alaska into the classroom, set it down, and then stand back as the girls descend upon it. As they sort through gifts and letters from their pen pals, I open a large cardboard envelope that arrived at the same time, from Tozen. Inside, there is an illustrated children's book with a cat on the cover. It is written in Japanese, and I work out "a million times lived cat," before arriving at the better translation, *The Cat Who Lived a Million Times*. On a slip of stationery there is only this explanation: "I lost the English version. Maybe this can be your Japanese study."

"Oh! That book!" says Naoko, taking notice of the pages turning in my hands.

"Is it a good book?"

"Yes, good book. I remember reading when I was child."

"What is it about?

"Very proud white cat, very beautiful, loves himself very much. He lives and dies and lives and dies many times. But he meets black cat and makes baby cats. He loves black cat and babies more than himself. Then, he dies."

"He dies happy?"

"No, very sad."

"Um, is this a good story?"

"A very good story, Tracy-sensei."

"Then I will do my best to read it."

"Hope you enjoy."

"Oh—Naoko, did you change your hair? Something is different. . ."

"Yes, black. We must return to natural color now. We will all have job interview soon, because we will graduate in February." She sweeps her arm around the room. "Do you see?" For the first time I do indeed see that almost everyone has "new" hair—shiny black, neatly trimmed. The highlights and fun dye jobs erased and returned to a monochromatic "natural." Somehow I had forgotten about this yearly ritual.

February. I've been waiting all year for this month to arrive, and now it is coming on too fast. "Oh Naoko, I am not ready for you to leave."

"We will miss you too, Tracy-sensei. Always remember you."

Thursday, January 20

Much of the day is spent editing stuff for Hiroe-sensei— seemingly mathematics-based linguistics papers that I understand only in terms of correct or incorrect grammar, and nothing more. "You are the only person who understands me," he tells me—not for the first time.

"Hiroe-sensei, you do realize that I don't understand the content of anything you write?"

"Yes, but I trust you. You are the only person I trust with my writing."

As I step out of his office, a throng of passing students circle around me. "Tracy-sensei, look! Look!" One by one I examine the sheets of professional photos in their hands, all taken for Coming-of-Age Day, a celebration of the year in which a person turns twenty. Gorgeously adorned in bright traditional kimono, elaborately styled hair and makeup, the young women are barely recognizable. "You all look so—glamorous and adult!" They laugh, tumble back down the hallway, repeating, "*Guramurasu . . . guramurasu . . . guramurasu.*"

When I return home, there is a letter from Yamada-san. It begins with cartoon sketches of me and Koun. There is also a two-tiered snowman, a line of mountains. A smiling bear. *If you move to Alaska, maybe I will visit you,* he writes. *I want to see white bear dancing under aurora.*

Friday, January 21

This afternoon, a long talk with Bryan on the phone. "Kathy and I are struggling a lot lately. More than usual. Maybe it's just all part of the process."

"Does the end point of that process mean that you'll be together?"

"Not necessarily. And the process never ends. Everything is process, an evolution. I'm a big believer in that."

"Is this process a line or a circle or a spiral or something else?"

"I'm not sure. I just know that I should be moving through it."

So, he tells me, he's taking the Feng Shui approach—clearing out the clutter and moving his bedroom to the smaller room because, after all, he doesn't want to be "spit off the continent" (the larger room is the "travel corner," apparently).

"The smaller room—that was where Koun and I stayed when we lived with you, right? I'm pretty sure we got 'spit off the continent.' Maybe *that's* why we returned to Japan. Mystery solved."

"Good point. But I think you both knew you'd go back."

"Well, would it be so bad for you? To just go to another place for a while?"

"There's probably some value to that, definitely. Maybe I'll take a week or two. I'm due for some vacation time."

"No, what if you did something more dramatic? What if you moved to Japan? Or, you know, some other totally crazy foreign place?"

"Well, that would be interesting, to be sure." Bryan, always diplomatic. "But I don't think that will be the best route for me right now. Someday—who knows."

"Sure, that's a crazy thing to do. Just up and leave it all behind."

"Well okay, maybe for *some* it's the right move."

"So how do you map out the different parts of your house?"

"Well, you start with the main door."

"The main door to your downstairs apartment? Or the main door of the house itself? They're opposites, right?"

"Oh, right."

After we hang up, I imagine him returning to the plan he's sketched out, tearing out the old and finding a new, clean sheet to map out a new and improved emotional geography.

Wednesday, January 26

Hiroe-sensei and I walk together across campus after classes—he on the way to his car, and I on my way home. "Oh, is this yours?" I say. The black sedan is usually parked here, in front of the gym, alongside my path to work each morning. "That long *juzu* hanging from the mirror always catches my eye."

"I'm a very pious man, you know. I was ordained many years ago, by my father."

"But—you are not a priest, are you?"

"Technically I am, but I chose the life of an academic instead."

"Well, you seem happy with your choice."

"I am happy, very happy. And I have good news. I am getting married in May."

"Wonderful—congratulations."

"I would have asked you," he says. "But you are already married."

"Well, at least we can still be friends."

"Yes," he says. "I would like that." There is a certain sadness to his voice, and I almost laugh, but then think better of it. Have we, I wonder, been engaged in some kind of invisible romance?

Saturday, January 29

"How is your husband?" I ask Yoko-san as she maneuvers her big white car through the narrow streets of a neighborhood that I do not recognize.

"Not good, not good," she replies. "But I can take care of him. I am still healthy and strong. . . ." Her voice trails off, and she waves toward our destination. "Oh! There is my friend! Shimamura-san." A tiny, bent old woman—she must be well into her eighties—bows in greeting as we pull into the parking space in front of a house that looks like all the others.

"Welcome!" she says as we get out of the car and follow her into the ample entryway. Her way of speaking is tinged with age and dialect, and I can see that I'll need to pay close attention to understand her. Inside, I remove my shoes and step up onto the main floor, carefully avoiding what looks to be a small quilt stretched across the wood.

"Oh, don't worry—you can step on it," says Shimamura-san.

I lean down to examine the intricate patterns. "But—it's so beautiful."

"Antique Japanese indigo cloth," Yoko-san explains. "Shimamura-san makes them by hand from old *samu-e* clothing. It is her hobby. Look." Yoko-san gestures around the room. Variations of the quilt adorn much of what I can see of her home. Years of work are represented in this dark and humble cloth.

"Oh—do you like Japanese quilts?" Before waiting for my reply, Shimamura-san disappears for a moment, and then reappears with two gorgeous quilts in her arms. She spreads both out on the floor. "Which do you like better?"

"They are both very lovely." I lean down to admire the stitching on cloth made to be durable, to last a lifetime. "Gorgeous."

"Then I will give you both."

"What? No, no, I can't. . . ." I look to Yoko-san, my hands in the air.

Yoko-san smiles at me as Shimamura-san beckons us both to sit at a low *kotatsu*. This too is covered with one of her lovely quilts. And then she disappears again, returning a moment later with a tray of Japanese sweets and tea.

"Ah, so you are an American. Tea is okay? You don't want coffee instead? Or a chair? I can get you a chair."

"No, no, I love green tea and *kotatsu*."

"Oh, you *do* like many Japanese things! And pottery too, I hear. Have you ever tried on a kimono?"

"Never, but I have often admired them."

"Come, come." We set down our tea and rise to follow her into a spare tatami room with nothing more than a *tokonoma* alcove and seasonal scroll, a chest of drawers, and a tall and narrow mirror. Afternoon light filters through half-open paper shoji. A glimpse of winter garden beyond that.

"*Saaahhh.* A very traditional Japanese room," says Yoko-san.

"Let me show you," says Shimamura-san, kneeling and opening one of the low drawers. "This is where I store my kimono. It is not necessary to wear traditional clothing so much anymore. And some of these are for a younger woman, like you, Tracy-san." She lifts one of the items from the drawer—a big slender square wrapped in thick, white paper—and places it on the tatami. She unfolds an edge of paper to reveal the bright, ornate silk beneath. "Ah, not this one. You are so fair. And this is *furusode*—it has the long sleeves of an unmarried woman." She returns the kimono and lifts another from the drawer—a pale yellow silk robe. "This will suit your complexion, the pink in your cheeks. Do you want to try it on?"

"Oh yes—may I?" I remove my sweater—just the American uniform of T-shirt and jeans beneath—and the two women dress me, discussing the proper way to wear kimono.

When they finish, Shimamura-san points to the mirror. "Please," she says, "it suits you very well." I move to the mirror. The transformation is remarkable. Who am I now?

"I will give this kimono to you. Just a moment please." She hastens out of the room.

"Yoko-san, I can't accept all of this. The quilts and now the kimono—it's too much."

"No, she wants to give these things to you. She is very old. She will be happy if you take them. Very, very happy." She smiles and moves across the room to the window overlooking the garden. "Oh—look!"

My body now bound in exquisite silk, I take small, delicate steps across tatami. In the garden outside, tiny yellow daffodils are in full bloom. The color of a kimono.

Sunday, January 30

A lonely day made more so, perhaps, by the heaviness of a dream I cannot shake: me, skiing some moonlit Alaskan trail alone in winter. A stillness pervading everything as I slip between the dark specter of trees. This vista of a far-off place overlays the Kumamoto kitchen in which I work clay all day, and I am there as much as I am here. Cups and bowls form beneath my fingers and fold back into themselves to begin again and again and again.

When I settle into my bedding at night, I follow a memory down that rabbit hole of sleep. It must have been just after my fifteenth birthday. I was getting off the bus for ski practice at Kincaid Park as snowflakes fell. That day, though, I'd forgotten my ski boots. One of the older boys said he had, too. So we sat across from each other at a table in the lodge for that hour and a half of practice while the others skied the trails in failing winter light. It was warm inside, but still I wore a big striped sweater—frumpy, like a thick hockey jersey—and he commented on it, my tendency to hide my body. And when I didn't respond, he leaned across the table and touched my hands, then my arms inside the sleeves of the sweater. I couldn't bring myself to pull away. I felt that for the first time I had been seen. That somebody recognized the darkness I carried. There was both cruelty and compassion in this moment that would not end. Then he released me and pulled a sketchbook from his backpack. "Look," he said, and I watched as he drew a timber wolf, starting from the line of the snout. I also loved to draw, but I had never seen anyone do so with such precision—nor from the center out. In this way, I saw him for the first time as well and that image seared into me: a boy in flow, a boy on the verge of becoming.

Strange, the memories we hold on to, that hold on to us.

Monday, January 31

A letter from Koun today. *There's something that comes up a lot in lectures here. 'Zazen no toki ni zazen o ikasu.' That is, 'When you do zazen you just let zazen be whatever it is.' 'Ikasu' in this case is active—an active 'letting be.'*

As I walk in the evening, I can't seem to escape a deluge of thought. All those past encounters. All of those things I could have said or not said. Actions I could have taken or not taken. That burden of karma given to me. Finally, I stop at the edge of the overspill area and stop trying to escape. I scoop up a handful of stones and throw them into the water one by one, thoughts rising again and again and again. I think about Koun, what I wish I could say in this moment: *There is a story I tell myself, that I have told myself for a few years now. About how I went to Lake Ezu and drowned my past there, all that misery unburdened. I wanted to be free of it so I could be with you. To live in nothing more than the story of our lives together. To be my very best self. But the truth is that it's all there still, just hidden beneath the surface. It's always been there. Maybe refusing memory is not the same as accepting and letting go.*

I pick up another stone, pull back my hand, and then stop. I lower my arm and inspect the object in my open palm. Ordinary, jagged, dirt-streaked granite. Flecks of gray, black, white. I tuck it into my pocket, give the water one last look before moving on. At the neighborhood statue of Jizo, I place my stone neatly, with two hands, and then bow and *gassho*.

Ikasu.

FEBRUARY
Beginnings

While drying one of my favorite tea cups this morning, I fumble and the cup flies free of wet hands and towel—shooting out neatly in an upward trajectory, pausing (it seems) in mid-air, and then completing the arc. The sound as it hits the floor is slight but decisive—a body exploding outward from the point of impact. For a few brief seconds, I believe I can preserve the cup by simply willing myself to get a better grip, to make a less aggressive pull with the towel. A course correction in the past tense. But this fallacy is quickly eclipsed by the forward motion of cause-effect logic. I cannot undo what has already been done, or not done. There is only this moment and then this moment and then this moment and then . . . this moment. *Well*, I think, *at least now I'm paying attention.*

The sky is brilliant blue and cloudless as I walk to work. It is almost an Alaskan sky, but absent that line of towering mountains. A fragment of thought arises as I walk, sharp as the edge of a favorite broken cup. It was in 2000, the summer Koun traveled to Alaska with me, to see the place where I came of age. The great adventure of that trip had been driving to Denali National Park, to visit the largest mountain in North America. We spent three days in a rustic log cabin with a reportedly fabulous view of Denali, "The Great One." Except there was no mountain—only an unyielding blanket of clouds. In the hotel gift shop, we bought postcards of a hypothetical view—a vision that I held only in distant childhood memory. Then, miles outside of the park as we drove back to Anchorage, the cloud cover lifted, burning away into blue sky, and a towering mountain appeared as if by magic, from nowhere. We pulled the car over and just stood, in awe. It had been there all along.

Thursday, February 3

It is an entrance exam day at our little university, and all regular classes have been canceled. After the completion of the assessments, the teachers disappear into their offices to huddle beneath the asthmatic groans of aging heaters while they mark student work or pore through books or compose research papers that matter. I pace the long unheated hallways, feeling unusually impervious to the cold. My breath is visible—a thin vapor ghost on every exhale—and my thoughts turn again and again to a flowering kaleidoscope of experience that opens out and out and out. The same pieces rearranging, juxtaposing themselves in new but still familiar ways. As I turn a corner in the hall near my office, I bump into Yukari and Sanae, the ever-*genki* ESS girls.

"*Bikkuri shimashita!* You surprised!" shouts Sanae, usually the less boisterous of this pair of friends.

"Are you okay, Tracy-sensei? You are looking a little . . . lost?" adds Yukari.

"Oh, I was just thinking."

"What thinking?"

"I was thinking about my very first weeks in Japan. About a lot of things."

"What was first impression?"

"Of Japan? That it is very different, very foreign."

"And now?"

I smile at the girls and consider the question. Puffs of breath rise from each of us. "I know that I still don't understand much, but this place is becoming a part of me. It's my home. One of my homes. I feel very lucky to know you all. Very lucky."

"I see. It's *ichi-go ichi-e*. Do you remember?"

"I remember."

"Oh! Tracy-sensei, do you know Setsubun? It is today. We want to show you."

"Setsubun? It's something to do with getting rid of evil spirits, right?"

"Yes, yes. Come with us to ESS room!" I follow the pair downstairs and along the corridor to the English club room, where the necessary items have been placed out on the table: a bowl full of beans, a bright red mask with fierce features.

"First, you must take hard soybean for your age." Yukari lifts the bowl and passes it to me. I count out 31 to their 21. "Eat for happiness, for this New Year." We pop handfuls of beans into our mouths, chewing with an air of thoughtfulness.

"Okay, now *janken* for the *oni*."

"What?"

"Do rock-paper-scissors now. We will take turns being the devil." We each hold out our hands, call out the necessary syllables to play the game.

"Ah—I am loser!" says Yukari. She grabs the red mask and pulls it over her face. "Now, I will go to building's door and you will chase me and throw beans."

Sanae adds, "And must shout, *oni wa soto fuku wa uchi!* Can you say it, Sensei?"

"*Oni wa...*?"

"It is 'bad luck out, good luck in!'" Explains Sanae as Yukari slips out the door.

I look doubtfully at the small, hard beans in my hand. "Wait—how do you say it again?"

"I am *oni* now!" shouts Yukari, her voice echoing from the other side of the building. "Chase!"

Sanae and I hurry after her, down the empty hall and out the door, and then we are racing across the campus grounds, shouting and hurling beans and laughing, like children held together in a moment.

Friday, February 4

Snow is falling outside this morning, a thin blanket of

white settling over everything. Students form tiny snowmen along the campus walkway to my building—miniature sentries guarding a fortress of knowledge. By noon, when the sun is at its highest, surely the snowmen will cease to be, leaving nothing behind but twigs and pebbles and a brief, damp memory.

After work, Yoko-san picks me up. Her youngest granddaughter, the five-year-old Ha-chan, sits in the backseat and clutches sweetly at a pink egg-shaped virtual pet. Twenty minutes later, we arrive at Hotel Castle, to a *shodo* calligraphy exhibition. "This is very fine work," explains Yoko-san as we enter the large gallery, its walls lined with scrolls of varying sizes. Many people move around us. Still, there is a reverent feeling to the room, a monastic air. Ha-chan—the virtual pet now on her wrist—moves silently between us, taking turns holding our hands as we walk through handwriting.

"What do you think?" asks Yoko-san, as we complete the loop.

"I don't understand anything. But I also can't look away."

"Oh. Then you understand."

Tuesday, February 8

Finally, it is our first day back to pottery practice after a too-long break. I feel the weight of Yoko-san's absence from our group. We all do. After the necessary pleasantries, we settle into our seats and begin opening our toolboxes. Each of us finds a wood *kote* inside, signed by Yoko-san. *Enjoy your pottery life!* reads mine. That elegant script of a master calligrapher.

"What a lonely sight . . ." sighs Baba-san, placing her new *kote* squarely in front of her work station.

"Oh! Look who's here. Yuko-san and baby!" says Sensei, leaping up and sliding open the glass door. Yuko-san, glowing with that ever-present warmth and a chubby new baby boy clutched to her chest, enters the workshop, into our outstretched arms. Women who create with nothing more than dirt and water.

Sunday, February 13

Even with the kerosene heaters on full blast, it is cold in the mountain monastery. I sit in many layers, a wool-and-cotton onion. Around me, the collective respiration of monks and the members of the *nichiyo sanzenkai* make it seem as if it is the building that is breathing. During *kinhin*, I slip out with Koun to prepare the meal for the others. We work in a dark and freezing kitchen. "I'll return to Zuioji in a few days, to wrap things up. I'll send my things in the mail to you before I go."

"I can't believe it's been a whole year."

"I can't either."

"Honestly, I'm a little nervous."

"Me too, T."

"It's a kind of beginning for us, isn't it."

"It's always a beginning. Every day."

After the meal has been served and consumed, Koun and I wipe down surfaces and put things in order in the kitchen. Three of the monks take turns washing dishes in the icy water. They gather the heat from each other's bare heads with their hands, laughing as they do this.

We finish our work and Koun points to the door. "We have a few minutes—come with me. I want to show you something." We walk behind the main buildings, to the frog pond. Clear ice edges the water and sunlight sparkles off everything. The sound of birdsong in the trees trickling down to us.

"Beautiful."

"Yes, in every season. The ice will be gone soon. Maybe by this afternoon."

I kneel next to the water, touch a fingertip to its clear, mirror-like surface and then watch as the ripples echo out. "My mother, you know, she used to be a teacher. I had some of her overhead projector markers—do you know the kind? I kept them in my coat pocket. I had a habit of searching out ice in winter. I drew things. I wrote on it."

"What did you write?"

"Anything. Everything. Mundane things. Beautiful things. Ugly things. All of my secrets."

"A kind of ritual?"

"Yes, and then later it all melted when spring came.... Koun, do you remember? At the gate, when you entered the monastery a year ago, you were asked, 'What is *shugyo?*'"

"Yes?"

"What was the correct answer?"

He laughs and steps toward me, toward the edge of the water that—now once again placid—reflects us both. "It was 'I don't know. I came here to learn.'"

~

Driving away from Shogoji toward home, I take in the view of a thawing landscape in sunlight. I am at the cusp of adolescence, leaning into snow, brushing it away from a smooth, opaque surface that reveals everything. Black or blue or red ink, all bright as blood.

Thursday, February 17

The phone rings shortly after sunrise, but I've been up for an hour or so already, trimming new bowls on the electric wheel in the kitchen. "Good news from the doctor so far," says my mother, who has just come home from a check-up.

"I'm happy to hear that."

She laughs, the sound transposing through the phone line into a digital music. "Well, it's all just moment-by-moment. One day at a time, right?"

"I guess that's true—for all of us."

I return to work at the kitchen table after our chat, return to my place at the electric pottery wheel while the morning light shines through the window and the glass sliding doors, and it occurs to me that I have been here before, in some previous iteration of window, table, kitchen, creation: my mother and I in a three-window rented breadbox of a house in Nome, just south of the Arctic Circle. A blizzard rages outside—a true whiteout—the most dangerous version of this kind of storm. In fact, everyone had stories of people getting lost just by stepping out of their homes, how some survived and some were found months later, in the thaw. So we—my mother and I—are held in a relative safety in this house, which is really nothing more than a frail wooden shelter shifting against the tide of permafrost beneath it. We stand or sit at the kitchen table painting, a six-year-old girl with her tablet of watercolors and her thirty-one-year-old mother with her many tubes of oil paint. Both of us create scenes of an imaginary sunlit summer—rainbows, birds, rolling fields of flowers and green. We take breaks at intervals, moving together to the one window in the living room that again and again shows only a blinding, horizonless white.

It is my mother, some hours later, who pulls me from my concentration and invites me to look out on what I felt could never return: a night sky filled with stars, the brilliant clarity of a full moon.

Saturday, February 19

"Are you up for a bit of a drive today?" I ask Satomi as she hops into my car.

"Okay. Where to?"

"Takamori. I want to find a place I discovered a long time ago."

"Ah, another mystery."

"Well, we are adventurers, aren't we?"

"What's in Takamori that you want to find?"

"A path in the woods, not far from the temple where Koun used to go every morning, when I first arrived in Japan. At that time, I was worried about many things—mostly, I was trying to figure out how to stay here legally. I was out walking—worrying and walking—while Koun was at his new job, and there was this trail into the bamboo, next to a pond. I didn't think about the dangers, the snakes, the bugs, anything like that. I just saw this overgrown path and followed it."

"Where did it lead?"

"At the end, there was a small cave—a hollowed out wall of rock, really. Inside was a stone Buddha. Weathered, very old. Most of the features of the face worn away. People had left things there—coins, flowers, *sake*."

"Ah, I see. Did you bring something to offer today?"

"Yes. One of my bowls, some bottled water to pour into it."

"Oh sorry—can you go back to my house?"

"Sure—why?"

"I need better shoes for this adventure."

Monday, February 21

It is final exams week at the university, and the campus is a bubble of collective concentration. The students with newly dyed black hair wear a somber seriousness in their faces, as if they've just stepped from childhood into the world of grown-up concerns.

Shortly after I return home from work, the postman delivers a large, heavy box addressed from Shogoji. After I thank him and close the door, I maneuver the box up the stairs, into the spare tatami room. There, beneath the watchful eyes of a small Buddha, I carefully slice through tape with a knife. The smell of incense fills the room as I unfold the cardboard flaps and begin to pull out the much-used belongings of a cloistered monk.

You're an *okesa* monk and a *rakusu* monk now, I think. Two sides of the same paper. I know Koun would agree.

Wednesday, February 23

Everyone is late to pottery class—"taking care of their late-home-from-work husbands," explains Sensei—so I sip tea and look at all the lovely work on display around the receiving room, asking questions about her creations in my halting, inadequate Japanese.

I also ask about her teacher, but she shrugs and is not so forthcoming: "What's to say? He was an old man, very strict. I studied with him for years, until it was time to move on and develop my own style." She moves to a display case, slides open the glass, and lifts out two of his *chawan*—tea bowls—a small, black-glazed vessel with hints of iridescent blue and the other larger, with a crackled, lumpy white glaze that only partially veils the pink-white rough clay beneath. When I pass one bowl and then the other back to her, I notice how she takes each carefully with two hands and gently, gently places it on the shelf as if it were a living being, perhaps an embodiment of the old man himself.

"Tracy-san, I have something for you. Or maybe it is a present for Koun-san." I follow her out of the room and jump down onto the concrete of the firing area. She points to a box on the ground. "I fired all of these this past weekend. I was a little behind on student work."

I crouch over the big cardboard box, turning cup after cup in my hand.

"So many! Did I make all of these?"

"Yes." She moves to my side and crouches next to me. "What do you see?"

"I don't know . . . cups?" I laugh.

"Look again."

"Maybe . . . *renshu*."

"No, not only practice. It's *shugyo*. It's training."

Friday, February 25

In the mail when I get home from my walk today there is a little package from Bryan. Inside is a DVD copy of the photos Dick has been organizing as well as some special chocolates that I had hinted at a longing for. A yellow sticky-note attached to the DVD reads simply, *Thought you might get a kick out of this*, which looks more like *Thugs yadda getcha kout otus*. (No wonder he was almost a doctor—his writing is another sort of foreign language.) The photos are a kind of retirement project for my father-in-law. I've been hearing a lot about it lately via the family e-mails.

I eat one of the too-sweet chocolates, wrap a blanket around my shoulders, and slip the DVD into the drive. Then I am transported to another era. Expansive scenery as backdrop to candid portraits of Dick and Viv in their twenties—younger than Koun and I are now—mixed in with a few photos from later decades. Family relatives (I can only assume) that I have never met in Montana and Texas. Pictures of the war in Vietnam: smiling buddies, tanks. Children there, too, hamming it up for the camera. Then hunting guns and broken birds, fishing and captured fish. A picture of Viv sleeping, angelic and child-like on a 70's-style bedspread. Fancy cars with men standing in front of them—all old classics now. Ornate European architecture—surely from the year Dick was stationed in Germany during the war.

Three hours later, when I close my eyes to sleep, I see vast American vistas and innocence and violence, lives that unravel like unspooled light, firefly trails that burn so brightly for a while before winking out. I can't sleep, so I get up to sit with it all. I understand. I understand. *This life, too, will pass.*

Saturday, February 26

In the dormitory courtyard out front, the last of the girls are being collected by their parents. Standing at the window, I watch car after car depart. Through thin walls and glass, the shouts of farewell and laughter drift into the room around me. A near-but-distant sound.

I close my eyes. It is my first week in Japan. Alone, I wander out into the streets of Takamori during a festival. A mass of people in traditional clothing moving around me. The sound of drums storm-like, rising and falling. A gaggle of children who all want to touch my long, brown hair—their small fingers in it as I crouch low. And then the parade of adolescent boys dressed as caricatures of women—too-bright make-up, wigs, flowing secondhand Western dresses. They pull me into their dance so that in my bright, strange foreignness, I am just another trick of the imagination. Who is mimicking whom? The dancers release me at a fork in the road, and a man in a burlap apron hands me a tiny wooden box filled with *sake* from a barrel. I hesitate, and then drink. "What is happening?" I shout. "What are we celebrating?" A woman next to me takes my arm and leans in close. Brilliant *sakura* bloom on her *yukata*, a fan is tucked into her wide belt. "It is an offering," she says in careful English. "*Okaze*. For the wind." "For the wind," I repeat, as she disappears—a stranger into a crowd of strangers. So that all I'm left with is the fork in the road. Right or left? Which way to home?

Monday, February 28

Koun called earlier in the day—he won't be able to return to me on time after all. Something to do with the paperwork at the monastery. "A few extra days. Maybe a week or two," he says in the phone message. "I can't be sure."

It is early evening. I am sitting at my kitchen table, sipping tea and sorting through the notes from my year of waiting for Koun. I do not know what any of it means, what it will reveal or fail to reveal in the rereading. Beyond my kitchen window, the plum blossoms have just begun to bloom around the townhouse, each knotted center uncoiling like a memory.

~

Garrett and I walk together outside the walls of the Japanese gardens in Spokane, white birds like ghosts scattering before our footsteps in the darkness, and a stone turning in my hand.

"So you're going to be a Zen monk."

"Yes. I believe that's what's right for me. That's my path. But, Tracy, what do you want to do with your life?"

I take a long time to answer, because this is the first time anyone has ever asked me this question.

Finally: "I want to be free."

Epilogue

July 2008—Anchorage, Alaska

Early morning. I am sitting zazen in a room with ten or twelve other people. It is summer in Alaska, in this small and familiar city where I now live. Koun is visiting Shogoji, serving as a translator for a handful of other foreign monks. I have not heard his voice for two weeks—my only way to talk to him is to wait for his call from a payphone at the base of the mountain. And so he does not yet know my secret: our child, this new life, unfolds inside of me from the dark, like a flame flickering into being.

Breathing in, breathing out—
in every moment,
here.

Note to the Reader

Timeline of Events

The arrangement of days and events in this journal may be somewhat imperfect. My original "journal" was not a single object, but many—small and large notebooks that lived on my bedroom floor or that traveled with me, loose sheets of paper, letters, an annotated calendar, the occasional computer file or even email, as well as memories that I failed to write down—or flesh out—until later.

Terminology and Names

For the sake of clarity and simplicity for readers less familiar with the language, I have presented Japanese words throughout in their simplest romanized forms. When introducing unfamiliar terms in Japanese, I've tried to integrate the definition in English. This can sometimes lead to redundancy, as in a *"kiai* shout" in karate—a *kiai* is a shout.

The usage of Japanese names and honorifics may present additional challenges. The family name is followed by the given name in Japan. But because I was writing in—or, at times, translating into—English, in the few instances in which both first and last names are mentioned I use the Western style of given name followed by the family name.

In Japan, people are generally addressed either by position/rank ("teacher," "mother," etc.)—or by family name with an appended honorific (*-sensei* or *-san*). A first name or a nickname may be used for children, but a child's diminutive, *-chan* or *-kun,* is often appended to it. A sibling, close friend, or student might be referred to only by his or her given name. When engaging primarily in English, the speaker may or may not drop the honorifics. So how names are expressed in Japan is highly contextualized, and the use (or not) of honorifics throughout this book is a simplified reflection of that.

Finally, some names in this text have been changed.

Acknowledgments

I am thankful to Peter Goodman for his willingness to take on this project—as well as for his keen eye and encouragement along the way.

I am also indebted to many of the people who appear in these pages—my teachers and students, colleagues, family, and friends.

My gratitude to Koun and to our children, Cormac and Norah, is boundless. Thank you, my wonderful family, for your constant love and support.

Stone Bridge Press books are available from booksellers worldwide and online.
SBP@STONEBRIDGE.COM • WWW.STONEBRIDGE.COM